Modern
Jewish
Morality

Modern Jewish Morality

A Bibliographical Survey

Compiled by
S. DANIEL BRESLAUER

G. E. Gorman, Advisory Editor

Bibliographies and Indexes in Religious Studies, Number 8

Greenwood Press
New York • Westport, Connecticut • London

Library of Congress Cataloging-in-Publication Data

Breslauer, S. Daniel.
  Modern Jewish morality.

  (Bibliographies and indexes in religious studies,
ISSN 0742-6836 ; no. 8)
  Bibliography: p.
  Includes indexes.
  1. Ethics, Jewish—Bibliography.   I. Title.
II. Series.
Z5873.B75   1986   [BJ1280]   016.2963'85   86-12145
ISBN 0-313-24700-5 (lib. bdg. : alk. paper)

Library of Congress Catalog Card Number: 86-12145
ISBN: 0-313-24700-5
ISSN: 0742-6836

First published in 1986

Greenwood Press, Inc.
88 Post Road West, Westport, Connecticut 06881

Printed in the United States of America

The paper used in this book complies with the
Permanent Paper Standard issued by the National
Information Standards Organization (Z39.48-1984).

10 9 8 7 6 5 4 3 2 1

Contents

Preface

This companion volume to <u>Contemporary</u> <u>Jewish</u> <u>Ethics:</u> <u>A</u> <u>Bibliographical</u> <u>Survey</u> (Westport, Conn.: Greenwood Press, 1985), is, like that volume, divided into two sections: an introductory review of the major moral questions considered by the sources followed by a bibliographical survey. The introductory review presents a theoretical model upon which to build an analysis of the data in the bibliographical survey, and it refers continually, as a guide and interpretation, to the entries in the second half. The six chapters comprising the bibliographical survey itself investigate biomorality, sexuality and the family, selected problems evolving from sexuality and the family, moral dilemmas associated with aging, death, and mourning, questions arising from interpersonal relationships, and aspects of political morality. Entries are culled from popular, professional, and theological writings (books and journals alike); a critical annotation describes both the contents of the entry and its relationship to modern Jewish moral reflection.

While <u>Modern</u> <u>Jewish</u> <u>Morality:</u> <u>A</u> <u>Bibliographical</u> <u>Survey</u>, like the earlier volume, focuses on writings drawn from the contemporary period (especially from 1968 to the present), it represents the modern rather than the specifically "contemporary" because the issues and agenda of Jewish moral reflection were already set in the eighteenth century. The background for this morality can be gleaned from a look at the section in the previous volume <u>Modern</u> <u>Jewish</u> <u>Ethics</u> as well as from later discussions in the introductory section of this volume. Jews were forced into an open society and had to take note of the scientific tradition, the sexual and moral codes, the business practices and political realities of that society; even dying meant a confrontation between traditional assumptions and modernity as the deaths of Spinoza, Heine, and Rachel Varnehagen demonstrated in the early modern period. Jewish identity could not be escaped even in as private a moment as death.

This agenda of concern is reflected in this present volume which looks at Jewish biomorality and questions of birth and

abortion arising from modern science and the mores of modern
society, at the breakdown in the family and selected issues
of moral dilemmas in that sphere of concern, at Jewish
interpersonal relationships among themselves, with the business community, and with the non-Jew, at the relevance of
political morality both in a modern democracy and in the
democratically organized Jewish state, and at the moral
questions arising from aging, death, and mourning in an age
in which traditions are being questioned and the very determination of death is problematical.

The traditional way of enumerating these areas of concern
reflects the human life-cycle, beginning with life itself
and culminating in death. The introductory survey argues
that this traditional view, while understandable, does not
adequately reflect contemporary realities. Instead six
crises form the core around which the investigation of
modern Jewish morality takes place.

The introductory survey will discuss these crises in
greater detail. Here they are sketched to provide an overview of the content to be found in this volume. The first
crisis has been caused by medical science and raises
questions of the physician's moral duties, the use of new
discoveries in preserving life through hazardous procedures,
the possibility of artificially stimulating procreation, and
the equally challenging temptation to terminate a human life
when medically required. This crisis forms the basis for
the first chapter of the bibliographic survey.

The crisis forming the basis for the next chapter has been
caused by the sexual revolution. Modern Jews have become
unsure of the balance between biological destiny and
cultural choice in their determination of selfhood. This
crisis is best illustrated by the feminist and gay liberation movements. The third crisis grows out of the first
two: it is the crisis of the family. The investigation of
this crisis includes consideration of the Jewish family,
intermarriage, and divorce. A fourth crisis arises when
rituals and symbols no longer reflect the reality of
people's lives and values. The moral dimension of this
crisis can be found in discussions of Jewish education, in
the inclusion of women in Jewish ritual and as ordained
rabbis, and in considerations of the Jewish approach to
aging, death, and mourning.

The roots of the fifth crisis can be traced to the openness of, Western society. Jews confront the political confusion of a dangerous and uncertain international situation.
The variety of Jewish response to the perplexities of political theory, war and peace, racism, justice, and human
rights reflects the problems caused by political crisis.

The final crisis is a crisis of evaluation. Jewish tradition insists on evaluating persons for who they are. The
consumer-oriented society evaluates on the basis of the

power to buy and sell. The crisis of values has sent Jews searching for new ways of expressing valuation and new modes of interaction that avoid treating human beings as commodities. Naturally one area of concern in response to this crisis has been the economic one. Associated with the economic crisis comes an ambivalence about charity, a sense of not knowing even who should be considered a needy person. In addition the pluralistic social order has compelled Jews to reevaluate their relationship to non-Jews-- both through interfaith dialogue and through efforts to convert the Gentiles to Judaism. The bibliographical survey looks at the crisis of values through a chapter devoted to business ethics, charity, truth, and interfaith relationships.

This volume seeks to be more than a compendium of interesting entries and annotations; it aims to present a unified picture of modern Jewish moral reflection. While recurrent themes emerge from Jewish discussion of such diverse issues as biomorality, women's rights, sexual mores, business ethics, political attitudes, the legitimacy of war, or confrontations with anti-Semitic black (in keeping with most recent usage this adjective is not capitalized) Americans, the pattern that makes all the thinking "Jewish" is not easily discernible.

The introductory survey takes up this challenge and suggests one way of dealing with the unity within diversity of Jewish moral thinking. A second purpose of the introductory survey is to demonstrate how Jewish moral thinking remains distinctive whether one is discussing a traditional or nontraditional author. Throughout the bibliographical survey, distinctions between representatives of tradition or of liberalism are drawn. Many times, however, those distinctions are misleading. The introductory survey provides a key to discovering when those distinctions are helpful and when they are not.

The bibliographical survey itself selects representative thinkers from differing Jewish traditions--both religious and secular. The original research for this work included a great variety of sources--some professional, some theological, some popular. The survey is "selective" in two senses. While the major areas of Jewish moral reflection are all included, isolated attempts to grapple with moral issues not commonly discussed are not included. The survey is also selective because of its choice of sources. Although popular writings are sometimes represented, the emphasis is on theological or professional sources. The reader will note that in many cases one or two individuals dominate the relevant literature. Such instances are true reflections of the situation in which particular Jewish thinkers carve out a reputation in a specific field. In such cases the Bibliography includes both popular and professional examples demonstrating the scope of the author's influence.

The double criteria of representativeness in content and representation of a broad spectrum of journals were used in determining what to include and what to exclude. With great regret it was decided to exclude Sh'ma magazine even though it is the best place for any reader to get a swift overview of the concerns animating the Jewish community. The reason for its exclusion despite this importance is that the articles in Sh'ma are short and the authors have usually published a more extended treatment of the subject elsewhere. Readers are still advised to refer to this publication for an exciting and provocative reflection of thoughtful Jewish moral reflection.

The citations include works originally written in languages other than English. Entries in Western languages will be left untranslated; Hebrew entries are translated, with the original language indicated in brackets. Where the Hebrew includes an English title page, that will be used for the translation; in other cases the translation is my own. Where entries are relevant to more than one section of the topical bibliography, cross references are provided, utilizing the entry number of the citation.

The three indexes provided are meant to guide readers in their use of the bibliography; access is to entry numbers, not page numbers. The index to authors refers to authors of the various entries rather than to authors mentioned in the annotations. Readers interested in the variety of writings by a single thinker will find this index useful. The index to titles also provides access to the enumerated citations. The actual title of the entry rather than, for example, the title of the anthology in which it appears, is cited. The third index is more general and concerns the basic subject matter included in both the introductory survey and the bibliographical survey. Subjects mentioned in the annotation as well as in the title of the entry are included.

A few words of acknowledgment must be added. The University of Kansas enabled the research for and preparation of this book through a sabbatical leave for the Fall Semester 1985. That support is gratefully acknowledged. The continual, careful, and critical guidance of the Reverend Gary E. Gorman, advisor to the Bibliographies and Indexes in Religious Studies series has improved this work at every stage. I am indebted to the editorial help of the entire Greenwood Press staff and most especially to Marilyn Brownstein. Finally I should note that my children, Don and Tamar, now in junior and senior high school, were a source of inspiration. During the preparation of this volume they were engaged in projects of their own covering the entire gamut of Jewish moral concern--doing research papers on war, racial tensions, and Israel and debating abortion, capital punishment, and other issues treated here. To them, and those who, like them, are continuing the Jewish moral discussion, I dedicate this volume.

Modern
Jewish
Morality

Introductory Survey

WHAT IS MODERN JEWISH MORALITY?

The distinction between morality and ethics, already discussed in Contemporary Jewish Ethics: A Bibliographical Survey, deserves repeating here. Morality concerns the specific decisions a person or a group makes during the course of existence. Ethics refers to the standard or yardstick, the general principles used in making this distinction. The first volume focused on the latter; this volume concentrates on the former. Less obviously the present survey calls itself "modern" rather than "contemporary" even though it utilizes entries drawn from recent publications. Although the issues raised in this volume have a particular poignancy and a specific orientation because of the twin events of the Israeli June 1967 war and the growing conservatism of American Jewry, the moral agenda reflected had already been set at the beginning of modernity. For a discussion of the periodization of Jewish ethical reflection and an investigation of modernity as such see the relevant sections of the previous volume. The shape of Jewish moral thinking had been established by the crises arising from Judaism's confrontation with the open society of the modern world. In this way the issues discussed while representing contemporary Jewish moral thinking are also characteristic of Jewish moral reflection throughout the modern period.

The simple distinction between ethics and morality needs to be expanded since a strict separation between them cannot be pressed too far. Understanding Jewish moral thinking entails recognizing that the ethical theories dividing Jews from one another influence the way in which particular moral issues are understood. Belief that Jewish morality depends upon a single ethical principle, for example, has enabled traditional Jews to recognize a plurality of moral responses as equally legitimate when looking at a particular concrete dilemma. While this volume looks at the concrete dilemmas that Jews have faced in the modern world, readers are advised to refer back to the previous work to comprehend the differing theoretical and theological positions involved.

Those theological issues, however, merely form the
background for the dicussions studied here. The important
question raised in this work concerns which specific
dilemmas have Jewish religious thinkers considered central
moral challenges needing a Judaic response. What makes a
particular dilemma of life a moral concern? Two elements
are involved: crisis and urgency. The first establishes the
need for thought and decision. When established ways are
challenged and accepted values are uprooted, people face a
moral dilemma. Moral questions arise from a crisis of
values, a sense that once- stable ideals are in need of
reexamination. The mere existence of a moral crisis, however, does not mean that moral reflection will automatically
follow. Human beings often deflect the crisis of morals
they face by ignoring it. A vital moral concern will not
allow such deflection; it possesses an urgency that demands
a solution. This bibliographical survey studies moral
dilemmas faced by Jews in the modern world, dilemmas that
have arisen in the crisis caused by a confrontation with
modernity and that have retained an urgency that could not
be denied. What these dilemmas were and how different Jews
sought to resolve them will be outlined in this introductory
survey and demonstrated in the bibliographical survey to
follow.

Moral reflection, then, begins in crisis, in a challenge
to the accepted way of thinking about the world and human
action. Modernity has raised six such crises. The first
occurs because science and technology have blurred the distinction between nature and culture. Human beings are able
to intervene in the natural order and dramatically alter the
course of natural processes. Science, since the seventeenth
century, has become humanity's tool for the manipulation of
the natural environment and even more significantly of human
beings themselves. This ability to control and alter nature
challenges modern people to define the limits of their
interference in nature. The problem remains the same
whether that interference involves the creative process of
stimulating birth or continuing life or the opposite process
of termination of life, whether fetal or adult. While
traditionalists of various types often regard the world as a
fixed natural order with which human beings should not tam-
per, the distinction between natural processes and human
intervention into them has become very difficult to make.
This crisis can be called the crisis of biomorality, challenging people to rethink the meaning of life and death, of
birth and conception, of the medical profession itself.

A second and related crisis concerns sexual roles and
personal identity. In a traditional world a person's bio-
structure determines cultural roles providing fixed tasks
and a clear identity. Modern men and women, however, think
of sexuality as a potential for selfhood to be developed on
their path to forging their own particular life not as their
destiny determining their roles and social status.
Traditional morality, therefore, finds it difficult to cope

with new views of personality that utilize sexuality as only a point of departure for self-realization. Human beings, however, are still social and cultural beings. The exact interplay of cultural role models with the search for personal identity needs definition and exploration.

The individualism characterizing the search for self creates still another crisis: that of the family. For traditional families certain economic, social, and personal advantages are attached to marriage and parenthood. In a modern society social and geographical mobility undermine the social benefits of family life; economic necessity as well as ideological concerns for women's equality render the traditional division of labor in a family untenable, and the quest for a personal, private and individual sense of identity makes the compromises demanded by marriage and parenthood problematic. When the individual person rather than the community becomes central, social institutions such as the family may be perceived as irrelevant.

The three crises discussed so far threaten presuppositions about the outside world, about personal identity, and about community. These three realities have long been symbolized by religious images and rituals. With the demise of the values imaged, the symbols themselves become uncertain. A fourth crisis develops in regard to education, to rituals and symbols, and to the representations of community common within traditional structures. Education can bring a community together or it can separate it from the world at large; modernity poses this problem for any subculture. A fifth crisis can be associated with the modern phenomenon of nationalism. The creation of nation states has introduced questions of national loyalty, responsibility for national government and policy, problems of integrating minority populations, and the relationship of a system of justice to universal human rights. A democratic society exacerbates the questions by making all citizens equally responsible for solving social problems. The crisis of how to shoulder this responsibility represents one of the major challenges of modernity.

The crisis of nationalism includes reference to minority populations. Every nation struggles to reconcile the conflicting minorities within it. At the heart of this struggle is another crisis: that of evaluation. Democracies are predisposed to favor majorities. They attach value to that which appeals to the greatest number. Traditional societies have other standards of evaluation. For them, intrinsic worth, moral rectitude, or cultic proficiency, provide greater benefit to society than does sheer quantity of productivity. Confronting that crisis of evaluation, modern men and women have learned to distrust insular, self-serving, modes of evaluation. For a religious group in particular, that crisis provides an opportunity for greater openness in relationship to others from differing religious communities.

The problem of valuation, however, encompasses more than merely national or intergroup problems. When the worth of a person becomes determined by productivity or achievement, human life loses its sense of inherent value. The success-oriented society threatens a traditional system that judges worth as an intrinsic human quality. The implications of the crisis arising from the new value system extend to how business is carried out and the perception of charity.

These six crises form the backdrop of modern Jewish moral reflection. This introductory survey, drawing upon the data found in the bibliographical survey to follow, will explore how Jews respond to each crisis and what particular moral dilemmas are associated with each.

Before progressing to that survey, however, another question needs to be addressed. This being a study of Jewish morality, the reader is entitled to know in what ways the selections are specifically Judaic. The companion volume to this survey discussed the ingredients in a modern Jewish ethics. These included the two characteristics of recourse to the sources of Jewish learning from the Bible to the present and a confrontation with the ethical challenges of modernity. The distinction between ethics and morality was also discussed in that volume: ethics investigates theoretical issues, theology, and the general rules governing decision-making; morality refers to concrete decisions, to practical issues.

This volume investigates certain challenges to Jewish decision-making, chosen because they exemplify the confrontation of normative Jewish thought and modernity. The term "normative Jewish thought" is taken to refer to the halakha, the set of specific and detailed decisions making up Jewish law. Changes in Jewish moral action cannot occur without confronting the traditional law. Differing groups of modern Jews view that confrontation differently; the section on ethics and halakha in the companion to this volume demonstrates the spectrum of possible responses. The Jewish moral stance may still be pieced together from the fragments of Jewish response to the modern situation. A survey of Jewish morality in the modern world can reveal that despite radical divergencies because of competing views of halakha, a pattern of Jewish moral action can still be discerned. Basic to the morality of the halakha is a two-fold concern: for the preservation of life and for its enhancement.

At first glance these two principles seem straightforward and uncomplicated. On closer inspection, however, both refer to an entire complex of ideas, to a hierarchy of values. The dimensions of Jewish morality in the modern world can be charted by noting the way these complex value judgments are applied to specific situations. The imperative to preserve life, for example, cannot be taken in a simplistic way. On the most basic level, life refers to all created beings. According to Judaism each living being

gives praise to God and fits into the divine scheme; therefore it is precious and must be respected. At the same time
it is clear that choices between one living being and another are constantly being demanded. When confronted with
such choices, the Jewish tradition modifies its basic principle. While all life is sacred, an adult human life takes
precedence over all other forms of life.

Such a view has far reaching implications. One example is
that of the choice between saving the life of a fetus and
that of an adult human being. This view suggests a certain
attitude to political problems, especially to the problem of
war and to social and economic dilemmas as well. The sanctity of personhood can be a principle used to cope with the
crisis of evaluation, providing both openness to others and
a standard for judgment.

While concern for human life provides a certain universalism, Judaism also recognizes that among human beings, distinctions can still be made. Self-protection offers one
clear case in which the life of one person, that of the
intended victim, takes precedence over that of another, the
attacker. War and the problem of acceptable or unacceptable
targets offers another case in which distinctions are often
made. The battlefield situation itself is an extreme example of a circumstance in which one must decide which victim
to treat and which to leave untreated. In a world of scarce
resources, however, such decisions must be made daily even
in the most peaceful of settings.

Jewish tradition has not hesitated in the past to make the
distinctions needed for such decisions. Jews have been told
that they have a primary obligation to preserve the Jewish
people, to continue the life of the community of Israel.
The imperative to preserve life extends beyond respect for
all living creatures or even reverence for human life; it
includes a specific injunction to work for the survival of
Jewry, of Jewish religion, and for the distinctive society
which Jews envision.

While Jewish peoplehood is a central moral category, the
Jewish individual is the basic component of that envisioned
Jewish society. The overriding imperative is that of pro-
tecting each Jewish individual. The preservation of life in
general, of human life in particular, of the life of the
Jewish community, can be set aside for the saving of the
life of an individual Jew. The various moral questions
related to the saving of life--choosing between the advancement of science and the risk of surviving an operation,
choosing between the life of a fetus and the life of a
mother, choosing between political capitulation and the
waging of war--bring this hierarchy of concerns about life
into sharp focus. Despite the uniformity of Jewish thinking
in this regard division still characterizes Jewish moral
decisions. Jews conflict in controversy over the hierarchy
of life and the nature of particular choices.

While the saving of life is always primary in Jewish morality, the enhancement of life is equally valued. The second moral imperative in Judaism is the enhancement of the quality of life. This additional moral imperative brings a radical perspective to Jewish morality. Judaism denies that any act is morally neutral: an act can either enhance or degrade human life, it is never insignificant. Thus Jewish morality compels thoughtfulness before every deed. One chooses not only between life and death but between the good and the better, between the bad and the worse, in every action. While decisions may often involve questions of life and death, they are more often concerned with choices between alternative ways of enhancing life.

How can Jews determine what enhances and what does not enhance life. Two alternatives are possible. The first looks to an absolute yardstick, an ideal pattern of what life should be like. For many Jews, traditional Jewish law, the halakha provides that yardstick. Detailed legal decisions guide Jews in their specific actions and suggest the ideal life, in the name of which an act is to be performed or avoided. Other Jews, however, find halakha to be an imperfect vision of the ideal life. They use modern culture as a tool, drawing from it inspiration and guidance in their evaluation of what is or is not life-enhancing. Naturally, the latter often diverge from the former in their moral choices. The former group, however, tends to be no less fragmented than the latter. The exact application of halakha to a modern problem can be tricky. Traditional interpreters of Judaism often disagree. While, as in the case of the first principle, most Jews agree with the general value (the enhancement of life), they differ as to how that principle should be applied in specific cases.

The two principles of Jewish morality can be applied to the six crises mentioned earlier. The crisis of medical science directly confronts the principle of the preservation of life. Jews apply that principle when seeking solutions to questions of medical morality and the professionalism of the physician, when advocating the duty of healing and of seeking healing, when making decisions concerning abortion, artificial insemination, and euthanasia. The principle of the enhancement of life, however, is equally applicable, especially to decisions concerning genetic engineering, hazardous medical operations, and the use of addictive substances (narcotics, alcohol). The crisis of sexuality can be approached from the standpoint of its implications for the preservation of the human species--both feminism and Gay Liberation might seem to imperil that value. The same crisis, however, can be approached from the standpoint of the enhancement of life and the ways in which human self-fulfillment depends upon sexual self-satisfaction.

The crisis of the family focuses attention on the interplay of individualism and the community. Without community, the continuity of life, and perhaps even its survival,

would be impossible.   Without freedom for the individual,
without allowing for solitude and privacy in the midst of
the family, the essential quality of human life may well be
threatened.   Intermarriage and divorce express the individual's needs in contrast to the concerns of society.   Can
the value of the enhancement of personal life be applied   in
these   cases while retaining the family as the basis for the
preservation of the life of the Jewish people itself?

    The   symbols and rituals of Judaism emphasize   traditional
values; these often conflict with the openness of modernity.
The   crises of sexuality and the family are closely   related
to   Jewish   questioning of their   ritual system.   No less
problematic   is Jewish education,   its intent and its   form.
Traditionally, Jewish education focuses on the internal concerns   of the Jewish people and on the parochial history   as
well as literature of the Jews.   Is Jewish life enhanced by
this separatism? Might not a more open acceptance of general
culture   be   appropriate?   On   the other hand might   not   a
Jewish   acceptance of general education be signing   a   death
warrant for Judaism?   Jewish education raises the problem of
enhancing   the life of a subcommunity without alienating   it
from   the general community.   Associated with education are
the ideals it imparts, particularly the ideal of truth.

    The moral implications of this debate extend beyond educa-
tion to every sphere of Jewish ritual observance and symbolism.   While the morality of religious images and ceremonies
may seem a strange topic,   it takes on relevance when understood   as   questioning whether those images   or   ceremonies
enhance life or not and of whether changing them   threatens
the   existence of the religion in question.   One central
moral   problem concerns determining whether traditional ways
of   observance are inherently discriminatory and   need
changing.   A second moral issue,   however,   focuses on   the
question of Jewish survival.   Some Jews argue that changing
ritual life defeats the purpose of Jewish religion entirely.
They claim that the introduction of female rabbis, inclusive
worship   (with men and women worshipping together),   and new
modes of expressing Jewish values threatens   the   continued
existence of Jewish religion.   The question has urgent relevance in the modern State of Israel since,   as it seeks   to
create a Jewish state,   it must resolve the dilemma of impo-
sing   a traditionalism on secularists or abandoning its particular mission.

    Another threat to the survival of Jewish religion and   to
the way in which religion enhances human life comes from the
society   at large and its view of death and aging.   Modern
society   has placed a premium on youth.   Judaism,   both by
symbol and religious law, values the experience of the aged.
Jewish moral thinkers have sought to reestablish traditional
priorities by reviving Jewish views concerning the aged.
The   elderly are often shunted to the margins of society.
Death and dying are relegated outside of the communal boun-
daries as well.   Jewish thinkers emphasize the inherent value

in every person's life and the importance of community for
the enhancement of every life. By focusing on the rituals
of mourning, many thinkers demonstrate how a moral concern
for life and its enhancement can integrate aging, death, and
the cycle of life itself.

Social awareness, represented by the rituals and symbols
surrounding aging and mourning, brings with it responsibilities. Community enhances life and must be valued; communal
duties, however, often bring with them obligations that
conflict either directly or indirectly with one of the two
major moral principles. Nationalism or political ideology
can lead to human conflict; whether Jewish survival depends
upon supporting one political view or another can be debated. The outcome of that debate may determine the morality of a particular political choice. Jewish views on the
issues of interracial relationships and on war and peace
divide over just this question of whether Jewish survival is
at stake or not. The general question of whether certain
forms of justice enhance or detract from life, on whether
certain policies in the State of Israel can be justified as
either preserving or enhancing life, occasions much discussion among Jewish moral thinkers. The scope of Jewish
political concern, it must be mentioned, has widened beyond
either a parochial focus on the State of Israel or on the
fate of Jews in various nations to include that of human
rights throughout the world wherever they are endangered.

Naturally Jews differ in their response to various political problems. Religious Jews differ on the political implications of their Jewish commitment. Not only in the Diaspora but even more strikingly in Israel, Jewish politics
presents a picture of competing perspectives. Sometimes
Jews see their religious tradition as essentially liberal,
sometimes as conservative. These varying self-definitions
impinge upon practical matters such as the relationship
between Jews and other minority groups (in particular,
American blacks and Israeli Arabs), upon Jewish response to
war (whether in the United States or in Israel), and the
demands for a just society and an equitable legal system.
What remains is a commitment to political action as one tool
in creating an environment for the preservation and enhancement of life.

Human life is inherently valuable, according to the view
of Jewish morality. Modern business life threatens that
assumption by assigning value based upon the market worth of
an individual's work or product. Modern Jewish thinkers
seek to reestablish the traditional mode of valuation by
challenging modern business thinking and reminding Jews of
obligations to the poor. Another implication of this
approach has been an emphasis on truthfulness, economically
in terms of advertising and personally in terms of everyday
living. This attempt to restore the human individual as the
center of value has implications beyond the economic sphere,
shaping the Jewish approach to non-Jews. Thus when human

has supreme value, external differences between persons appear less significant. Modern Jewish morality has explored relationships between Jews and non-Jews, seeking to discover what duty Jews have to encourage such relationships, to engage in dialogue, and to teach Judaism to those who are not Jewish. A particularly pressing question in this regard has been the role of Jewish proselytism of the non-Jew. While Jews differ in their final conclusions regarding these matters, they nonetheless agree that Jewish morality demands involvement in them.

The crises of modernity can, therefore, be related to Jewish morality and its response to contemporary issues. A study of each set of issues will reveal both the agreement and disagreements that characterize modern Jewish moral thinking. The relationship of modern Jewish morality to the two principles of the preservation of life and its enhancement has just been sketched; the specific themes involved and the differences among Jews remain to be discussed below.

The following discussion draws upon Jewish theological reflection, informed by the halakhic or legal process and by the experiences and observations of students of the Jewish religious community. While this introductory survey, like the bibliographical survey to follow, includes reference to popular journals and sociological studies, its central interest is in Jewish religious morality. The various source material illuminates the way in which Jewish religion understands, copes with, and is challenged by modernity. Many contemporary Jews embrace a secular, ethnic, or cultural Judaism. While their expression of morality has intrinsic significance, the definition of "Jewish" ethics and "Jewish" morality given here excludes their thought from the present analysis. Such a definition should be understood as stipulative, not essential. Traditional Judaism affirms that Jews, even if they stand outside the religious tradition, remain Jews.

MODERN JEWISH BIOMORALITY

Modern science has challenged Jews to reconceive their understanding of life and death, of birth and conception. Five biomoral problems emerge as particularly crucial: first, the interaction between the moral imperative toward life and health and other, often competing, moral values; second, the moral implications of the risks involved in utilizing experimental techniques and scientific knowledge; third, the emotional and attitudinal effect of technology on human beings; fourth, the relative values of adult and fetal life in a world in which both contraception and fertility pills, abortion and artificial insemination, are daily realities; and, finally, the choices between life and death demanded when technology can extend bodily existence by the use of mechanical and scientific devices that render the traditional concepts of death irrelevant.

Jewish tradition unambiguously affirms the necessity for life and health (see entries 001, 003, 004, 006, 007, 013, 014, 019, 020, 022, 025, 026, 030). This unambiguous affirmation, however, is challenged in a number of cases. One such area is that of truth telling to those with a potentially terminal illness (note of course that life itself is terminal). The value of truth is an important one in Jewish morality. Can it be put aside in the case where knowledge of the truth might worsen the condition of a patient? The overwhelming consensus of Jewish thinkers is that withholding the truth is indeed acceptable in such a case (see for example, entries 018, 027, 054, 162, 166, 189, 190).

Another conflict of values occurs concerning the professionalism of the physician. Questions of privacy and confidentiality compete with the necessity for screening to discover carriers of a disease. Physicians have considerable responsibility in traditional Judaism, even though their legal liability is not extensive (their judgment is left to the "hands of heaven"). The obligations incumbent on the physician are balanced by responsibilities of the physician. This balance, however, is changed when the medical practice involved is also a religious precept (for example, ritual circumcision, see entries 010, 012, 015, 017, 023, 029).

The choice between alternatives is not always easy. Judaism demands respect for a corpse. Science, however, uses the dead to advance knowledge and for experimentation. Jewish thinkers often reject the claims of science in this regard considering disrespect for a corpse a powerful attitudinal impetus against respect for human life in general. The value of the primacy of life does not always lead to unambiguous answers (see entries 034, 035, 044, 046, 050, 052, 058, 060, 062, 065 on the use of a corpse and 033, 034, 035, 037, 041, 042, 044, 054, 059, 061, 063, 064, 068, 070 on medical experimentation).

An even more problematic choice is that caused by the lack of resources plaguing modern society. Decisions must be made about who shall live and who shall die. The problem of triage or "life-boat ethics" arises when more potential patients exist than resources to cure them. The Jewish moralist finds two key principles in the tradition to guide such decision-making. The primacy of one's own life is unquestioned. One never has an obligation to save another human at the cost of one's own life (even though the ways of piety and mercy might encourage such an act). The good of society as a whole, however, mitigates the self-centeredness of this principle with responsibility to others. While society may not demand that an individual or individuals sacrifice themselves for the common good, guidelines need to be established for individuals when faced with such difficult choices. The life of the individual gains meaning from being within society, and society must provide the individual with moral help (see in particular entries 011, 013, 016, 024, 043).

Individual pleasure often conflicts with the social good. The individual who chooses to indulge in one or another pleasure may be harming both self and the social order. Jewish morality emphasizes personal health and responsibility to society when making such choices. Debate on the permissibility of smoking and use of narcotics focuses on the putative harm to self and society each involves (see entries 071-082).

The potential conflict between society and the individual is nowhere more evident than in the tension between Jewish feminists and traditional Judaism. The feminist sees her body as her own property; she resents men who tell her that she must bear children, that she cannot choose an abortion, that only certain means of contraception are open to her. While each of these concerns with birth and the prevention of birth has its own moral dimension, the tension between men and women has a moral quality of its own. The moral value of feminine independence and a woman's self-fulfillment together, often oppose the dogmatism of traditional Judaism, its assumption of fundamental values, and, above all, its understanding of the role of women in society. Here, as in the previous question of triage, the common good and the good of the individual conflict. Contemporary Jewish morality suggests that only that society which enhances the life of its members is entitled to require personal sacrifice from them. Naturally, different thinkers diverge in defining what it is that enhances the life of society's female members (see entries 083-154).

The crisis of birth and birth control has arisen because science enables women to control their natural cycle in ways unforeseen in earlier times. The benefits of modern science are often purchased at the price of great risk. Contemporary Jewish moral thought investigates that price to discover under which circumstances the risk may be accepted and when rejected. Hazardous operations are often undertaken for less than pressing reasons. Cosmetic surgery may pander to pride without being medically required. Screening for being a carrier of a disease can be a book to science but also a problem and a risk for the patient. Fetal examination may be dangerous for both the fetus and the mother. While Jewish thinkers agree that the benefit from hazardous operations outweighs the risks, the discussion involves long and complicated argumentation (see entries 033, 035, 041, 048, 050, 061, 063).

Technology as such, without regard for the particular use to which that technology is being put, has presented a challenge to contemporary Jews. Some thinkers contend that using technological techniques to heal human beings or to define human beings undermines a sense of the spiritual, of the image of God expressed by humanity. The patient becomes an object instead of a person, the process of birth becomes a technique not an outgrowth and expression of love between two people, and the individual becomes a pawn in the hands of community.

The experience of Jews with Nazi technology and experimentation cannot be forgotten. Jewish morality cautiously
questions human creativity lest it be used irresponsibly
today as it was once before. A number of interrelated
questions arise from questioning scientific experimentation.
The moral problem of using human beings for experimentation
becomes critical when the benefit is only putative and
uncertain. Should individuals sacrifice themselves for a
possible good for others? The good of society may represent
a valuable and worthwhile rationale for risk-taking, but it
may also be an unjustifiable endangering of the self.
Jewish reflection on this subject shows ambivalence about
the usefulness of both asking for volunteers and for volun-
teering to engage in such experimentation (see entries 028,
041, 043, 045, 061, 063).

One of the most experimental and technologically threatening areas of science for Jewish morality is that of
birth. Science has enabled families to decide how many
children they wish to have, when they wish to have them,
and to examine the fetus for genetic defects. Families
formerly sterile can find artificial means of conception;
men and women can become voluntarily sterile. The blessings and the curses of technology become painfully obvious
when dealing with the process of birth (see entries 083-
102, 140-154).

Traditional Jewish morality considers the life of the
species and the life of the individual to be of utmost
importance. The first commandment that Jews find in the
Bible is that of propagation of the species (see entries
100, 102, 211). While feminists sometimes chafe at this
concern (see Frank, 098), the consensus of Jewish male
scholars is that Jewish fertility is the key to Jewish
survival. Because many families have physical impediments
to bearing children, the advances of science can be hailed
as an important benefit for Jews (see entry 099).

At the same time, many Jews are wary of technology when
it interferes with the natural process, even for the
seemingly positive purpose of enabling Jews to fulfill this
commandment. Artificial insemination, host mothers, and the
transplanted ovum create special problems from a Jewish
standpoint. Life alone is but the raw material; the meaning
of life lies in shaping it according to the divine decree.
Jewish law permits sexual intercourse only when certain
strict regulations and requirements are fulfilled, requirements that extend to a definition of feminine purity and a
prohibition against a man's "wasting semen." This view of
licit sexuality raises questions about artificial generation
or gestation. The host mother as well as the biological
mother, have moral rights; the institution of motherhood
itself seems in jeopardy by the artificial process. Jewish
scholars feel impelled to raise questions about the benefits
of scientifically induced births. While they are not
unambivalently opposed to such techniques, they demand a

serious study of the details involved. The creation of
children is not an end in itself, and Jewish morality insists that the true end of life--the fulfillment of God's
commands--be a restrictive force in even the most positive
of scientific discoveries (see entries 140-154).

If Jewish thinkers are uneasy about artificial means of
initiating fetal life, they are even more disturbed at the
prospect of interrupting that life. The Talmud discusses
contraception in terms derived from the scientific theories
of its time. No Jewish thinker denies that when a woman's
health is in danger, contraceptives are allowed. Jewish
law, however, restricts the nature of allowable contraceptives. The obligation for propagation of the species falls
upon the man; any device that interferes with the male
sexual act is suspect as both deviating from this obligation
and as an intentional wasting of seed. Women, as well,
cannot use all forms of contraceptives since mutilation of
the body is forbidden. Again, in accordance with the basic
principle advocating health and life, sterilization done to
save a life--in the case of a cancerous growth, for
example--is permitted by all authorities (see the discussions in entries 083-097).

Traditional Jewish leaders oppose contraception since they
claim that people become morally insensitive if they
conceive of their offspring in materialistic terms. This
same concern extends into the discussion of abortion. Certainly biblical precedent, as most Jewish thinkers admit,
distinguishes between fetal life and the life of a human
adult. In this way Judaism should be distinguished from
other religions, for example, Roman Catholicism. Jews do
admit a hierarchy of life in which the life of an adult Jew
is more precious than fetal life. Interestingly, while Jews
are permitted abortions in life-threatening cases, a strict
interpretation of Jewish law could imply that non-Jews are
not entitled to such abortions. Despite the permissiveness
in the tradition for Jewish abortions, however, most Jewish
thinkers treat this leniency gingerly. While admitting that
sometimes psychological as well as physical danger to the
mother justifies abortion, they call for caution.

Debate on the morality of abortion is particularly instructive for this study since the distinction between Reform, Orthodox, and Conservative thinkers lies clearly less
in their official affiliation than in their reading of the
facts of the case--what is truly danger to the mother and
what abortions are only due to the whim of the moment?
Different Orthodox thinkers, as J. David Bleich clearly
shows (entries 103-105), utilize the principles of life and
life enhancement to come to different conclusions in similar
cases. Bleich notes the variety of factors that Jewish law
considers before permitting an abortion. His discussion of
the possibility of aborting a fetus shown to have Tay-Sachs
disease demonstrates the complexity with which Orthodox
rabbis debate when and under what circumstances a fetus may
be aborted.

Reform Judaism's moral thinkers show an equal caution when approaching the subject. While some thinkers advocate the prohibition against abortion, arguing that the law only gives the "right to do wrong" but that religion should discourage people from using that right, others find the needs of the mother so pressing as to be primary (note the exchange of ideas in entries 106, 107, 126, 137). Solomon Freehof, an exponent of Reform Jewish moral thinking on these issues, writes with clear ambiguity (entry 116). While admitting the lower status of the fetus and the primacy of the mother's life, he decries any permission for wanton destruction of life. With regard to governmental legislation, Reform advocates that the woman be given the right to her own choice. This view must be put into the proper context. Reform leaders trust the intuition of the woman. The facts of the case--whether a woman's life is in danger or whether she is merely following a prudential whim--are left to the woman herself. Unlike the Orthodox who seek an independent assessment of the facts and who are suspicious that people pander to themselves, Reform leaders take individual decision-making seriously. While agreeing with the Orthodox that an abortion is warranted only in the most serious of cases, these thinkers tend to allow the participants in the decision-making process to decide upon its seriousness.

The spectrum of ideas found among both Orthodox and Reform Jewish thinkers about abortion is also found among Conservative Jews (see entries 067, 114, 115, 117, 123, 124, 128). Seymour Siegel, however, provides unique insight into this approach when studying whether fetal experimentation is permitted (entry 067). His introduction to this essay emphasizes that one must take very seriously the reservations of those who consider feticide murder. The views of these people should be taken into account since Judaism has a "bias for life" that does not end with a bias for adult Jewish life. This willingness to listen to a variety of authorities continues throughout the essay in which Siegel points to the views held by the parents, the physician, and the researcher as well as by Jewish authorities.

A discussion of abortion cannot conclude without mentioning the perspective of women. As primary participants they are most directly affected by any moral decision concerning abortion. The concern of Jewish moral thinking has been with both the seriousness with which women should approach the question and the seriousness with which women take the Jewish concern with life. An interesting variation on this theme comes in the essay by Annette Daum (entry 111) which claims that Orthodox Judaism has as high a stake in the abortion debate as do women themselves. If Orthodoxy aligns itself with an inflexible opposition to abortion, she avers, it will have betrayed Judaism itself. By not taking the needs of women seriously it will have undermined its religious seriousness (see entry 119).

The same problems with technology and its relationship to the Jewish concern for life raised by questions of birth, contraception, and abortion reoccur in connection with death, most particularly in connection with euthanasia (literally, beautiful death). The double burden of technology--its ability to keep the dying alive longer and its threat of identifying death more easily--is clearly apparent in Jewish thinking. The bimoral question of when the primacy of life should be set aside for the sake of other considerations is raised with particular poignancy in connection with euthanasia. The Jewish tradition has an ambivalent attitude that is more complex than would appear at first glance. While no active steps to promote death may be taken, the removal of obstacles to dying is sometimes permitted. Again, as in earlier cases, Jews do not disagree concerning the principle involved. Disagreement arises when Jews seek to determine the exact definition of what is passive or what is active, what is removing an obstacle and what is hastening death, and of who decides difficult cases (see entries 156, 157, 160, 161, 164, 166, 168-172, 174, 177, 179-182, 185, 186, 191, 192).

Traditional Jewish law considers it crucial to determine the exact criteria to guide decisions concerning organ transplantations and the continuance or termination of treatment. The concept of "brain death" in contrast to cessation of the heart beat occasions much debate among traditional and Conservative Jewish thinkers. As technology extends bodily functions, the question of whether that extension should be considered "life" must be answered. The answers given take on added significance because government often seeks to intervene with legislation providing an external definition of the time of death (see entries 155, 158, 159, 165, 167, 173, 176, 184).

Euthanasia or the determination to cease treatment often occurs on the advice of an expert, not on the basis of a decision of the patient. The patient's choice for death, the choice that is for suicide, raises problems because Jewish law forbids such an act. Is it permissible to violate Sabbath law for the sake of a suicide? Judaism, whether interpreted by liberals, conservatives, or traditionalists, seems to emphasize compassion for life over Jewish ritualism in this case (see entries 157, 175, 178, 180, 183, 187). Respect for human life includes respect for one's own life.

Respect for life, however, may involve difficult questions over whose life is respected. The transplantation of organs from the dying to the living raises complex problems of priority. The legitimacy of "brain death" would permit a rapid transplant of organs; respect for the humanity of the dying and of a corpse protects against such haste. Traditional Jews are less likely to permit the desecration of a corpse for the sake of of the living; liberal Jews are more likely to push the time of death earlier to enable the

the transplantation of vital organs. While no Jewish thinker would argue that the dying must sacrifice their lives for others, disagreement centers on the criteria of death and of the meaning given to respect for human dignity. The corpse is understood in Judaism to remain a symbol of humanity. It must be treated with respect. The essential point of Jewish laws concerning the treatment of dead bodies is to insure such respect. In Israel considerable controversy has arisen over the practice of autopsies. Many traditional Jews consider such a practice anathema to the dignity that must be afforded to a human corpse. The central conflict focuses on whether the potential benefit derived from studying a corpse outweighs the desecration involved in its mutilation. The nature of that putative benefit, whether to society, to certain individuals, or to humanity as a whole, requires detailed study before any final determination can be given. Whether the question is one of transplantation or autopsy Jewish morality asks whether the possible enhancement of human life in the future is worth the desecration of a symbol of life here and now (see entries 038, 039, 044, 046, 048-053, 058, 060, 062, 065, 542, 551).

SEXUAL MORALITY

Not only science but social and cultural forces challenge Jews to rethink their self-image and their morality. Birth and procreation, traditionally controlled by a tight familial morality, have become the province of the individual. More importantly, Jewish men and women have learned to understand themselves less through their biological fate than through choices they make about themselves. Personal identity and sexual choices in the modern world grow out of the individual's struggle toward selfhood. Jewish thinkers, both traditional and non-traditional, have been compelled to take account of this phenomenon, even when they disapprove of it. The general conflict occurs between the individual who seeks an enhancement of personal life and the religious community that feels its corporate existence is endangered. Specific problems can be superficially related to three different types of questions arising from sexuality and family life. The first problem arises when values clash. Modern views of sexuality threaten the traditional understanding of sexual morality as the learning of self-discipline. While traditional writers reaffirm that the purpose of human life is self-restraint, that human fulfillment comes only through gaining control over the wayward impulses of sexuality, and that marriage is the only appropriate context for the expression of sexual intimacy (see entries 197, 203-207, 210, 213, 214), other Jewish thinkers affirm a more creative approach to human sexuality. Some present a review the strengths and weaknesses of sexual options (see Borowitz, 194); others mediate between culture and tradition (see Gordis, 201; Green, 202; Matt, 208). Others suggest their own response to the crisis of contemporary sexuality (Elkins, 196; Friedman, 200).

Because of the competing value systems suggesting contra-
dictory ways of expressing human sexuality , a number of
Jewish writers confront the problem of sexual education. In
the controversy of where such education should be given,
Orthodox Jews often affirm that the Jewish day school provides the best environment. Jewish learning embraces every
aspect of human existence; Torah demands knowledge of even
the most intimate of human behavior (see Lamm, 207). Traditional leaders also acknowledge the need for counseling on
sexual matters (Tendler, 215). Perhaps the most extraordinary approach is that of Steinberg (214) suggesting that
Judaism utilizes the wayward impulse and strives after the
golden mean through educating people how to channel their
sexuality creatively.

Sexuality presents a problem for Judaism not only because
modern values conflict with traditional ones. The increased
self-awareness of Jewish men and women often makes them
impatient with traditional sexual roles assigned by Jewish
law. Modern individuals define themselves by their contributions to human life as a whole, not merely by their biological contributions. The symbols of productivity assigned
to men and women by the tradition seem to clash with the new
identities Jewish individuals have forged for themselves.
Armed with a new self-confidence in their sexual identity,
dismayed by their exclusion from the general power structure, and restless with what appears an antiquated value
system, many Jews reject the sexual definitions given in
traditional Judaism. They challenge the truthfulness of
Judaism's construction of the world. Thus Jewish feminists
and homosexuals charge traditional Jewish life with an au-
thoritarian and discriminatory policy. Both demand that
Judaism be more responsive to their needs and include them
in their power structure.

Jewish feminists raise a number of important challenges
to traditional Judaism. In the first place they demand
recognition in their own right. The very titles of some of
the articles--"The Jew Who Wasn't There" (Adler, 216), "Can
a Woman be a Jew" (Brin, 224), "Time for a Change" (Gendler,
236), "Conflict in Identities" (Plaskow, 264)--suggest their
uneasiness and concerns. Jewish women feel excluded from
the very definition of being a Jew. Sometimes their
response takes a nationalistic turn and is combined with
Zionism (217) only to be disappointed by the reality of
discrimination against women in the state of Israel (270,
278). At other times they take a more conciliatory approach
noting that Judaism itself will suffer if it excludes one
half of the creative element it might utilize (see Greenberg, 239-241; Hyman, 245; Ozick, 260). In response Orthodox Jewish men continue to repeat the traditional justification for the separation of the sexes: women have a different
destiny and task; they must accept their place in the divine
scheme, a place that is different but no less important than
that of men (see entries 221, 225, 246, 249, 257, 262).
Even traditional Jewish women reiterate that view (232).

The traditional viewpoint resonates even within the writings of more liberal authors (see Gittelsohn, 237), while
some traditional Jews voice the need for changes (Berkovits,
218; Berman, 219). The Conservative movement, in general,
reflects this tension with some of its members advocating
change in the status of women (entries 222, 231, 238, 242,
258) with others voicing a warning against radical changes
(entries 230, 259, 275, 276). The Reform movement is just
as conflicted. While it boasts the first woman rabbi (see
Preisand, 269), its history has not been exemplary (see
entries 266, 267).

In the midst of this controversy, the real predicament of
Jewish women may become obscured. On the one hand Jewish
males are advocating an extreme modesty for women (see
entries 220, 250). On the other hand life forces them into
the work force and out of a closed society (see entries 226,
235, 268, 271). Feminism itself offers only temporary com-
fort since the anti-Semitism of the movement alienates many
Jewish women (see entries 263, 265, 272). If Judaism can
offer only compendiums of laws written by men (see for
example Ellinson's masterly summaries, entry 229, then women
find themselves trapped with nowhere to turn. The balanced
view of Maurice Friedman (233, 234) suggests an alternative
to either extreme position.

The Jewish homosexual, whether lesbian or Gay--although
Jewish traditional law is harsher on the male homosexual--
faces a different predicament. Jewish response attempts to
be compassionate. Every article written insists that crimi-
nal proceedings against homosexuals are undesirable. At the
same time the alternative views are far from positive. Many
Jewish moralists condemn male homosexuality unconditionally
(see Lamm, 293, for an Orthodox response and Freehof, 287,
for a Reform view). Others define the problem more as
complex including as elements to be considered aspects of
compulsion, disease, and disability within the condition
(see Bar Zev, 284; Feldman, 286; Gordis, 290; Lehrman, 295;
Matt, 298). Only a few Jewish analysts view Gay liberation
as a symbolic challenge to Judaism, demanding a changed
understanding of its values (but note Miller, 300). The Gay
Jewish community, however, creates its own Judaism, a particularly vibrant alternative to the established forms of
Jewish life (see entries 296, 299, 301, 302). The moral
challenge lies not merely in coping with the homosexual
person but with the transformed Judaism evolving from the
homosexual's new self-acceptance.

MORALITY AND THE FAMILY

The clash of values occurring when the enhancement of an
individual's life conflicts with that of the community as a
whole characterizes the crisis of the modern Jewish family.
As individuals seek to express their inward selfhood, they
find the constraints of social behavior, best exemplified by

the restrictions growing out of family arrangements,
intolerable. Ideally,the family can be a context for
personal growth in which an individual discovers how to be
alone in the midst of others, how to be a unique self
through interaction with other selves. In the modern
family, however, personal identity often seems thwarted by
the social demands relayed through the familial structure.

The contemporary Jewish family looks beyond the tradition
to find role models for interaction. New conceptions of
fatherhood, of parent-child relationships, and of familial
responsibilities have arisen from new situations.   Families
must cope with a single parent, with shrinking support from
extended familial ties, with a new ethics on the part of
contemporary youth. These new models for personal development have convinced some thinkers that the Jewish family may
be an endangered institution (see entries 306,   311,   314,
328-330,   336,   343, 344, 348, 352, 356, 357, 360, 366, 368,
372).   One response, raised by traditionalists in a similar
manner to their response to feminism noted above, solves the
dilemma by suggesting that the structure of family life
identified with Orthodox Judaism and the halakha provides
the best model for human development (see entries 317,   335,
339,   346,   349-351,   353, 362, 369). Another response contends that the life of the Jewish single needs to be considered a viable alternative to traditional models of family
life (see entries 309,   354, 372). Creative views of family
structure and of the meaning and purpose of the family add
to the options from which Jews can choose (see entries 328-
331,   371).   The decision about ideal models of the family
has more than theoretical importance; as civil governments
become involved in legislating familial morality, representatives of the Jewish community have been forced to articulate a public stance (see Siegel, 364).

The contemporary Jewish family usually comes into being
through affirming at least the rudiments of social commitment in a ceremony of marriage. That ceremony itself,
however, shows signs of the moral tensions within the Jewish
community.   Couples often demand that the marriage formula
itself be changed to reflect equality between the marriage
partners (325). Many traditional Jews reject the modernized
marriage ceremony, contending that only halakhically valid
marriages are acceptable. Such a view leads to conflict
over which marriages are to be considered binding (see
entries 318, 319, 327, 332, 359, 363, 370). This discussion
demonstrates why marriage cannot be understood as merely an
individual decision. Children may also be victims in these
cases as the number of technical bastards, mamzerim, may
increase because of non-halakhic marriages (see entries 307,
324, 338, 363, 370, 393, 418, 439).

An even more serious challenge to Jewish morality comes
from cases of divorce.   Here personal growth and individual
self-expression threaten the fabric of social life (contrast
the individualism in entries 428, 436, 437, with the social

concern found in entries 416, 426, 429, 432, 440, 447). The
problem for traditional Jews is compounded because of the
detailed legislation concerning divorce and the regulations
to be followed before permitting the woman to remarry.
While Jewish marriage laws are fairly liberal, the laws of
divorce and remarriage are rigorous. At its inception this
rigor provided security and material benefit to the wife;
some would argue that this holds true even today. Because
the civil government, today, holds a coercive legal power to
protect the wife, however, many couples ignore the requirement for a Jewish divorce as well as a secular one. Such a
move, however, will leave the woman unable to remarry.
Traditional Jewish law forbids a woman to remarry unless she
has a valid Jewish divorce. Without an official divorce,
which can be initiated by the husband or by the court but
not by the wife and which must be obtained from the husband
voluntarily, a woman is stranded, often without recourse to
any action. The term used for such a woman is _aguna_, a
woman bound in marriage with no hope for release. Sometimes
a vindictive former husband will refuse to give a Jewish
divorce as a means of harrassing the woman; sometimes such a
divorce is impossible to obtain since the husband may be in
a foreign country or dead.

The condition of the _aguna_ has proven a difficult one to
solve. In Israel, where marriage must be strictly according
to rabbinical law, the problem of the _aguna_ receives considerable attention as a contemporary moral problem (see entries 410, 411, 413, 414, 419-421, 430, 433, 434, 438, 445).
While Orthodox Jews seek a solution to the problem, they
refuse to use drastic measures. They do look for ways of
compelling a divorce or declaring a previous marriage annulled without recourse to drastic alteration in Jewish law
(see entries 409, 412, 413, 414, 419, 420, 430, 441, 443,
446). Conservative Jews have engaged in various strategies
to relieve the condition of the _aguna_. One such tactic
modifies that marriage contract (or _ketuba_) so that it makes
provision for such a situation (see entries 433, 438-440,
444, 447). Orthodox authorities, however, do not recognize
the force of these tactics. Reform Jews ignore the entire
question and accept civil marriages and divorces as legal.
There are two problems in this approach of the Reform movement. The first is that it solves the problem of the _aguna_
by ignoring it. A woman is redefined so that she cannot be
classified as bound in marriage if the secular courts consider her unmarried. That approach may solve the problem for
a few women, but it is not accepted by traditional Jewish
authorities. The second problem is that a Jewish writ of
divorce (_get_) is the requirement for an Orthodox remarriage.
If a woman remarries with a civil divorce but not a _get_,
there are disastrous consequences for the children of that
second marriage (see entry 332). The non-Orthodox claim
that Orthodox leaders utilize Jewish law to gain power for
themselves at the expense of innocent victims. The solution
of Reform, however, does not confront this power-play but
ignores it.

A similar situation of mutual incrimination between traditionalists and non-traditionalists occurs over the question
of Jewish intermarriage with non-Jews (entries 374-408).
While there is no clear division on this issue between
traditionalists and non-traditionalists, the rhetoric often
makes it appear that way.   The actual problem lies in how a
particular author understands reality and the threat to
Judaism.   Some Reform Jewish leaders, it is true, consider
intermarriage a way of strengthening the Jewish people (see
entries 388, 394, 405).   Others from the he Reform movement,
however, condemn it out of hand (entries 390, 402).   Perhaps
the most honest response is that calling the problem a
"Catch-22" (entry 385). Conservative Jews as well vacillate
between compassion for the individuals involved and the
rigorous demand of halakha for endogamy (see entries 374,
396, 399).   Orthodox leaders divide between strident calls
denouncing intermarriage as the consequences of assimilation
(entries 383, 393, 398) and sensitive responses to the
personal needs of the intermarried (entries 384, 386).   Social scientists confuse the moral picture by suggesting that
intermarriage may not be as much of a threat to Jewish
survival as often imagined.   Intermarriage may integrate new
perspectives into the Jewish community (see entries 375,
379, 387, 391, 392, 406).

MORALITY AND JEWISH IMAGES

At first glance it may appear strange that religious
images and rituals should be considered in a survey of
Jewish moral concerns.   While these events bring the
experience of the sacred into human life, they are not often
associated with ethical issues.   From the very beginning of
Jewish life, however, religious symbols and precepts have
pointed to the ethical dimension of human life.   The covenant ceremony, cementing Israel into a religious nation,
included certain moral and ethical precepts as part of an
entire blueprint for human and communal living.   That blueprint expressed concrete values and views of human nature
through rituals and symbols.   The images of Jewish ritual
life have been integrated with the larger program of Jewish
behavior and have, therefore, in the modern period raised
ethical questions that are important for any understanding
of Jewish morality.

Four areas of concern stand out as most important: education of Jewish youth, images of women, images of aging, and
images of human life associated with death and mourning.
These four areas are particularly problematic because the
modern world has challenged the traditional views of Judaism
with regard to them. Education, traditionally conceived, is
both experiential and doctrinaire.   Jewish education serves
to integrate Jewish children into a specific subculture, to
develop their sense of special identity, to equip them with
skills needed to live as a distinct group in the midst of a
majority culture.   Modernity has challenged that idea, demanding Jewish integration into society as a whole.

Two moral dilemmas arise from the crisis in education. The first is the decision whether to demand government support for Jewish parochial education. The moral issue involved is that of whether, either in the United States or in Israel, the common good is served through the creation of separatist schools. The arguments for government aid suggest that all children benefit and the society as a whole improves when parochial education is supported. The arguments against such aid focus on the need for broadening experiences and an inclusive rather than exclusive context for learning. Jewish response to the question of such "parochaid" has been clearly mixed. In America, for example, the initial response was to cherish separation of religion and government as the basis for Jewish acceptance in the non-Jewish society. As that acceptance became second-nature, Jews began to demand that the government support Jewish institutions through funding for Jewish day schools and through tax exemption for Jewish religious bodies (see the historical sketch given in entries 462 and 463). Not every American Jew agreed with this change in direction. The question raised both by those who supported the new approach (entries 453, 454, 460, 489, 494) and by those who opposed it (entries 485, 488, 492) concerns whether such intermixture of Jewish religious life and American federal aims would enhance Jewish life. The argument most often used for supporting federal aid was that the survival of Judaism depends upon Jewish education and that the Jewish day school can survive only with the help of governmental funding (see entries 479, 489). While the commitment to the Jewish day school has been unquestioned by Orthodox Jews and while many Reform Jews still support separation of religious and secular education, Conservative Jews have contested the various options in heated controversy (see entries 471, 473, 483, 485, 488, 489, 491). A similar moral debate took place in Israel as traditional Jews sought to know whether civilian education was permissible to those most involved in religious learning (see entries 496, 497).

A second debate focuses on the ideas and values transmitted through Jewish education and the means of their transmission. A major concern has been the techniques used to transmit Jewish values, with many educators contending that only an experiential approach can provide the in-depth Jewish commitment needed for Jewish survival (entries 449-451, 467-469, 473, 482, 484, 486, 493). Jewish education can be understood as an act of worship (entry 455) and thus as a form of religious living (452). As such, many contend that indoctrination in Jewish values rather than an experience of democratic living is needed (see entries 459, 472, 480, 484). One value that requires investigation is that of honesty and truthfulness. The practical implications of this virtue involve school practice itself (see entry 457), while the theory evokes intricate debate (see entries 461, 470, 474, 477, 481). Another challenge Jewish schools must face involves the child with special learning needs.

Judaism does not, contrary to popular belief, value the intellect above all else. Every individual's life is precious and schools must confront the case of children with special learning requirements (see entries 458, 466, 475, 478). In meeting each of these challenges, Jewish education projects images of value, models of ideal human behavior.

Judaism faces still another demand on its value system. The problems of women and their needs suggest that Judaism may have a false image of human nature. Jewish rituals and symbols tend to be oriented toward males. Jewish women have suggested that without an inclusive structure that opens synagogue boards, the honors of reciting the public blessings before the reading of the Torah (the aliya), or the inclusion of women in the prayer quorum Judaism has betrayed its principles of equality (see entries 498, 500, 501, 502, 504, 524, 527). By rejecting women in these instances, Judaism forfeits an important creative resource in its midst (see entries 503, 508, 509, 511). In recent times the question of whether women may be ordained as rabbis has become a focus for feminist concerns. The Conservative Jewish movement in America, after long and acrimonious debate, finally admitted women into its rabbinical program. The image of a woman as the ideal Jew, as a teacher, a witness, and a decisor of Jewish law seems to many a travesty of traditional Judaism; to others it seems a logical, if belated, expression of Jewish commitment to human equality (see entries 506, 507, 510, 516, 520, 523, 526, 528). How Jews conceive of women reflects their conception of humanity in general; their images of the feminine expose their moral stance on human equality and its religious significance.

Although the oppression of women has received considerable attention, other groups in the population are equally ignored. Modern western society values youth over age. Society often segregates the elderly and places them at the fringes of community life. Jewish moralists, however, insist that treatment of the elderly reflects the way society views the human being generally. Honoring the aged demonstrates a respect for the human person over and above the material contributions that person may make to the economic order. Jewish writers stress the need to respect the aged and to honor their intrinsic worth (see entries 529, 530, 532, 534, 535, 537, 538, 540). Practical problems threatening that honor and respect demand moral response based upon Jewish theory (see entries 533, 536, 541).

The meaning of respect for life can be communicated clearly through symbols and rituals associated with death. Just as behavior toward the elderly articulates a culture's view of the human, so too its manner of coping with dying and its rites of mourning testify to its view of life. Forms of burial and mourning are ways of integrating an affirmation of life even in the presence of death. The morality of such practices, however, depends upon how mourners are treated since they are often victimized by those who minister to them. needs. Jewish moral writers focus on the process of mourning, appropriate signs of mourning, and on the life-orientation entailed by Jewish ritual. This focus helps place the ritual in proper perspective and demonstrate the basic moral principles underlying chief priority. Respect for a corpse, illustrated by Jewish burial rituals, communicates respect for the human person (see entities 542, 543, 545-549, 551, 560, 561, 563). The central prayer of mourning, the Kaddish affirms life, thereby reintegrating the mourner into the community as a whole. Since this prayer can be said only when ten Jews are present (in an Orthodox setting ten men are needed), ritual can be said to create the very community into which the mourner reenters. The measured degrees of mourning provide a further integration into life as a whole according to a graded plan (see entries 544, 550, 552, 554-559, 561, 562, 565, 568-575). Judaism considers the rituals of death and mourning a moral affirmation of life.

MORALITY AND POLITICS

Since modern Jews live in an open society, they insist that civil and political life must be approached from a Jewish standpoint. Issues facing the body politic are judged using the same standards that Jews use when solving problems concerning science, birth, or Jewish rituals, and the same dilemmas arise.

A paradigmatic case involves the nature of Jewish politics altogether. Some thinkers contend that a Jewish politics must be a liberal one. Only the liberal approach, it is argued, enhances life, gives freedom to both the individual and the group, and encourages that integration into modernity that modern life requires. Such a view, although no longer widely spread and a source of bitter controversy within modern Jewry, finds its exponents today (see entries 576, 578, 584, 589, 590, 594, 595, 597, 603, 609, 611, 612, 630, 634, 636). Others argue that not liberalism but only the radical left expresses an authentic Judaic concern with the enhancement of life (see entries 591, 604, 614, 617, 621, 622, 635). Changing Jewish needs have led others to talk either of a new conservatism or of a Judaism beyond any political description (see entries 596, 597, 609, 621, 630). The questions involved focus on the implications of any political stand for the survival of individual Jews, for the preservation of Judaism and the Jewish people.

An important political problem concerns the state of Israel. In so far as it is a "Jewish" state, certain obligations toward traditional religion exist. Their exact nature and meaning must be defined. Orthodox religious groups contend that a "Jewish" state must be one in which time and action is shaped by Jewish tradition. Religious political parties seek legislation to enforce the observance of the

Sabbath   and other Jewish holidays.   The legitimacy of non-
Orthodox Jewish celebrations is denied (see the   discussions
in entries 577,   579, 586-588, 592, 593, 602, 608, 610, 613,
618, 619, 623-628, 633, 638). On one level the argument
appears   to be between freedom of conscience and   religious
dictatorship.   On the other hand, however, it can be argued
that   a   nation exists on the basis of a broad ideology of
consensus.   The Orthodox insist that in Israel that ideology
must be Jewish tradition.   The existence of the state of
Israel as   a Jewish state depends upon fidelity to that
tradition.   In this way religious legislation can be seen to
express the communal will or national identity; as such it
is not in contradiction to freedom of conscience.   The
controversy centering on Meir Kahane and his extremist position demonstrates the problem (see entries 588,   599,   600,
601,   617,   626, 629, 637). Kahane sees clearly that Israel
cannot survive without compromising either its Orthodox view
of Judaism or its commitment to democracy.   Since he refuses
to relinquish the first ideal,   he calls for an end to democracy.   This   extreme position appeals to Israelis   on the
fringes of society and should not be taken as representative
of   mainstream thinking; Kahane,   nevertheless,   provides a
clear example of the tensions within Israeli politics between those supporting a Judaic theocracy and those   advocating freedom of conscience.

One   might think that the question of war answers   itself.
If   the   preservation and enhancement of   life are primary
values,   then war cannot be justified.   Self-defense, however,   has long been recognized as a legitimation of war in
Jewish tradition,   a legitimacy that takes precedence over
all other considerations.   Willingness to die for the   sake
of Jewish ideals is likewise an approved moral choice.   The
debate among Jews about war is exacerbated because different
wars seem to demand different choices: the Arab-Israeli war
is almost unanimously recognized as a fight for survival and
therefore, to some extent, justifiable.

Various wars pursued by other powers, notably the American
involvement in Southeast Asia, seem less justifiable.   Those
who insist upon a pacifist tradition claim that in the
modern world all war, even those that Judaism legitimized in
the past,   are indefensible and immoral (see entries 651,
659,   661, 665, 669, 672).   Other writers legitimize wars on
the basis of their justification in terms of Jewish law (see
entries 640,   643,   645, 646, 656, 658, 662, 664, 673).   The
case of war in Israel presents a special case.   Can pacifism
be justified if it places the very existence of the Jewish
state in danger?   War may be a commandment when the land of
Israel is involved.   Again,   however,   Jews differ.   Some
contend   that   war for the sake of the land of Israel is a
religious commandment (see entries 641,   644, 647, 648, 653,
670).   Others, however, question the morality of an Israeli
war of attrition and trust in God,   not the Israel Defense
Forces,   to   save the Jewish people (see entries 657,   663,
671).

The conflict of perceived interests noted in the question of war is also present when confronting the relationship between Jews and black Americans. Some observers contend that Jews, who traditionally supported blacks in their struggle for equality, have only been hurting themselves. The establishment, by applying the "affirmative action" of numerical guidelines for the hiring of minorities, brings the spectre of "quotas" together with memories of how such quotas excluded Jews in the past. The fears engendered by these memories convince many Jews that they Jews are the victims of the new coalition between American whites and blacks. Others disagree and find that anything that enhances the life of any group within America enhances the life of all. From this perspective Jews, even at the expense of their own security, should support the efforts of blacks to gain equality (see entries 674-679).

Jews have contested the value of capital punishment from the earliest debates in the talmudic period when Rabbi Akiva declared that a court that sentenced a person to death once in seventy years was "blood thirsty," and his colleague Rabban Gamliel responded that if such were the case the world would be overrun with murderers. Jews disagree over the correct way to punish criminals and to have a safe and just penal code. The question of what is just punishment and what is torture cannot be answered easily. Jews refer to their classical texts, but defining what type of penal legislation enhances life cannot be neatly answered. The division among Jews on this issue reflects a division on the facts of the case, on the efficacy of different forms of punishment, and on the effectiveness of rehabilitation. The current discussions focus on capital punishment but range in content and scope through the entire spectrum of issues concerned with the justice of the judicial process (see entries 698-711).

Jews have an overriding concern for the preservation of human rights and have focused their attention on two issues in contemporary Jewish life: concern for human rights for Jews in the Soviet Union and concern for Arab minority rights in the land of Israel. There is unanimity among Jews of all denominations in each case. Traditionalists and liberal Jews agree that Soviet Jewry must be at the center of the contemporary agenda of Jewish concern. The tactics used to ameliorate the condition of Soviet Jewry has elicited some debate (although the organized Jewish community has unanimously rejected terrorism and violence), but rallies and demonstrations for Soviet Jews have united world Jewry as no other issue. Jewish moral writers claim that the example of Jews seeking their freedom, gaining their rights for free expression of religion and for emigration has inspired others in the Soviet Union to seek their rights as well. The moral outrage occasioned by the discrimination against Soviet Jews serves to stimulate a moral questioning of Soviet policy generally (see entries 712-716, 719-721, 723, 724, 730).

Modern Jews agree that the non-Jewish minority in the
state of Israel must be granted complete rights. While
human rights issues in Israel exist, they are placed in the
perspective of a country at war. Traditional Jewish moralists in Israel have defined the rights of non-Jews in broad,
liberal terms, although important exceptions do exist to
test this rule (see particularly the writing of Meir Kahane
in entries 599, 600, but note that he is not widely accepted
among Israeli moral thinkers). This liberal attitude demonstrates a commitment to enhancing life even when confronted
with tremendous obstacles (see entries 717, 718, 722, 725).

THE MORALITY OF VALUATION

The political sphere demonstrates dramatically the broad
sweep of Jewish moral concern. That concern springs from a
commitment to the value of every human life. Modern western
civilization challenges such a valuation of the human individual. That civilization often rejects those without
money, property, or economic value. Jewish thinkers confront this crisis of valuation on a number of levels. At
the most obvious level, Jewish writers emphasize the needs
of the poor and their importance for society. Sometimes
this emphasis entails restating the basic concerns Judaism
has for the economic well being of all people and insisting
that the poor have a right to sustenance: zedaka (the word
for philanthropy) literally means simple justice, not
charity (see entries 732, 739, 741, 742). Other authors
point to the real practical tasks necessary to help the poor
(entries 733-739, 743-745).

On a less obvious level, the very concept of business and
commerce needs refinement. The purpose of labor, the
morality of business relationships, and the religious dimension of economics should be spelled out so as to provide a
theological foundation for economic life. Jewish law supplies a rich resource of theological and moral material;
some laws are concerned with commercial and economic obligations and with political attitudes (see entries 754, 758,
763, 768, 772, 784). Some laws address the possible conflict between Jewish morality and a successful engagement in
contemporary economic endeavors. The observance of traditional holidays, for example, may entail economic hardship
(see entries 747, 752, 777). The rights of workers together
with the rights of owners as understood in Jewish law restrains each from exploiting the other (see entries 751,
762, 764, 772, 773, 794). Another tricky question concerns
interest (ribit). From the biblical period onward, the
charging of interest (ribit) has been strictly governed and
regulated. Such regulation, today, raises questions of the
halakhic legitimacy of such enterprises as savings banks,
interest-bearing checking accounts, and perhaps most importantly, home mortgage loans. The solution has often been in
the creation of a legal fiction of partnership through a
document called a hetter iska. The moral dimension of

contemporary banking and finance has often become, for the Jew, a discussion of that document and how it should be utilized (see entries 750, 783, 786, 788). The morality of enhancing personal life at the expense of others is a central principle involved in this debate. Two other areas of conflict between private gain and public morality are hotly debated--gambling as a means of raising revenue for a worthy cause (see entries 755, 759, 760, 770) and general honesty in advertising, competition, and general sales presentations (see entries 751, 754, 761, 762, 779, 782, 786, 787, 791, 792).

Beyond these two fairly obvious areas of valuation, Jewish theory includes the valuing of non-Jews. To view worth in terms of the groups to which an individual belongs demonstrates the most obvious type of prejudice. Jews confront this prejudice in themselves and seek new ways to share themselves with others and to learn from non-Jews. Interaction with the non-Jew has opened new doors for Jews, but has also established new challenges. An ancient dictum preventing the Jew from doing anything to benefit the non-Jew has been reinterpreted and so limited as to be nonapplicable to the modern world (see entry 817). A more difficult problem to solve has been that of Jewish exclusivity. Jewish tradition prohibits teaching Torah to the non-Jew. While some contemporary Jewish thinkers find this prohibition morally repugnant, others defend its importance in preserving Jewish life. The question turns out to be whether Jews feel that their corporate life is threatened by interfaith dialogue and teaching or whether they feel that that life is enhanced. Those who support dialogue and teaching Torah to the non-Jew emphasize the ecumenicity of the modern world. While the non-Jew has not entirely forsaken anti-Semitism, the signs are hopeful for its future eradication (see entries 799, 800, 802, 807, 808, 811, 816). This hopefulness, however, is mixed with a certain wariness (see entries 796, 797, 805, 814, 815, 818). These cautious thinkers recall the history of anti-Semitism and the reluctance of non-Jews to support the State of Israel or other specifically Jewish concerns. They feel that Jewish life is not enhanced by interfaith dialogue and may even be endangered by it.

This volume concludes by surveying the recent debate on Jewish proselytism (entries 819-840). From the frankly pragmatic views of Peter Berger (821) to the lyrical evocation of traditional Orthodoxy's welcome to the convert (832 and 840), a new energy motivates Jewish conversionary activity. The moral question rests on two points: does conversion represent a voluntary, informed decision (see entries 819, 822, 825, 827, 831, 833, 836, 837, 838), and are conversions done by non-Orthodox rabbis valid (see entries 820, 823, 824, 826, 829, 835, 839). While the latter problem would seem to divide Jews along denominational lines, the moral dilemma remains the same. How are proselytes evaluated? While not disputing value of every human being, Jews debate whether conversion to Judaism should be encouraged for its own sake.

CONCLUSIONS

Jewish morality faces concerns that extend from birth to death. The connecting link between these various concerns is their focus on life and its enhancement. Modern human beings face many difficult dilemmas presented to them by science and technology, by sexuality and its contemporary expression, by the challenges to family life and to religious observance that modernity offers, by an open society that places interpersonal relationships in an ecumenical setting and that conveys political responsibility to general citizens, by a process of aging and confrontation with death that requires a rethinking of older traditions. Jews select from those challenges the dilemmas that focus on life and the choices that must be made in order to enhance life. Whether the dilemma arises from new scientific discoveries or the politics of war and peace Jews reduce the basic issue to a choice between life and death, or between life's enhancement or degeneracy. Individual Jews differ on their final decisions; often such differences cut across the lines dividing Reform, Conservative, or Orthodox Jews. Jewish agreement comes in the agenda of issues to be decided, in the process of moral decision-making, and in the principles used to make the decision. Beyond this area of agreement the variety and division are considerable and instructive.

This selected and annotated bibliography offers a critical guide to both the considerable division and the equally significant agreement of Jewish moral thinkers on the issues discussed above. It is hoped that the reader will be able to trace the trends and patterns of Jewish moral deliberation through this bibliographical survey and build upon it a better understanding both of contemporary Jewish morality and of the tradition that informs it.

Bibliographical Survey

1
Jewish Biomorality

BIOMORALITY

1 Abraham, Abraham S. <u>Medical Halacha for Everyone</u>
New York: Feldheim, 1980.

Abraham defines the needs of the sick, discusses the duty of
seeking and giving medical care, considers conflicting medical advice, and reviews the variety of cases in which Jewish
law impinges on medical concerns (including marriage, birth,
contraception, abortion, and death). Like many of the other
general and introductory surveys of Jewish medical morality
(see entries 001, 003, 004, 006, 007, 013, 014, 019, 020,
022, 025, 026, 030) this work compiles information gathered
from a number of sources.

2 Adler, Mark. "Religious Commitment in Medical Practice:
A Jewish Perspective." <u>Yale Journal of Biology and Medicine</u>
49 (1976): 295-300.

Adler uses Jewish law to solve dilemmas arising from euthanasia, abortion and experimentation on human beings. His
approach defends traditional Judaism and its specific direc-
tives as well as its orientation toward life. Compare
Bleich (004, 006), or Rosner (022) and contrast Baruk (003),
Kavesh (020), Siegel (028) or Wolf (031).

3 Baruk, Henri. "La Medecin et La Torah." <u>Revue
d'Histoire de La Medecine Hebraique</u> 138 (1981): 35-39.

Baruk claims that Judaism opposes both idolatry of human
technology and interference with nature and idolatry of
natural instincts that permits no such interference.

4 Bleich, J. David. <u>Judaism and Healing: Halakhic Perspec-
tives</u>. New York: Ktav Publishing House, 1981.

This book summarizes Bleich's review of Jewish morality on
the entire range of health issues including general and
specific concerns. Compare entries 005-007, and 025.

5 Bleich, J. David. "Ethico-Halakhic Considerations in the Practice of Medicine" Dine Israel (1976): 87-135.

Bleich examines questions facing the physician, stresses the primacy of life in Jewish morality, the religious legitimacy of the art of healing and its limitations, and investigates the cases of the moribund patient, hazardous operations, and prayer's relevance in medical decisions.

6 Bleich, J. David. "Medical Questions." In his Contemporary Halakhic Problems 2, 54-56. The Library of Jewish Law and Ethics, 10. New York: Ktav Publishing House, 1983.

Bleich has compiled here and in a similar chapter in his Contemporary Halakhic Problems (The Library of Jewish Law and Ethics, 4.   New York: Ktav Publishing House, 1977, 93-96) a number of reflections on moral issues in medical practice and summaries of rabbinical decisions on them.

7 Bleich, J. David. "The Obligation to Heal in the Judaic Tradition: A Comparative Analysis." In Decision Making and the Defective Newborn, edited by Chester A. Swinyard, 512-561. Springfield, Illinois: Charles C. Thomas, 1978).

This essay, reprinted in entry 025 surveys Anglo-American law in the context of Jewish values and finds the latter distinguished by an emphasis on the primacy of life.   It considers the importance of prayer in the healing process, the acceptability of hazardous medical procedures, and the need for a religious ethics to guide contemporary society.

8 Bleich, J. David. "Physicians' Fees." In his Contemporary Halakhic Problems 2, 68-74.   The Library of Jewish Law and Ethics, 10. New York: Ktav Publishing House, 1983.

This essay, reprinted from Tradition 19 (1981): 354-358, focuses on the obligation of treating patients, with special regard to the obligations of the physician (the physician's responsibility to heal and the patient's duty to seek out a physician for healing is also a central concern in other studies of the medical profession, see entries 010, 012, 015, 017, 023, 029). Compare Faur (015) on physicians' fees.

9 Bleich J. David. "Physicians' Strike." Tradition 21 (1984): 80-84.

Bleich contends that physician's have a sacred duty to save lives.   Because of this duty they have no right to go on strike.   This view is supported by traditional Jewish sources and argued with particular fervor. Compare the previous essay as well as the one that follows.

10 Bleich, J. David.   "Professional Secrecy." In his Contemporary Halakhic Problems 2, 74-80.   The Library of Jewish Law and Ethics, 10. New York: Ktav Publishing House, 1983.

Bleich notes the biblical obligation against spreading gos-
sip.   Since, however, truth may often be required, the bet
din may compel disclosure.   There are some restrictions on
such compulsion.   Jewish ethics of disclosure, especially in
matters of life and death are complex and intricate.

11   Dichowsky,   Shlomo.   "Rescue and   Treatment: Halakhic
Scales of Priority" [Hebrew].   Dine Israel (1976): 45-66.

Dichowsky reviews priorities between saving the self and
saving the other, remarking on the prohibition against placing oneself in danger, concluding that religion must have a
say in such matters.   The question of priority also includes
deciding which patients are to be treated and which are to
be left untreated.   Compare entries 013, 016, 024, 043.

12 Eliash, Yehiel.   "The Physician in Halacha" [Hebrew].
Sinai 75 (1974): 259-276.

This general work (compare entries 007-009) examines the
imperative for healing found in Jewish writings from the
Bible to the present.   Eliash studies questions   of
physician's fees, qualifications, and authority in questions
of Jewish practice.

13 Elon, Menahem.   "Jewish Law and Modern Medicine."
Israel Law Review 4 (1969): 467-478.

Elon provides a legal background for understanding the Jewish approach to medical ethics, probing questions of medical responsibility, of the physician's duties, of organ
donation and transplantation, and of choosing from among
possible patients the one most likely to be healed. Compare
entries 001, 008, 011.

14 Falk, Zeev W.   "Forensic Medicine in Jewish Law." Dine
Israel 1 (1969): xx-xxx.

In a survey of Jewish medical concerns (comparable to those
indicated in entry 001) Falk examines the historical and
contemporary use of medical knowledge in Jewish legal cases.
He studies its relationship to charges of murder, divorce,
and insanity. Compare his essay "Problems Medicaux Dans Le
Droit Hebraique et Israelien" in Revue D'histoire De La
Medecine Hebraique 24 (1971): 49-51.

15 Faur, Jose.   "The Physician's Fee in Jewish Law"
[Hebrew]. Dine Israel (1976): 79-98.

This essay looks at the physician's responsibility to heal
as a religious obligation and the need for good relationships between the physician and the patient.   The question
of fees must be understood in this regard rather than as a
purely professional matter. Compare Bleich (entry 008).

16 Freehof, Solomon B.   "Choosing Which Patient to Save."
In his Modern Reform Responsa, 203-216. Cincinnati: Hebrew
Union College Press, 1971.

Freehof captures Jewish agonizing over the problem of
triage.   He cites talmudic examples to conclude that the one
who will benefit the most is to be saved.   Compare the way
more traditional authors view the problem of establishing
priorities for treatment in entries 011, 013, 024, 054.

17 Goren, Shlomo.   "The Physician's Responsibility for the
Life of His Patient" [Hebrew]. Dine   Israel (1976): 13-24.

Goren begins by noting the equality and holiness of every
person.   He then focuses on the responsibilities of the
physician to the patient and whether he is commanded or
merely allowed to heal.   After reviewing the physician's
dilemma he concludes that caution must be used in deciding
medical responsibility. Goren, while representing the traditional viewpoint, has an individual approach and should be
compared to other authors discussing the centrality of life
and healing in the items noted in entry 008.

18 Herring, Basil F. "Truth and the Dying Patient." In his
Jewish Ethics and Halakhah For Our Time: Sources and Commen-
tary, 49-66. The Library of Jewish Law and Ethics, 11.
New York: Ktav Publishing House, 1984.

Herring summarizes the biblical and rabbinic sources dealing
with truth telling to the patient.   He recognizes that
concern for mental pain may entail benefiting another without his consent.   He concludes that from the Jewish standpoint a person even in death can be affirming life.On the
dying patient in general see entries 027, 054, 164, 166,
189, 190.

19 Jakobovits, Immanuel. "Medicine and Judaism: An Overview." Assia 4 (1983): 289-310.

Jakobovits, a leading authority on Jewish medical ethics,
summarizes the historical antecedents of Jewish morality.
He cites ancient authority and precedent to emphasize the
duty to preserve life and health, the sanctity of life and
the limits to which one must go to preserve it. Compare the
other works noted in entry 001 and 002.

20 Kavesh, William.   "Medicine." In The Second Jewish
Catalog, edited by Sharon Strassfeld and Michael Strassfeld,
123-150.   Philadelphia: Jewish Publication Society of
America, 1976.

Kavesh investigates the major health issues facing Jews and
examines the problems of dangerous operations, of abortion,
of organ transplants, and of genetic screening.   Contrast
Abraham   (001)   and   Tendler   (030).

21   Roberts,   Hyman J.   "Jewish Perspectives in Medicine: A
Reconstructionist   Appraisal."   The Reconstructionist   46,10
(1981): 15-21.

This   impressionistic essay resembles those of Adler   (002),
Siegel (028),   Wolf (031), or Bokser (041) in its generality
and lack of specificity.   Roberts focuses on general ethical
principles   of respect for the human being,   of concern   for
life   and the seriousness of medical decisions.

22   Rosner, Fred.   Modern Medicine and Jewish Law.
New York: Yeshiva University Press, 1972.

This book contains previously published essays by Rosner   on
healing, cigarette smoking, contraception, abortion, artificial   insemination,   euthanasia,   and   organ   transplants.
Relevant   essays are found in entries 023,   062,   080,   090,
131, 151, 178, 179, 551.

23   Rosner, Fred.   "The Physician and the Patient in Jewish
Law."   Tradition 11 (1971): 55-68.

The question of professionalism in the healing arts and   the
general   Jewish   attitude toward interfering with nature   is
examined   here.   God's role in relationship to   the   physician's   is   raised.   Rosner notes that while God heals   the
physician has an obligation to help another person in   need.
The   patient as well has the obligation to seek out a physician for help.   This essay should be compared to the   items
noted in entry 008.   It is reprinted in entries 025 pp. 45-
55 and 022, pp. 11-24.

24   Rosner, Fred.   "Rationing of Medical Care: The Jewish
View."   Journal of Halacha and Contemporary Society 6 (1983):
21-32.

Rosner   claims that medicine reflects God's distribution   of
resources.   Human beings,   he contends, must take this into
account when establishing medical priorities.   He discusses
the   relevance of religious status,   personal   dignity,   the
choice of which patients should be treated,   the question of
a   patient's curability,   and the physician's obligations to
society   as   well as to   the   individual   patient.   Compare
Dichowsky (011)   and the annotation there.

25   Rosner,   Fred,   and   Bleich,   J. David,   eds.   Jewish
Bioethics.   New York: Sanhedrin Press, 1979.

This anthology addresses bioethics from a   traditional,   Orthodox,   Jewish standpoint.   The articles express a   basic
conservatism   of outlook and are highly weighted toward   the
works   of the two editors.   Some important theoretical studies concerning the ethics of research and behavior   arising
from modern biological technology are included.   See entries
007,   023, 032, 060, 064, 065, 073, 090, 097, 103, 122, 142,
150-152, 158, 160, 177, 178, 551.

26 Schindler, Ruben. "Illness and Recovery: A Jewish Hala-khic Perspective."   Journal of Jewish Communal Service 56 (1980): 129-134.

Schindler surveys the need for communal support and personal relationship with service professionals.   In the process he demonstrates the concern that traditional Jews have note only for healing as such but for the commandment to foster life as a means of fulfillng God's will.

27 Schindler, Ruben. "Truth Telling and Terminal Illness: a Jewish View." Journal of Religion and Health 21 (1982): 42-48.

Schindler holds that if health requires it, the patient should not be told about a terminal condition. He considers the imperative for life the most basic of commandments; even truth must be sacrificed for the sake of even the possibility of increasing life in however small a measure.   Compare the items in entry 018 and 163.

28 Siegel, Seymour. "The Ethical Dilemmas of Modern Medi-cine: A Jewish Approach." United Synagogue Review 29, 2 (1976): 4-5, 30.

Siegel, a major Jewish theologian, presents the problems of medical ethics clearly and popularly. Issues raised include abortion, euthanasia, use of organs from a corpse, and genetic engineering.   He concludes that the most important task is that of educating those who deal with the issues of life and death to be sensitive to the ethical dimension. As a Conservative Jewish thinker he emphasizes both fidelity to the halakhic process and a keen awareness of the modern moral predicament.   Compare his survey to the more tradi-tional ones by Bleich (entries 004-007) Rosner (022) or Tendler (030) and to the more liberal view of Wolf (031). See his extended treatments of specific issues found in entries 067, 184, 185, 212.

29 Silberstein, Arthur J. "Liability of the Physician in Jewish Law." Israel Law Review 10 (1975): 378-388.

Silberstein summarizes talmudic and midrashic views of the physician's duty to heal, of standards of conduct, and of the physician's responsibility for the death of a patient. This traditional approach emphasizes not only the duty to heal but the obligation to take responsibility for per-forming that duty faithfully.   He concludes that, while a physician is not legally liable in Jewish law, God will not waive the responsibility for healing.   Compare the way in which medical responsibility is discussed in the items in entry 008.

30 Tendler, Moshe D. Medical Ethics: A Compendium: Jewish Moral, Ethical, and Religious Principles in Medical Practice 5th ed.   New York: Federation of Jewish Philanthropies, 1981.

This compendium reviews the duty for healing, studies problems relating to Jewish religious observance in hospitals,
moral dilemmas arising from obstetrics, gynecology, circumcision, human sexuality, genetic screening and engineering,
treatment of the critically ill, and the Jewish opposition
to autopsies. An appendix added in 1981 studies issues in
the treating the critically ill. Beyond this general review
Tendler examines specific cases as in entries 096, 189, 190,
and 215.

31 Wolf, Arnold J. "Judaism on Medicine." Yale Journal of
Biology and Medicine 49 (1976): 385-389.

This theological essay, approaching the question of medical
ethics much in the way of Adler (002), Bleich (005), Jakobovits (019) Roberts (021) or Siegel (028), seeks to find the
basic values of Jewish medical ethics and understand them
through investigating particular moral cases. Wolf looks at
specific issues in Jewish medical ethics to derive five
basic principles that guide Jewish moral decision-making in
bioethics: the primacy of life, the assumed harmony of body
and mind, the presupposition that people should be healthy,
and a demythologization of the curing process. He illustrates these principles through specific examples such as
abortion and makes clear the practical as well as theoretical concerns of Jewish medical morality.

EXPERIMENTATION, TRANSPLANTS, AND HAZARDOUS PROCEDURES

32 Bleich, J. David. "Experimentation on Human Subjects."
In Jewish Bioethics, edited by Fred Rosner and J. David
Bleich, 384-386. New York: Sanhedrin Press, 1978.

Since Judaism disapproves of taking unnecessary risks (see
entries 033, 034, 037, 054, 059, 061, 063, 064), Jewish law
is also ambivalent towards experimentation on human beings.
Experimentation is approved only if the benefit outweighs
the risk (note the different views in entries 035, 041, 042,
044, 061, 063, 064, 068, 070. Here Bleich contends that
since human life is an absolute good the chance to save life
must always be taken. The same principle, however, determines that experimentation must be performed with volunteers
and only in extreme situations. Since all human life is
valuable the lives of criminals, prisoners, and defectives
cannot be sacrificed for the sake of other human beings.
Experimentation on animals is given unqualified approval.
Bleich also notes the prohibition against a patient's refusal of medical treatment. This essay provides a good introduction to the problem of experimentation and the more
general one of hazardous medical treatment.

33 Bleich, J. David. "Hazardous Medical Procedures." In
his Contemporary Halakhic Problems 2, 80-84. The Library of
Jewish Law and Ethics, 10. New York: Ktav Publishing House,
1983.

This reproduces Bleich's essay in Tradition 16 (1972): 113-117, and emphasizes that Judaism is a hopeful religion. Because of this hope a limited life span may be jeopardized for the sake of a cure. The question is less that of risk than of medical procedures of the day. The debate on the value of risk noted in the previous entry should be read in connection with this one and the following entry as well.

34 Bleich, J. David. "Induced Labor." In his Contemporary Halakhic Problems 2, 84-86. The Library of Jewish Law and Ethics, 10. New York: Ktav Publishing House, 1983.

In this essay from Tradition 16 (1977): 123-125, Bleich contends that neither the convenience of the physician nor the observance of Jewish laws justifies such a risk to human life. Since induced labor is a risk to life it should not be taken even to sanctify the shabbat. Judaism's concern with the safety of the patient demands that when not required by reasons of health neither caesarean birth nor induced labor should be permitted. Compare entry 059.

35 Bleich, J. David. "Medical Experimentation Upon Severed Organs." In his Contemporary Halakhic Problems, 126-128. The Library of Jewish Law and Ethics, 4. New York: Ktav Publishing House, 1977.

In this essay, reprinted from Tradition 12 (1971): 89-90, Bleich raises the ethical question of defiling a corpse in order to benefit humanity as a whole. He distinguishes sharply between removed organs and a fetus as objects of experimentation. His generally positive attitude toward experimentation for the sake of human progress progress demonstrates the Jewish approval of medicine and his acquiescence to the use of organs if utilized for purposes of scientific study followed by appropriate burial shows the realistic and flexible approach of Judaism to science. The items mentioned in entry 032 are relevant to this essay.

36 Bleich, J. David. "Pituitary Dwarfism." In his Contemporary Halakhic Problems 2, 64-68. The Library of Jewish Law and Ethics, 10. New York: Ktav Publishing House, 1984.

Bleich rehearses the prohibition against making use of a cadaver. He notes that, in this case, elements are used as catalysts and not as essential parts of the cure. In that case, respect for the dead may be consistent with the use of material from a corpse. Compare entries 034, 035, 044, 046, 050, 052, 058, 060, 062, 065. This essay appeared in Tradition 18 (1980): 371-373.

37 Bleich, J. David. "Plastic Surgery." In his Contemporary Halakhic Problems, 119-123. The Library of Jewish Law and Ethics, 4. New York: Ktav Publishing House, 1977.

This article, first appearing in Tradition 14 (1974): 126-129, begins with the moral reflection that body is not the individual's property but must be held in trust for God's purposes. The risk of endangering one's life must be taken very seriously; corrective plastic surgery is to be regarded very differently from cosmetic plastic surgery. It notes Jewish hesitancy to permit risk-taking but points to a lenient tendency for the facilitation of religious observances. Compare entry 047.

38 Bleich, J. David. "Study of Anatomy I: Dissection." In his Contemporary Halakhic Problems 2, 56-60. The Library of Jewish Law and Ethics, 10. New York: Ktav Publishing House, 1983.

Bleich reaffirms Jewish hesitancy about utilizing a corpse, even for humanitarian purposes. This article, originally appearing in Tradition 19 (1981): 266-269, notes that while physicians need to use an actual corpse for their studies, Jewish law forbids disrespect to the dead. Can such a violation of halakha be justified on the grounds that the learning so gained saves human lives? Bleich suggests that non-Jewish cadavers are considered usable by many authorities. Beyond this, non-Jews are under no restriction from dissection of a corpse, even of a Jewish cadaver. The following entry should be read in connection with this one together with entry 036.

39 Bleich, J. David. "Study of Anatomy II: Observation." In his Contemporary Halakhic Problems 2, 60-64. The Library of Jewish Law and Ethics, 10. New York: Ktav Publishing House, 1983.

This study, reprinted from Tradition 19 (1981): 269-272, reviews the permissibility of deriving benefit from a non-Jewish cadaver. He notes that while a Jew cannot waive the right to burial, indirect benefit from such an act is permissible. Torah knowledge is not a "benefit" and if the study of anatomy provides that knowledge it is permitted.

40 Bleich, J. David. "Tay-Sachs Disease." Tradition 13 (1972): 145-148.

Jews of Eastern European extraction are most susceptible to Tay-Sachs Disease, an always fatal affliction of newborns. Considerable Jewish thinking has been done on whether the abortion of a fetus known to have Tay-Sachs Disease or even screening for the disease is Jewishly permitted (see entry 056 and items noted there). In this essay Bleich worries about the inherent problems in the screening procedures for Tay-Sachs Disease carriers. The moral issues raised include concerns about whether such screening is for the purpose of abortion and about the possibility of victimizing those being screened. In general screening before marriage is permitted.

41 Bokser, Ben-Zion. "Problems in Bio-Medical Ethics: A Jewish Perspective." Judaism 24 (1975): 134-143.

This is a very general but perceptive article that explores
the questions raised by scientific technology. Such technology depends upon experimentation and challenges the status
quo. Jewish ethics, according to Bokser, favors both technology and experimentation since interference with nature is
one way humanity helps God liberate the world. This survey
of bio-medical ethics combines general theory with specific
example in the way of a number of essays included in this
bibliography (see the items in entry 001).

42 Carmi, Amnon, ed. Medical Experimentation. Ramat Gan:
Turtledove Publishing Company, 1978.

Experimentation on human beings and concerning human health
brings two Jewish values into conflict: the rights of the
individual and the welfare of the community. Differing
opinions reflect different evaluations of which principle
has priority in any particular case. This anthology of
essays on the rights of the unborn, on the ethical problems
involved in experimentation on human beings, and on the need
for informed consent brings together valuable insights into
Jewish ethics. Entries drawn from this anthology include
043, 054, 132; compare these works with the items cited in
entry 032.

43 Carmi, Amnon. "The Challenge of Experimentation." In
his Medical Experimentation, 1-14. Ramat Gan: Turtledove
Publishing Company, 1978.

Carmi analyzes the current predicament for both the researcher and the patient who hopes for some good to come out of
an affliction. The chaos concerning how experimentation is
done and how volunteers are treated demands attention. Carmi rejects reliance only on private initiative and calls for
a planned approach to provide moral authority to physician.
Moral questions include the nature of the subjects, the
compulsory or voluntary nature of the experiment, the value
of experimentation and the importance of preserving life
and health. See the entire anthology (entry 041) to which
this is an introduction.

44 Dresner, Samuel H. "A New Heart, A New Life?" United
Synagogue Review 21,2 (1968):12-13, 28-30.

Dresner, a Conservative Jewish rabbi, raises religious and
moral questions concerning organ transplants. Since the
process is hazardous, the decisions to be made are fateful
ones. He suggests that they be made only after self-purifi-
cation and religious self-searching. These issues of risk,
the need for religious self-examination, and the conflict of
values are expressed as well by the Reform Jewish writer
Freehof (entries 052, 053) in connection with organ transplantation. For most traditionalists the basic questions
arise concerning the problem of determining death and its
criteria (see the items in entry 155).

45   Elovitz, Mark H.   "The Bio-medical Challenges to Law and
Morality."   Judaism 24 (1975): 144-156.

Elovitz   suggests that bio-experimentation raises moral   and
religious   questions.   The human being is both the   subject
and the object of experimentation and must retain a   subjective   center in order to remain human.   He sees a danger in
such   experimentation as   dehumanizing the process of   creation   and   personal uniqueness.   In such a   case   religious
leaders should advocate a refusal to proceed on much experimentation.   See the discussion and items in entry 032.

46   Fink,   Reuven.   "Halakhic Aspects of Organ Transplantation."   Journal   of   Halacha   and   Contemporary   Society   5
(1983): 45-64.

Fink reviews the basic prohibitions against mutilation of a
corpse,   of benefiting from it,   or preventing burial.   He
looks at the theological presuppositions involved,   specifically   those concerned with the world to come and   resurrec-
tion,   as obstacles to utilizing organs from a cadaver.   See
the references in entry 036.

47   Freehof,   Solomon B.   "Cosmetic Surgery."   In his Reform
Responsa For Our Time,   287-290.   Cincinnati: Hebrew Union
College Press, 1971.

Freehof,   unlike Bleich (entry 037),   unambiguously approves
of   cosmetic   surgery.   He finds that it enhances life   and
should not be considered self-injury.   He claims that Jewish
girls   are permitted to beautify themselves for the sake   of
finding a husband but,   again unlike Bleich, does not mention
cosmetic surgery for men.

48   Freehof,   Solomon B.   "Kidney Transplants."   In his New
Reform Responsa,   62-66.   Cincinnati: Hebrew Union College
Press, 1980.

Freehof   examines the obligation of a relative to donate   an
organ   so that a patient can live.   He suggests that   where
the   operation is experimental and where the   donor   becomes
endangered by the operation that duty is relieved.   Compare
the   question   of   scarce resources discussed   in   Dichowsky
(011)   and   the items mentioned there concerning   the   moral
dilemma of when donors are or are not obligated to sacrifice
themselves for others. The discussion in entries 036 and 042
and the items mentioned there are also of importance here.

49   Freehof,   Solomon   B.   "Remains of Bodies   Donated   To
Science." In his Modern Reform Responsa,   278-280.   Cincinnati: Hebrew Union College Press, 1971.

While   allowing   the   burial of bodies donated   to   science
Freehof, it should be noted, does not justify such an act on
either   scientific   or humanitarian grounds.   He   seems   to
share the concerns discussed in entry 058.

50 Freehof, Solomon B.   "Surgical Transplants."   In his
Current Reform Responsa,   118-124. Cincinnati: Hebrew Union
College Press, 1969.

Freehof notes that if the dead can cure the living and there
is a matter of life and death, Judaism is lenient.   The
stricter the criteria of death, however, the better from the
Jewish standpoint.   He also acknowledges the abhorrence of
desecrating a dead body. The consistency of Freehof's liberal viewpoint with that of the tradition itself should be
noted by comparing his views with the other entries noted in
the annotation to entry 032 and 036.

51 Freehof, Solomon B.   "Transplanting a Pig's Heart Valve
into a Human Body." In his Modern Reform Responsa, 217-222.
Cincinnati: Hebrew Union College Press, 1971.

The Jewish prohibition on pork products extends to all
benefit from such products (not merely the eating of them
but use of the bristles for brushes and other types of
benefit.   In this essay Freehof raises the general problem
about transplanted organs but suggests that for Judaism
healing takes precedence over all other considerations except for idolatry, murder, immorality. He therefore permits
using an unclean animal for the healing of a human being.

52 Freehof, Solomon B.   "The Use of the Corena of the
Dead." In his Reform Responsa For Our Time, 152-158. Cincinnati: Hebrew Union College Press, 1971.

The various parts of a corpse are treated differently in
Jewish law. Use of catalysts from such a body, for example,
are permitted even by Orthodox Jews (see entry 738 and the
references in the annotation there). Freehof wonders how
much defilement actually occurs. He claims that the eyeball
is not a limb and therefore permissible for removal from a
corpse.

53 Freehof, Solomon B. "Using the Blood of the Dead." In
his Current Reform Responsa, 242-246. Cincinnati: Hebrew
Union College Press, 1969.

While admitting that tradition objects to benefiting from
the dead, Freehof notes that the saving of a life takes
precedence. In the matter of defilement, he claims, blood
is not included.

54 Goren, Shlomo. "The Religious and Ethical Dilemma in
the Case of the Critically Ill." In Medical Experimentation, edited by Amnon Carmi, 141-148. Ramat Gan: Turtledove
Publishing Company, 1978.

This thoughtful article concludes that the sanctity of human
life overrides all other considerations. The physician must
be relied upon just as a court is relied upon when judging

a capital case. He supports this view with classical Jewish
texts from the Bible, Talmud, and Responsa. In the extreme
cases he decides that it is better to risk experimentation
rather than have certain death. Compare the other essays in
entry 011 and the items noted in the annotation there.   The
discussion of the critically ill includes consideration of
the problem of truth telling found in entries 018, 027.

55   Jacobs,   Steven B.   "A Religious Response to Tay-Sachs
Disease Screening and Prevention." In Tay-Sachs Disease:
Screening and Prevention, edited by Michael M. Kaback, 75-
80. New York: Alan R. Liss, 1977.

This view does not represent an organized Jewish communal
response but rather a general religious overview of the
problem of Tay-Sachs Disease and its implications.   The
moral and religious questions of screening for disease as
well as the rationale behind that screening are discussed.
The religious and moral dimension of intentionality must be
taken as seriously as the health consequences. See the
discussion and items mentioned in the following entry.

56 Kaback, Michael M., ed.   Tay-Sachs Disease: Screening
and Prevention. New York: Alan R. Liss, 1977.

Tay-Sachs Disease, which afflicts Jews of Eastern European
descent, presents moral questions concerning screening and
use of the information it provides. This anthology brings
together representative views from the medical community,
from Orthodox, Conservative, and Reform Jews, and from interested laity.   See other entries from this anthology 055,
057, 069 and compare 040, 066, 105, 125.

57 Lamm, Maurice.   "Control of Tay-Sachs Disease: An Orthodox View." In Tay-Sachs Disease: Screening and Prevention,
edited by Michael M. Kaback, 85-92. New York: Alan R. Liss,
1977.

Lamm represents the cautious Orthodox view and considers the
different possibilities involved.   If health is the primary
concern then screening is appropriate; a problem arises if
the testing involves a decision for an abortion.   See the
previous entry and the references given there.

58 Nathan, Hilel.   "On Body Donations-Factors and Motiva-
tions." In The Dying Human, edited by Andre de Vries and
Amnon Carmi, 53-56. Tel Aviv: Turtledove Publishing
Company, 1979.

The question of donating the body to science can be answered
in many ways. In this essay, the psychological dimension of
such an act is investigated. Nathan contends that such an
act is both a conscious and often unconscious breaking with
tradition. It must be understood psychologically as well as
rationally.   See other essays in this anthology (entry 190)
for views that examine the halakhic rather than the psychological or social aspects of organ donations.

59 Poleyeff, Israel. "Induced Labor." Journal of Halacha
and Contemporary Society 5 (1983): 84-91.

Poleyeff raises the traditional Orthodox opposition to risk.
Induced labor is only permitted in a life threatening situation either for the mother or the child. The moral dimension of this decision should be noted. Compare the discussion in entry 034. The general discussion of risk in hazardous medical treatment should also be considered; compare
the discussion and items in entry 032.

60 Rabinovitch, Nachum L. "What is the Halakha for Organ
Transplants." In Jewish Bioethics, edited by Fred Rosner
and J. David Bleich, 351-357. New York: Sanhedrin Press,
1979.

This useful essay presents in concise form the various
principles used in making decisions concerning the permissibility of organ transplantations. Rabinovitch reviews the
three prohibitions: against mutilation, against benefiting
from the corpse, and against delaying the burial. He demonstrates how the use of organs from the dead can easily be
exploited to become a use of organs from the dying. He also
notes that questions of ritual defilement can occur in such
a situation. Compare the annotation in entry 036.

61 Rasiel, Moshe. "Can a Patient be Forced to Undergo
Medical Treatment?" [Hebrew]. Tehumin 2 (1981): 325-336.

Rasiel raises the case of a patient in critical medical
condition for whom an operation will be of doubtful success.
He concludes that the imperative to heal outweighs medical
doubt. Death and life are in the hands of God; even a short
life of less than twelve months is sacred to God and physicians must struggle to preserve even such a life as long as
possible. Compare entries 013, 033, 054.

62 Rosner, Fred. "Heart and Other Organ Transplantations
and Jewish Law." Jewish Life 37,1 (1969): 38-51.

This popular article reviews the criteria for donation of
organs to others and the difference between live and dead
donors as well as the criteria for death. Rosner's awareness of the moral issues involved, as well as of the aspects
of Jewish law involved, proves instructive in this simple
but clear article. See the annotation to entry 036; the
article appears in entry 022, pp. 135-176.

63 Rosner, Fred. "Jewish Ethical Issues in Hazardous Medical Therapy." Tradition 19 (1981): 55-58.

Rosner comments that patients in desperate situations may
need risky treatment. He summarizes the disagreements over
the amount of risk that is allowed. The theme of the
primacy of life is clearly sounded when he declares that an
act that can save a life supercedes all biblical laws.

The concern of Jews to avoid risk is clearly evident
throughout the literature, combined with a tendency to relax
this concern when saving a life is involved. See entry 032
and the items noted there.

64 Rosner, Fred. "Judaism and Human Experimentation." New
York State Journal of Medicine 75 (1975): 1439-1444.

Rosner notes all the complexities involved and the ethical
issues which make even informed consent an ambiguous solution. He agrees that risks must be taken for the preservation of life, but suggests many problems involved in both
genetic engineering and genetic screening. Compare the
discussion in entry 033 and the items mentioned there. This
essay is reproduced in entry 025 pp. 387-397.

65 Rosner, Fred. "Organ Transplantation in Jewish Law."
In Jewish Bioethics, edited by Fred Rosner and J. David
Bleich, 358-374. New York: Sanhedrin Press, 1979.

This well developed and technical article explores the various decisions in Judaism as to when an organ transplant is
permitted and when it is forbidden. Differences between
live and dead donors and distinctions between different
types of organs are carefully delineated. Rosner shows an
awareness of the moral complexity of the problem of choosing
when desecration of a corpse is justified and when it is
not. Respect for the dead is never given priority over the
survival of the living. The question, then, concerns the
enhancement of life and not its preservation.

66 Rosner, Fred. "Tay-Sachs Disease: To Screen or not to
Screen." Tradition 15 (1976): 101-112.

Rosner provides a description of the disease, clinical mani-
festations, detection of carriers, and the moral problems
presented by screening. He considers the question of abortion and notes both the general rigorous refusal to grant
permission for such action as well as the exceptional lenient rulings. This essay is reproduced in entry 025 pp.
178-190. Compare the various studies in entry 056 and the
items noted there.

67 Siegel, Seymour. "Fetal Experimentation: A Bias for
Life." In Contemporary Jewish Ethics, edited by Menahem
Marc Kellner, 285-295. Sanhedrin Jewish Studies. New York:
Sanhedrin Press, 1975.

Siegel, a Conservative Jewish theologian, while disagreeing
that feticide is murder, respects those who oppose abortion.
Refusing to be recklessly lenient, he demonstrates the complexity of the Jewish approach to fetal research, emphasizing the Jewish bias toward life and in favor of the rights
of a fetus as potential life. He summarizes views about
fetal death, the necessity for a physician's consent, and
the rights of the researcher as well. Although focused

on the problem of fetal experimentation the essay has implications for the question of abortion (see entry 116).

68   Stern, Kurt.   "Experimentation on Human Subjects: A
Search for Halakhic Guidelines." Tradition 17 (1978): 41-
52.

Stern approves of much of the experimentation now performed,
pointing to both immediate and long term benefits that come
from new knowledge.   He does, however, raise Jewish moral
questions, suggesting the need for guidelines to establish
the conditions of humane experimentation and to monitor the
motivation, evaluation, and implementation of planned experimentation. Compare entry 032 and its annotation.

69 Tenenbaum, Edward M.   "A Conservative Jewish View of the
Tay-Sachs Screening Procedures."   In Tay-Sachs Disease:
Screening and Prevention,   edited by Michael M.   Kaback, 81-
83. New York: Alan R. Liss, 1977.

The Conservative viewpoint summarizes Jewish law and emphasizes the bias toward life and the betterment of human
beings.   Conservative Jewish thought is characterized by the
positive view of screening and the sympathetic attitude
exemplified in this essay.   See entry 50 and compare the
other essays listed there.

70 Warhaftig, Itamar.   "The Ethics of Using Prisoners for
Experimentation" [Hebrew]. Tehumin 1 (1980): 530-536.

Warhaftig reiterates the primacy of Jewish respect for life
with references to the way such considerations override
other laws, to the negation of suicide, and to the debates
over acceptable risks in medical experimentation.   He insists that prisoners are to be accorded the rights of human
beings and that, while they are coerced bodily, they have
free will.   Since choice is involved they cannot be morally
enticed into becoming experimental victims even for the good
of society as a whole.   Experimentation and its value is
discussed in entry 32; see the items noted there.

FOOD, DRUGS, AND MEDICINE

71 Aberbach, Moses.   "Smoking and the Halakhah." Tradition
10 (1969): 49-60.

Aberbach argues that the Jewish commandment against endangering life forbids cigarette smoking and cites rabbinic
the precedent for prohibiting even a suspected health hazard.   He rejects contrary arguments as irrelevant when
saving a life (pikuah nefesh).   Compare his view with that
in entries 077 and 082 and contrast it with those in 072,
078, 080.

72 Bleich, J. David.   "Smoking." Tradition 16 (1977): 121-
123.

Bleich provides ambiguous guidance on the morality of cigarette smoking. While he acknowledges the prohibition
against harming the self, he suggests that there is enough
doubt about smoking to consider it in the realm of the
permissible risks of life. This view, while shared by some
thinkers (as in entry 078), is clearly a minority opinion;
see entries 071, 077, 080, 082 for the majority view.

73 Brayer, Menachem M. "Drugs: A Jewish View." Tradition
10 (1968): 31-41.

Jews for a long time ignored the problem of drug addiction.
Recent Jewish moral thinking has grappled with the issue and
offered different solutions to it. In this important essay
Brayer surveys the problem of new drugs and the adolescent
mentality. He suggests that Judaism considers the use of
such drugs a danger both to health and religious growth.
The answer, he suggests, is not medical but moral: Jews must
correct the deficiencies of love in the present society.
Compare the approach found in entries 074, 075, 076, 079.
The essay is reproduced in entry 025 pp. 242-250.

74 Diskind, Meyer H. "The Jewish Drug Addict: A Challenge
to the Jewish Community." In The Jewish Family in a Changing World, edited by Gilbert S. Rosenthal, 122-135. New
York: Thomas Yoseloff, 1970.

Diskind contends that the Jewish community has hidden from
the reality of the contemporary situation. According to
him, Jewish morality demands that problems be addressed and
taken seriously. He calls for new social agencies designed
for the treatment of the addict. He also suggests attempts
to ameliorate the cultural deprivation that creates the
climate for addiction. Other essays in this anthology
(entry 358) are relevant here (075, 081).

75 Einstein, Stanley. "The Use and Misuse of Alcohol and
Other Drugs." In The Jewish Family in a Changing World,
edited by Gilbert S. Rosenthal, 81-121. New York: Thomas
Yoseloff, 1970.

In a complementary essay for the previous essay (also found
in entry 358), Einstein declares that drug misuse is not a
new fact of life but merely one that has been ignored by the
professionals. Even the rabbis, his research shows, see the
human problem but not the moral and ethical dilemma involved. He calls for a Judaic approach to the problem.

76 Freehof, Solomon B. "Psychodelic Drugs." In his Current Reform Responsa, 247-250. Cincinnati: Hebrew Union
College Press, 1969.

Freehof's liberalism does not include sanctioning the abuse
of drugs. He notes that while Jewish tradition does not
discuss addiction to drugs or alcohol as such it does prohibit drunkenness in the Temple and forbids a reckless

risk of life and health. In this way he suggests that Jewish morality stands against abuse of drugs and alcohol. His approach should be compared with that of Novak (079) whose conclusions are similar but whose investigation is more measured.

77 Greenberg, Sidney. "Does Judaism Permit Smoking-On Weekdays?" United Synagogue Review 23,2 (1970): 16-17.

This view by a Conservative Jewish writer reaffirms the moral stance against endangering ones own life taken by both Orthodox and Reform Jewish thinkers. Greenberg cites parallel cases in which the halakha prohibits substances that might be dangerous. His view should be compared to entries 071 080, and 082 and contrasted to 072 and 078.

78 Herring, Basil F. "Smoking and Drugs." In his Jewish Ethics and Halakhah For Our Time: Sources and Commentary, 221-243. The Library of Jewish Law and Ethics, 11. New York: Ktav Publishing House, 1984.

After a comprehensive summary of the contemporary controversy within Orthodox Judaism on smoking, Herring sides with those who are lenient on the basis of precedent. While the moral principle involved, he suggests, is the choice between halakha and instant gratification the details of that choice are often unclear. The variety of viewpoints on smoking can be found in entries 071, 072, 077, 080, 082.

79 Novak, David. "Alcohol and Drug Abuse in The Perspective of Jewish Tradition." Judaism 33 (1984): 221-232.

Novak offers a vigorous defense of the use of alcohol in Jewish religious life, combined with caution about its misuse. Because of long standing tradition, however, he refuses to concede the permissibility of marajuana. Although he admits some precedent for its acceptance he insists that since that precedent does not have the same Judaic pedigree as the use of alcohol it must be rejected. Contrast his approach with that of Freehof (076)

80 Rosner, Fred. "Cigarette Smoking and Jewish Law." Journal of Halacha and Contemporary Society 4 (1982): 33-45.

This essay presents a strong case against the permissibility of cigarette smoking according to Jewish law. Rosner notes not only that health hazards are forbidden by the sages but also recent precedent, that of the Chafetz Chaim who opposed smoking on those grounds in the nineteenth century, for prohibiting cigarettes. Many modern Jewish scholars agree with that evaluation. Contrast other traditional thinkers who take a lenient view such as Bleich (072), and Herring (078) and compare the other strict interpreters such as Greenberg (077) and Weiss (082). The essay is reprinted in entries 085, pp. 265-287 and 022, pp. 35-41.

81 Schachet, Richard I. "The Rabbi and the Addict." In
The Jewish Family in a Changing World, edited by Gilbert S.
Rosenthal, 136-144. New York: Thomas Yoseloff, 1970.

Schachet's case history demonstrates his own developing
awareness of the problem, its causes, and possible ways of
coping with them. His personal description of the Jews who
become addicted to narcotics and of how a rabbi finds he
must minister to them. Compare the other essays in entry
358; especially entries 074, 075.

82 Weiss, Zvi I. "Smoking." Tradition 17 (1978): 139-140.

Weiss concludes that there is enough evidence to show that
smoking is detrimental to health and so should be forbidden
by the halakha. He challenges the views of J. David Bleich
(entry 072) that the situation is ambiguous and inconclu-
sive. Bleich responds (pp. 141-142) that it is forbidden to
prohibit that which is permissible. This dispute shows how
even Orthodox scholars differ on particular moral decisions
despite agreement on the basic moral principles.

BIRTH AND FAMILY PLANNING

83 Aviner, Shlomo Hayyim HaCohen. "Establishing a Family
and Contraception" [Hebrew]. Assia 4 (1983): 167-182

This essay stresses that the primary imperative for propagation falls on the male and that the prohibition against
wasting semen must be considered. Also considered are the
number and sex of children required for a Jewish family.
Moral questions concerning family planning are also studied
to show the general approach of Jewish law. The traditional
Jew evinces greater concern for discovering a sanction for
contraception as can be seen since the majority of essays on
this subject (084, 086, 087, 089-097) are from Orthodox
thinkers with only one (088) from a Conservative Jew, and
even that provokes controversy!

84 Bleich, J. David. "Sterilization of Women." In his
Contemporary Halakhic Problems, 96-99. The Library of Jewish
Law and Ethics, 4. New York: Ktav Publishing House, 1977.

In this essay, first appearing in Tradition 13 (1972): 143-
145, Bleich notes the distinction made in Jewish law between
the obligation and that of women for propagation of the
species. is addressed to men, not women. Women, however,
are under obligation to care for their bodies and not to
mutilate themselves. Therefore, while sterilization of men
is clearly forbidden that of women is disputed can be allowed only where health is at risk. Compare the discussion
at entry 089.

85 Cohen, Alfred S. editor., Halacha and Contemporary
Society, 265-287 (New York: Ktav Publishing House, 1983)

This selection of essays from Journal of Halakha and Contemporary Society includes important contributions to questions of medical morality, social morality, business morality, aging, and family life. Since a majority of the entries involve bioethics the collection is entered here. The essays included in this bibliography are entries 080, 081, 094, 531, 815.

86 Ellinson, Getsel [Elikim]. Procreation in Halacha. Jerusalem: World Zionism Organization, 1977.

The command to be fruitful and procreate is central in Jewish thinking and moral teachings (see entries 98-102, and 211). Here Ellinson summarizes the basic moral commitments of Judaism concerning birth. He presents a traditional Jewish view on such questions as the primacy of life, the command for propagation, abortion, birth control, and artificial insemination. Compare the following entry and his entries 087, 112, 113, 229, 318.

87 Ellinson, Getsel [Elikim]. "Birth Control and Abortion in Halakha." Dine Israel 9 (1978-1980): 97-118.

This essay reviews David Feldman's book (entry 088), objecting to its use of Jewish sources and reliance upon conjecture. According to Ellinson, Feldman's approach is both liberal and biased; in particular, the view that a woman's anguish is a rationale for an abortion must be rejected. Compare his views on abortion in entries 112, 119, and the items noted there.

88 Feldman, David M. Marital Relations, Birth Control and Abortion in Jewish Law. New York: Schocken Books, 1974.

Feldman shows sensitivity to moral issues while focusing on permitted and forbidden methods of contraception and the circumstances under which abortion can be allowed, and the various laws concerning marital obligations. See the critique by Ellinson (087). See also the annotation at entries 114 and 197 suggesting the range of subjects covered in this insightful book.

89 Halibard, G. B. "Sterilization." The Jewish Law Annual 1 (1978): 192-195.

Sterilization contradicts the commandment to propagate and mutilates the body. This essay focuses on issues of Jewish law, explaining that while men are never to be sterilized except as by-product of a life-saving medically needed operation, women, may be permitted this option in limited cases. This essay makes the moral principle of the primacy of life and health evident. Compare Bleich (084)

90 Rosner, Fred. "Contraception in Jewish Law." Tradition 12 (1971): 90-103.

Rosner clarifies values, laws, and options in the Jewish approach to conception. He reviews the biblical commandment for procreation and the prohibition against useless emission of semen. The essay is reprinted in entries 025 pp. 87-97, and 022, pp. 32-52.

91 Schachter, Herschel. "Halakhic Aspects of Family Planning." Journal of Halakha and Contemporary Society 4 (1982): 5-32.

Schachter's examination of Jewish law shows by example how the primary command for propagation takes on concrete form. He provides a moral rationale for a variety of traditional Jewish laws concerning birth and contraception. The essay is reprinted in 085, pp. 3-30.

92 Spero, Moshe Halevi. "Psychiatric Hazard in the Halakhic Disposition toward Contraception and Abortion." In his Judaism and Psychology: Halakhic Perspectives, 168-180. New York: Ktav Publishing House, 1980.

Spero rejects the argument that psychological hazard represents a rationale for contraception or abortion (see entries 088, 108, 115, 119). His cautious approach represents the traditionalist's suspicion that halakhic permissiveness may be misused. The moral question for Spero must be answered in terms of the motivation for contraception and combined with a recognition of the seriousness of the decision to be made. For support of this view see entries 106, 107, 120, 123, 130, 131, 134.

93 Steinberg, Avrahom. "The General Jewish Approach to Contraception" [Hebrew]. Assia 4 (1983): 139-160.

This useful summary of Jewish thinking on the permissibility of contraceptives adds a comparative orientation making it particularly useful as a study in Jewish morality. The moral basis for Judaism's emphasis on large family size and its opposition to the general use of contraception is contrasted with that of Roman Catholicism. Judaism is said to be more life-affirming in its approach to the question. The general principles involved should be compared to those expressed in entry 083.

94 Steinberg, Avrahom. "Natural Childbirth: May the Husband Attend." Journal of Halakha and Contemporary Society 2 (1981): 107-122.

Reproduced in entry 085, pp.54-69, this seminal study of the enhancement of life shows how a woman's pain and suffering mitigates the strict separation of men and women. If only the husband can ease his wife's suffering in childbirth then he may be permitted to be present even though with all else being equal it is preferable to have a woman as helper.

95 Steinberg, Moshe Halevi. "The Use of Contraceptive
Devices" [Hebrew]. _Assia_ 4 (1983): 161-166.

Steinberg summarizes the legal tradition that permits contraception when pregnancy would endanger life, noting permitted devices in the light of the competing values of the
importance of the woman's life, the relevance of the pain
she feels, and the problem of a man's wasting of his seed,
and the commandment to propagate the species.

96 Tendler, Moshe. D. "Obstectrics and Gynecology." In
his _Medical Ethics: A Compendium of Jewish Moral, Ethical
and Religious Principles in Medical Practice_, 5th ed., 31-
37. New York: Federation of Jewish Philanthropies of New
York, 1975.

Tendler summarizes the Jewish concerns about family planning. He notes the concern for life, for the avoidance of
unnecessary risk, and the variety of sexual and moral problems raised by abortion, sterilization, prostate surgery,
Jewish laws of feminine purity, contraception, semen
testing, and artificial insemination. See the annotation for
the compendium of which this is a part in entry 030 for this
and the following entry.

97 Tendler, Moses D. "Population Control -- The Jewish
View." In _Jewish Bioethics_, edited by Fred Rosner and J.
David Bleich, 97-104. New York: Sanhedrin Press, 1978.

While Tendler considers the morality of population control
suspect, he does allow family planning under certain conditions. These conditions include a prior compliance with the
command for procreation and a careful examination of motives. He does not reject out of hand motivations based
upon the personal finances and the situation of the couple
involved.

FERTILITY AND ITS STIMULATION

98 Frank, Shirley. "The Population Panic: Why Jewish
Leaders Want Jewish Women to be Fruitful and Multiply."
Lilith 1,4 (1978): 12-17.

Ms. Frank contends that Jewish religious leaders urge Jewish
women to propagate the species are not motivated merely by
concern for Jewish survival but also by the sexist ideal of
keeping women at home. She contends that Judaism can survive only by becoming more adaptive to modernity. Quality
of Jewish life, not quantity of Jews is necessary for Jewish
survival. Her feminist perspective should be compared with
the views of women on abortion in entries 111, 119, 139.

99 Freehof, Solomon B. "The Fertility Pill. In his _Reform
Responsa For Our Time_, 205-211. Cincinnati: Hebrew Union
College Press, 1971.

Freehof claims that traditional sources do not discuss the possibility of a fertility pill, but notes the Jewish emphasis on the imperative to be fruitful and multiply as implicit sanction for it.   He suggests caution concerning side-effects since Judaism forbids taking of risks.   The discussion on risk taking in entry 032 should be reviewed as well as the entries on family planning, entries 083-097.

100 Gordis, Robert.   "Be Fruitful and Multiply: Biography of a Mitzvah." Midstream 28 (1982): 25-32.

Because of the crisis of modernity, Gordis urges Jews to have larger families and uses the occasion to sketch the stages in the development of the commandment from biblical to modern times, showing how morality fits the needs of particular times and places.   In the modern world there is new urgency for Jewish population growth and Gordis provides organizational suggestions for promoting growth.   Compare the theological treatment of this commandment (entry 211), the feminist critique (entry 098), and a critical response to his approach (entry 102).

101 Ofseyer Jordan S.   "The Need for Larger Jewish Families." United Synagogue Review 30,2 (1977): 12-13.

Ofseyer responds to the feminist critique (entry 088) of the call for larger families.   While women suggest that Judaism depends upon quality and not quantity of Jews, sheer numbers are essential for survival.   He claims that when Jewish survival becomes problematic, fertility becomes a Jewish duty.   Jewish women as well as men, therefore, have a moral obligation to have larger families.

102 Rackman, Emanuel. "Large Jewish Families." Midstream 29 (1983): 39-41.

Rackman, while agreeing with Robert Gordis (entry 100) on the critical nature of the decline in Jewish population, chastises him on ignoring traditional Orthodoxy and using a historico-critical periodization to cloud the discussion. Rackman also claims that Gordis' realization of the crisis is a belated one.   Gordis replies defending both the timing and approach of his suggestions, pp. 42-43.

ABORTION

103 Bleich, J. David. "Abortion in Halakhic Literature." In his Contemporary Halakhic Problems, 325-371.   The Library of Jewish Law and Ethics, 4.   New York: Ktav Publishing House, 1977.

This seminal article from Tradition 10 (1968): 72-120, (reprinted in entry 025, pp. 123-177) has influenced many Jewish writers. Bleich's in-depth discussion not only reviews the current controversy over when and under what conditions abortion is permitted, but also shows the moral importance of both the principle of life and concern for human pain in Jewish thinking. In an important contribution he discusses why different standards concerning abortion are applied to Noahides (non-Jews). Compare other Orthodox views in entries 109, 110, 112, 113, 118, 120, 121, 127-112, 129-130-132, 134-136, 138; Conservative views in 067, 114, 115, 117, 123, 124, 128, Reform views in 106, 107, 108, 116, 126, 137, and feminist views in 111, 119, 133, 139.

104 Bleich, J. David. "Post-Mortem Caesareans." In his Contemporary Halakhic Problems, 123-125. The Library of Jewish Law and Ethics, 4. New York: Ktav Publishing House, 1977.

This study focused on fetal life, reprinted from Tradition 12 (1971):114-115, suggests that a fetus receives the same consideration as all other human life. Bleich points out that this question also involves the criterion of death since some might argue that such an act hastens the death of the mother. Compare Siegel (067) and Freehof (116).

105 Bleich, J. David. "Tay-Sachs Disease." In his Contemporary Halakhic Problems, 109-115. The Library of Jewish Law and Ethics, 2. New York: Ktav Publishing House, 1977.

In addition to questions raised concerning medical screening and experimentation (see entry 056 and references noted there), the disease raises the question of choosing between the pain of the mother and the inevitably short life-span of an infant born with a quickly terminal and degenerative disease. Bleich contends that pre-marital screening is to be preferred. He summarizes the rabbinic debate with one view suggesting that abortion is not appropriate in these cases, another view, however, disagrees. He notes that Israeli Rabbi Eliezer Waldenberg stands against the majority in his permission of abortion in this case. The essay first appeared in Tradition 16 (1976): 160-163.

106 Block, Richard Alan. "The Right to Do Wrong: Reform Judaism and Abortion." Journal of Reform Judaism 28 (Summer 1981): 3-15.

This is a remarkable essay for a Reform Jewish leader since it urges caution and restraint in the approval of abortions. It received an urgent reply in a following article (see entry 137). Block stands against the liberalism that contends women should have complete control over their own bodies. He notes that men no less than women have a stake in determining the morality which governs social life. He agrees that the definition of the fetus is ambiguous and that this ambiguity gives the law sanction to allow abortions. The religious person, he argues, must act morally in places where the law is unclear. Compare the following entry and those noted in entry 103.

107   Block, Richard Alan "A Matter of Life and Death: Reform Judaism and the Defective Child." Journal of Reform Judaism 31 (1984): 14-30.

Block notes the multidimensional aspects of the abortion question and discusses a variety of methods for solving it. He includes among the debated subjects the definition of a dying person and the Jewish bias for the continuation of life. See his views in the previous entry.

108 Brickner, Balfour. "Judaism and Abortion." In Contemporary Jewish Ethics, edited by Menahem Marc Kellner, 279-283. Sanhedrin Jewish Studies. New York: Sanhedrin Press, 1978.

While approaching the question of abortion from a Jewish standpoint Brickner's main focus is upon the rights of individuals. He deplores the situation in which the federal government must intervene in medical and moral decisions and appeals for the right of the woman to decide the fate of her own body based purely upon of personal conscience. He relies on the passage in Exodus 21:22, where the fetus is clearly not understood to be a full human being. Given this view he feels that the enhancement of a full human life is more important than the consideration of nascent life. In that way abortion does not decrease the value of life but expresses belief in its sanctity. Compare the items noted in entry 103 and particularly the controversy among Reform rabbis in entries 106, 107, 126, 137.

109 Carmy, Shalom. "Halakhah and Philosophical Approaches to Abortion." Tradition 16 (1977): 126-147.

Carmy contrast Judaism with its view that fetal life while important does not exemplify the sanctity of human life as fully as that of the mother with philosophical views seeking absolute consistence. The halakhic view shows a greater realism and sensitivity to human needs. Compare the philosophical issues in entries 096, 104, 107, 108, and 116.

110   Carmy, Shalom, and Weiss, Roslyn. "Abortion and Halakhah." Tradition 17 (1979): 112-115.

The authors raise the questions of when a fetus is considered human in a relevant way for the halakha? In order to answer this problem they make a distinction between rights and between ethical duty, noting that Jewish law embraces both concepts. They conclude that respect for the fetus as a potential human life is an ethical duty in the halakha even thought Jewish law does not establish absolute rights of life on behalf of the fetus. The approach taken reflects that of traditional Jewish law; compare entry 103 and the items listed there.

111   Daum, Annette. "The Jewish Stake in Abortion Rights." Lilith 8 (1981): 12-17.

Daum notes that abortion rights are not high on the agenda
of contemporary Jewish ethics. Since the abolition of abortion, would would affect Orthodox Jews as well as the non-
Orthodox, she suggests that they have an obligation to help
prevent such legislation. They, not the Reform, misrepresent Jewish tradition. Compare the items noted in entry
103 with particular reference to the feminist critique of
traditional Orthodoxy. The philosophical essay by Lubarsky
(entry 126) complements this statement well.

112 Ellinson, Getsel [Elikim] Family Planning and Contraception [Hebrew]. Jerusalem: 1978.

This study explores the various Jewish laws concerning the
fetus, conception, and family planning. Ellinson's vast
knowledge of the subject (see his entries noted in 86) and
his traditional viewpoint make his works valuable resources
for discovering how halakha understands the question of
procreation, contraception, and abortion.

113 Ellinson, Getsel [Elikim]. "The Fetus in the Halakha"
[Hebrew]. Sinai 66 (1970): 20-49.

This indepth study of how Judaism understands the status of
the fetus has direct and indirect implications for the
permissibility of abortion. The human quality of the fetus'
life is clearly established, even if the mother's life
sometimes takes precedence.

114 Feldman, David M. Marital Relations, Birth Control and
Abortion in Jewish Law. New York: Schocken Books, 1974.

Feldman notes that first question to be answered is whether
an abortion is murder. He then distinguishes the moral
principle of a right to life from the right to be born,
clarifying how Judaism sees the mother's welfare to be an
aspect of the right to life. He contrasts the warrant for
therapeutic abortions in Judaism with the opposition found
in Roman Catholic theology. Despite his rather traditional
conclusions his view from Conservative Judaism contrasts
with both the Orthodox and the Reform approaches; see the
items noted in entry 103. See also entries 088, 197.

115 Feldman, David M. "Abortion and Ethics: The Rabbinic
Viewpoint." Conservative Judaism 29 (1975): 31-38.

This essay reviews the major ideas included in Feldman's
book cited in the previous entry.

116 Freehof, Solomon B. "Abortion and Live Fetus Study."
In his Reform Responsa For Our Time, 256-260. Cincinnati:
Hebrew Union College Press, 1971.

Freehof's unambiguous liberalism can be clearly discerned in
this essay. He states without qualification that the fetus
is not a person and that the mother's life takes precedence

over that of the fetus. Nevertheless he acknowledges that
there should be no destruction without reason, and that if
the fetus emerges alive from the womb it should not be put
to death. Despite this admission his stress that during the
first forty days of pregnancy the fetus is only as if water
and that upon abortion there are no burial and mourning
rites for the fetus, implies the primacy of the mother in no
uncertain terms. Contrast Siegel (067) and the other items
noted in entry 103.

117 Gordis, Robert. "Abortion: Major Wrong or Basic
Right?" Midstream 24 (1978): 44-49.

Gordis provides a clear historical summary of the rather
sparse classical materials. He supplies a lucid explanation
of the different moral implications of therapeutic and non-
therapeutic abortions. He significantly rejects the argument that a woman's body belongs to herself alone and draws
from that rejection the conclusion that the spirit of Judaism is against abortion on demand.

118 Green, Ronald M. "Genetic Medicine in the Perspective
of Orthodox Halakhah." Judaism 34 (1985): 263-277.

Although this essay begins with a sketch of bioethical
problems in general, its major emphasis is on the problem of
abortion. Green declares that Judaism opposes the liberal
tradition of individualism. The mother's pain is not the
first concern but rather with moral standards.

119 Greenberg, Blu. "Abortion: A Challenge to Halakhah."
Judaism 25 (1976): 201-208.

Greenberg offers a sympathetic treatment of both Jewish
moral concerns and the needs of contemporary women. She
concludes that Judaism should give reluctant support to
legalized abortion. While she recognizes both the lenient
and strict tendencies within Jewish moral thought about
abortion she suggests the need for a widened area of discussion that will evolve a new approach consistent with both
Judaism's reverence for life and with absolute concern for
the welfare of women. She insists that women no less than
Judaism need to be prepared to compromise if morality is to
be more than merely lip-service to ideals. This essay is
reprinted in entry 239, pp. 147-155. Contrast her views
with other feminist positions in entries 111, 126, and 133.

120 Grumet, Seymour M., and Rosner, Fred. "The Morality of
Induced Abortion." Jewish Life 38 (1971): 5-12.

This popular article arguing against abortion musters the
various arguments of the halakha. The Jewish view on abortion is contrasted with what are regarded as two extreme
views: reform and repeal. The question is not one of literal murder but of moral murder. The latter while certainly
allowed in the case of extreme necessity -- to saving the

life of the mother, can be dangerous if used too freely. To allow abortion for potentially deformed children undermines the hopeful theology of change and growth which, the authors argue, characterizes Judaism and might lead to toleration for other offenses such as genocide, euthanasia and abortion merely for the sake of fetal research. Compare entry 067.

121 Herring, Basil F. "Abortion." In his Jewish Ethics and Halakhah For Our Time: Sources and Commentary, 25-48. The Library of Jewish Law and Ethics, 11. New York: Ktav Publishing House, 1984.

Herring studies the moral complexity in the Jewish tradition concerning abortion. He notes that, while the biblical text in Exodus does regard the fetus as less than a full human being, abortion does imply that the marriage act was accomplished in vain. Recognizing the moral principle of sexuality for the sake of propagation, he claims that even when the fetus is "only water" it should not be aborted except in cases of danger to the mother's life. This essay should be read together with the other items noted in entry 103.

122 Jakobovits, Immanuel. "Jewish Views on Abortion." In Jewish Bioethics, edited by Fred Rosner and J. David Bleich, 118-133. New York: Sanhedrin Press, 1979.

In this statement of traditional Jewish Orthodoxy, Jakobovits looks at varying moral claims associated with abortion. He holds up the primacy of life in Judaism to defend the right of monster births and to oppose the destruction of defective embryos. He recognizes that considerations of cruelty to women and to fetuses must each be taken seriously. Above all, however, he sees the moral standards of society as a moral challenge to contemporary Jews. While, therefore, agreeing that in case of a threat to the mother's life an abortion is permitted he is far more cautious than many other Jewish thinkers in giving such permission (compare the other items in entry 103).

123 Klein, Isaac. "Abortion and the Jewish Tradition." In Contemporary Jewish Ethics, edited by Menachem Marc Kellner, 270-278. Sanhedrin Jewish Studies. New York: Sanhedrin Press, 1978.

This erudite article considers rabbinic precedent to be more important than hellenistic Jewish precedent in determining the morality of abortion. By looking at the Mishna, Talmud, and medieval Jewish thinkers Klein defines when a fetus is a threat to human life, when it is a murderer against which the woman must defend herself. Klein, although not an Orthodox Jew, has reservations about the arguments for abortion based upon the mother's mental anguish. He contends that giving a carte blanche to abortions spells moral defeatism. Compare other Conservative authors Gordis (117) and Novak (128);this essay first appeared in Conservative Judaism 24 (1970): 26-33.

124   Klein,   Isaac.   "Teshuvah on Abortion." In Conservative Judaism and the Law,   edited by Seymour Siegel with   Elliot Gertel, 258-263. New York: Rabbinical Assembly, 1977.

This   "teshuva"   or   responsa looks at   various   traditional Jewish   texts to conclude that approval is given,   but   with caution   in only a few,   very specific cases.   Compare   the previous entry and Feldman (entries 104 and 105).

125   Kukin,   Marrick.   "Tay-Sachs   and the   Abortion   Controversy." Journal of Religion and Health 20   (1981):   224-242.

While   Kukin   presents a very general summary of Jewish   law this   essay is exceptional for including non-Orthodox   viewpoints.   The debate among Orthodox thinkers over the   decision   of Eliezer Waldenberg to permit the abortion of a Tay-Sachs   fetus   is reported together with the   statement   that Torah interpretation is various,   like sparks flying from an anvil, and that the question is less that of the morality of abortion on demand but on the respective needs of the mother and the fetus.

126   Lubarsky,   Sandra B.   "Judaism and the Justification of Abortion   for Non-Medical Reasons." Journal of   Reform   Judaism 31 (1984): 1-13.

Using   an approach that includes both a feminist and process theology   perspective   Lubarsky   argues   that   anti-abortion interpretations   of Jewish law are   misguided.   These   views misrepresent both biblical precedent and rabbinic thought by making   six unwarranted assumptions.   Despite her   argument Richard   Alan Block (107) remains unconvinced. Compare   her philosophy   to   that of Carmy (109) and her feminism to   entries 111, 119, 133, and 139.

127   Maeir,   David M.   "Abortion and Halakha: New   Issues" [Hebrew]. Dine Israel 7 (1976): 138-150.

Maeir   notes the new legislation occurs as moral   principles and   social development interact.   While the halakha has an inviolable core,   he   suggests that it responds   to   modern reality. He surveys recent halakhic decisions that seem   to give a positive response to the possibility of abortion.

128   Novak, David.   "A Jewish View of Abortion."   In his Law and Theology in Judaism, 114-124. New York: Ktav Publishing House, 1974.

Novak   recognizes the complexity of the question of abortion and uses the variation in the prohibition as applied to both Jews and non-Jews to demonstrate it.   He notes the   difference   between a threat to life and running the risk of self-mutilation and seeks to place abortion within the context of these two dangers.   He inculcates respect for human life as the basis for modern moral reflection.

129 Rackman, Emanuel. "Violence and the Value of Life: The Halakhic View."   In Violence and Defense in the Jewish Experience, edited by Salo W. Baron, 113-141. Philadelphia: Jewish Publication Society of America, 1977.

Rackman provides a general discussion of violence in Judaism which includes an analysis of violence against the self encompassing a study of abortion. The discussion of abortion shows that despite an abhorrence of violence, the tradition clearly conceives of a hierarchy of life in which the mother's life is superior to that of the embryo. The realism of this essay should be carefully noted.

130 Rosner, Fred. "Induced Abortion: Jewish Law and Jewish Morality." Man and Medicine: Journal of Values and Ethics in Health Care 1 (1976): 213-226.

This essay clearly reiterates the basic views of traditional Jewish law (see the items in entry 103). Rosner begins by reflecting on the moral implications in the theological statement that the human being is created in the image of God. Because of this image he agrees with the Israeli Chief Rabbi Unterman who calls abortion an 'appurtenance' to murder although not murder itself. He acknowledges the traditional view that there are stages in fetal development but concludes that the moral dilemma which includes the fact that no one speaks for fetus demands a rigorous opposition to abortion at all stages. His essay is followed with a critique by Robert R. Reeves, 225-226.

131 Rosner, Fred. "The Jewish Attitude Toward Abortion." In Contemporary Jewish Ethics, edited by Menahem Marc Kellner, 257-278. Sanhedrin Jewish Studies. New York: Sanhedrin Press, 1978.

Rosner reviews the Jewish view on the fetus and its various stages of development, the traditional rationale for abortions when the mother is threatened, and the relevance of the limitation of this rationale to Jews. He considers the case of defective births and considers abortion in such a case to be an 'appurtenance to murder.' The original essay appeared in Tradition 12 (1968):48-71, and is reproduced in entry 022, pp. 54-79. See the French translation of this article in Revue D'histoire De La Medecine Hebraique 25 (1972): 53-56, 69-76.

132 Seer, David M., and Zohar, Eli. "The Rights of the Unborn." In Medical Experimentation, edited by Amnon Carmi, 117-124. Ramat Gan: Turtledove Publishing Company, 1978.

The authors summarize the biblical and rabbinic data on miscarriage and the abortion. They conclude that while feticide is morally less onerous than destroying sperm the line between feticide and infanticide is drawn too sharply to be realistic. They urge parents not to feel guilt at a handicapped child but to trust God. Compare entry 042.

133 Shapiro-Libai, Nitza. "The Right to Abortion." Israel
Yearbook on Human Rights 5 (1975): 120-140.

Shapiro-Libai summarizes the Israeli controversy on abortion
and comments that the conflict is between right to shape
one's life and the obligation to respect nascent life. She
considers the conflict to be that between the need to protect the individual's welfare and the welfare of the society
and advocates the liberal, individualistic approach.

134 Silber, Tomas J. "Abortion: A Jewish View." Journal
of Religion and Health 19 (1980): 231-239.

Silber recognizes the problem in defining a "Jewish" view
because Jewish thinkers diverge and because Judaism itself
is composed of divergent strands of moral thought. He sorts
out the historical data and the foundations of Jewish law to
establish the basic principles of the centrality of life and
the primacy of the mother's health. He cautions, however,
that a mother's instincts can be wrong and that she can
regret actions once taken . This article includes a useful
appendix on the sources of Jewish ethics, the structure of
Jewish law, and major principles of morality such as lifnim
mishurat hadin, as well as contemporary Israeli law.

135 Sinclair, Daniel B. "The Legal Basis for the Prohibition on Abortion in Jewish Law." Israel Law Review 15
(1980): 109-130.

Sinclair traces the moral issues involved through Jewish
history from the Bible and rabbinic sources through the
sectarian movements as well. His analysis shows that the
prohibition is of rabbinic origin but he notes that the
Hasidic rabbi Schneur Zalman says that the fetus is potential life and must be respected as such. Despite this
dissenting view Sinclair finds the general trend of Jewish
morality to be life affirming and in that way distinctive
from other views, particularly that of Roman Catholicism.
Compare this view with that in Steinberg (094).

136 Steinberg, Avrahom. "Induced Abortion According to
Jewish Law." Journal of Halacha and Contemporary Society 3
(1981): 29-52.

This essay, also found in International Journal of Medicine
and Law 1 (1979):187-203, reviews Jewish legal decisions
concerning the status of a fetus in the first trimester, the
relevance of parental anguish in permitting an abortion in
the first 40 days of a pregnancy and rabbinic differences on
the meaning of the fetus as an "endangered limb" in terms of
the principle of the primacy of human life.

137 Washofsky, Mark. "Abortion, Halacha and Reform Judaism." Journal of Reform Judaism 28 (Fall 1981): 11-19.

Washofsky argues against Block's call (entry 106) for a more cautious approach to abortions by suggesting the precedents for seeing the fetus as non-person and for making the mother's health primary. Block responds (pp. 19-22).

138 Weinfeld, Moshe. "The Genuine Jewish Attitude Toward Abortion" [Hebrew]. Zion 42 (1977): 129-142.

Weinfeld contends that Judaism unlike either Christianity or Hellenism refuses to absolutize decisions about abortion. The Jewish approach makes the living individual primary and responds to need not personal whim or abstract ideals.

139 Yishai, Yael. "Abortion in Israel: Social Demand and Political Response." Policy Studies Journal 7 (1978): 270-300.

Yishai's sensitive article demonstrates how the ethics of abortion moved from a non-decision through diverse pressures from religious factions, Israel Feminist Movement, and public interest to become a social issue.

ARTIFICIAL INSEMINATION AND GENETIC EXPERIMENTATION

140 Address, Richard F. "Test Tube Torah." Central Conference of American Rabbis Journal 24 (1977): 59-63.

Address sees genetic engineering as creating the need for moral reflection. He looks at the traditional Jewish sources on eugenics and suggests that they stress the need to produce the highest quality children possible. This view by a Reform rabbi shows the general caution that all Jewish thinkers display towards tampering with the natural process (compare entries 143, 145, 147, 149, 150, 152). Address, however, does not investigate the particular halakhic questions of identity, inheritance, and sexual morality that concern traditional Jews when facing the challenge of eugenics (see entries 142, 148, 149, 151, 153, 154 in contrast to 144-146).

141 Bleich, J. David. "Host Mothers." In his Contemporary Halakhic Problems, 106-109. The Library of Jewish Law and Ethics, 4. New York: Ktav Publishing House, 1977.

Bleich explains that a transplanted organ becomes an integral part of the host body and that, therefore, while some identify the donor mother as the true mother, others say that the host mother is the true mother or that two mothers are involved. Although it is forbidden if done for the sake of convenience alone, such an act may be permitted to save the life of the fetus. This article first appeared in Tradition 13 (1972):127-129. Note the discussion in the previous entry.

142 Bleich, J. David. "Test-tube Babies." Tradition 17 (1978): 86-90.

Jewish   law demands propagation but also looks with   caution
on   conception   by a married woman in   unconventional   ways.
Bleich   concedes   that if the procedure is done   with   moral
sensitivity,   and   if   properly safeguarded with the   wife's
husband as the donor,   artificial insemination can   overcome
certain problems of conception.   Note how both this and the
previous   entry   focus on specific halakhic concerns   rather
than general theory.   The article is reprinted in entry 025
pp. 80-84.

143 Drori, Moshe.   "Genetic Engineering: Preliminary Discussion,   Legal   and Halakhic Aspects   (Genetic   Engineering)"
[Hebrew].   Tehumin 1 (1980): 280-296.

Drori summarizes the general process of the genetic   formation   of   a child and the distinction between this   and   so-
called"   test tube babies" as the background for his discussion, raising the moral question of whether such a procedure
disrupts nature, whether it can be construed as adultery, as
a   misuse of male semen,   or whether it is an   inhumane   activity,   and   the legal status of the child.   Contrast   the
specificity   of these concerns with the general moral   questions   raised in the following three entries representing   a
liberal Reform approach.

144   Freehof,   Solomon B.   "Insemination with Mixed Seed."
In his New Reform Responsa,   202-204.   Cincinnati: Hebrew
Union College Press, 1980.

Freehof   raises   the question of an infringement on   general
morality though scientific technique.   Thus artificial   insemination   might lead to an adulterous or incestuous   relationship based on ignorance of parentage.

145 Freehof, Solomon B.   "The Test-tube   Baby."   In his New
Reform Responsa,   205-212.   Cincinnati: Hebrew Union College
Press, 1980.

Freehof   approaches   the question of   artificial   conception
with considerable concern and hesitation.   He suggests that
tampering   with nature may result in the production of   mon-
strosities   and counsels caution.   His   response,   however,
raises none of the legal questions of inheritance,   implications for marriage,   or specifically Judaic moral tenets   of
Orthodox Judaism.

146   Freehof,   Solomon B.   "The Transplanted Ovum."   In his
New   Reform Responsa,   213-218.   Cincinnati: Hebrew   Union
College Press, 1980.

Although   not an Orthodox Jew,   Freehof does suggest caution
when   approaching artificial insemination.   He   objects   to
artificial generation or gestation, wondering whether impreg-
nation   without   intercourse is permitted or whether it   is
considered adultery.

147   Rabinowitz, Avraham Tzvi.   "Remarks Concerning the Halakhic Policy and its Implications for Genetic Enginee-ring" [Hebrew]. Tehumin 2 (1981): 504-512.

The Orthodoxy of this approach can be grasped by looking at the detailed halakhic questioning involved in contrast to the preceding three entries.   Rabinowitz notes the proble-matic nature of genetic engineering: its possibilities for both benefit and for misuse are reviewed.   Of particular interest is the way in which Rabinowitz demonstrates that the Halakha takes both possibilities into consideration in its approach to human interference in the world order.

148   Rosenfeld, Azriel.   "Generation, Gestation, and Ju-daism." Tradition 12 (1971): 78-87.

Rosenfeld analyzes the meaning of parenthood and the possible tension between the host mother and biological mother.   The first's right to accept the fetus and the latter's right to offer it are both questionable.   Family purity is also at stake as well as the status of the child from an Orthodox standpoint in ways that liberal Jews do not take into their considerations.

149   Rosenfeld, Azriel.   "Human Identity: Halakhic Issues." Tradition 16 (1977): 58-74.

Rosenfeld considers the creation of artificial life, of the Golem (homonuculus) in tradition, and various biblical and rabbinic definitions of life.   He reviews the different problems associated with differing types of artificial inse-mination.   The extent of this article makes it valuable for more than questions of procreation and enable it to be a guide to the Jewish view of human life in general.

150   Rosenfeld, Azriel.   "Judaism and Gene Design." Tradition 13 (1972): 71-80.

Rosenfeld illustrates the Jewish concern with life by empha-sizing the need for safe procedures, approval for organ transplants, even of sex organs, and discussion of the spiritual as well as biological basis of heredity.   The essay is reprinted in entry 025 pp. 401-408.

151   Rosner, Fred.   Artificial Insemination in Jewish Law." Judaism 19 (1970): 90-103.

Rosner reviews Jewish moral thinking about artificial inse-mination and concludes that it is only permissible under certain definite conditions.   The ideas expressed echo those of the other traditional thinkers listed in entry 130.   The essay is reprinted in entry 025 pp.   45-55, and in entry 22, pp. 89-106.

152   Rosner, Fred.   "Genetic Engineering and Judaism." In Jewish Bioethics, edited by Fred Rosner and J. David Bleich, 409-420.   New York: Sanhedrin Press, 1979.

Rosner reviews the problems of genetic engineering from a Judaic standpoint, including its relevance to an understanding of sexual process. He investigates questions of legislative involvement and of safeguards against irresponsible experimentation. Recognizing the moral dilemma of Judaism which emphasizes propagation but is wary of sexual license he summarizes the division of opinion on artificial insemination among Jewish thinkers (compare the previous entry as well as those listed in entry 140).

153 Rosner, Fred. "In Vitro Fertilization and Surrogate Motherhood: The Jewish View." Journal of Religion and Health 22 (1983): 139-160.

Rosner suggests the moral, ethical, and Jewish concerns arising from having surrogate mothers. He reviews the principle of the value of life in the context of the specific issues raised. The essay is a good example of how considerations of Jewish law can lead into general moral discussion. His generalizations should be compared to those of liberal thinkers such as Address (140).

154 Rosner, Fred. "Test Tube Babies, Host Mothers and Genetic Engineering in Judaism." Tradition 19 (1981): 141-148.

Using host mothers as an example Rosner demonstrates how Judaism transforms scientific questions into moral issues. He follows through the implications of such technology for the human questions of identity, of inheritance, of fulfilling the commandments, and of improving human life. This detailed analysis takes his considerations beyond the generalities of Address (140) and avoids the over generalizations that characterize Freehof (144-146).

DEATH, EUTHANASIA AND SUICIDE

155 "Discussion on the Criteria of Death." Conservative Judaism 30 (1976): 31-39.

While the Jewish community has been united in confronting the moral dilemma of aging in a youth-oriented world (see entries 529-541), the moral issues associated with death and dying have raised considerable controversy. Two central questions have concerned what constitutes death and when termination of life is permissible (euthanasia). These two concerns are often linked together (see entries 158, 160, 163, 165, 169, 173, 176, 184 and the various essays in 156). In this symposium the diversity of contemporary Jewish moral discussion concerning death and dying becomes clear. Seymour Siegel and Daniel Goldfarb and other rabbis exchange ideas concerning transplantation from dying patients, prolonging life, and the criteria of death. This symposium displays the variety of moral issues Jews face in relationship to death and dying and the primacy of life in Jewish morality.

156   Bar-Zev, Asher.   "Euthanasia: A Classical Ethical Problem in a Modern Context."   The Reconstructionist 44,9
(1979): 7-16; 44,10: 7-10.

The question of where Judaism stands on euthanasia is not as
easily   answered as a simple glimpse of the traditional lore
would suggest.   There, it appears, while passive euthanasia
is permitted,   active is not.   Jewish thinkers in the modern
age,   however,   have found a complexity in the heritage (see
entries 160,   162-164,   166, 168-172, 174, 177, 180-182, 185,
186,   191,   192.   Bar Zev notes that Jewish tradition emphasizes the primacy of life.   The technology that both permits
the consideration of euthanasia and makes it problematic   is
discussed.   The Jewish viewpoint takes on special meaning in
this   modern context in which the good of the individual   is
often sacrificed for family,   society,   or an anonymous person.   Judaism emphasizes that the individual's life must be
inviolable.   Bar   Zev contrasts this with other secular and
religious points of view.   He details the variations   found
in Jewish response to active and passive euthanasia.

157   Bardfelt, Philip A.   "Jewish Medical Ethics."   The
Reconstructionist 42,6 (1976): 7-11.

While   entitled "medical ethics," this essay focuses on   the
issue of euthanasia, the precedents found in Jewish history,
such   as the suicide of King Saul,   and the differences between   actively enabling death and passively removing   obstacles to it.   The entries concerning suicide listed in entry
175 and entries 161,   168,   174,   180,   193, 186 alternative
theological perspectives.

158   Bleich,   J.   David.   "Establishing Criteria of Death."
In his Contemporary Halakhic Problems, 372-393.   The Library
of   Jewish Law and Ethics,   4.   New York: Ktav   Publishing
House, 1977.

Bleich   summarizes the rabbinic views on criteria for   death
in   contrast   to modern medicine.   He claims   that   neither
brain death nor coma is irreversible.   He disputes the idea
of "death with dignity."   Of importance here is not so   much
the   question   of euthanasia as that of respect for   a   dead
body and the problems that arise from seeking to utilize the
organs of the dead for transplantation.   Compare the references   in   the   annotation to entry   155.   See   Tradition   13
(1973): 90-113 and entry 025, 177-195.

159   Bleich,   J.   David.   "Time of Death Legislation."   Tradition 16 (1977): 130-139.

Bleich refers to the variety of decisions found in contemporary   Jewish thinking including his own work (entry 158) and
the   work   of Moshe Feinstein.   He insists   that   religious
freedom   is   in   jeopardy if the   state   decides   upon   the
criteria   for death.   He emphasizes the importance   of   the
time   of death for Judaism and for the respect that must   be
given to the dead.   Compare the annotation to entry 155.

160   Bleich, J. David.   "The Quinlan Case: A Jewish Perspective."   In Contemporary Jewish Ethics,   edited by Menahem Marc Kellner, 296-307.   Sanhedrin Jewish Studies.   New York: Sanhedrin Press, 1978.

Bleich   contends   that Jewish morality is   distinctive   from that of American pragmatism.   Whereas the former makes life primary,   the second places self-interest first.   He argues that,   in the case of deciding when to remove life-support systems, Judaism is always more cautious than American pragmatism.   See entry 155;   this essay is reprinted in   entry 025, pp. 266-276.   Compare Weisbard (192).

161   Dagi,   Teodoro Forcht.   "The Paradox of   Euthanasia." Judaism 24 (1975): 157-167.

Dagi asks who is ultimately responsible for death--the physician   or   God.   Since   some interference with   nature   is permitted,   the question of when that interference is prohibited   is   difficult to answer.   The paradox   is   that   the ability   to   cure   also provides an opportunity for   taking life.   The individual physician may have a difficult choice in   deciding   what   action is in the best   interest   of   the patient.   Compare the annotation at entry 156,   and   especially entries Bardfelt (157) and Silver (185).

162   Dorff,   Elliot.   "Rabbi I'm Dying."   Conservative Judaism 37 (1984): 31-51.

This   essay   addressed to rabbis suggests that   one   should never infantalize the dying person.   Respect the individual and offer prayer,   study,   and encouragement.   Dorff reviews Jewish   bioethics and the primacy of life in Jewish thought. This is a valuable essay not merely to those who counsel the dying but to anyone interested in both the human   compassion and principled approach Judaism takes when approaching death and dying.   The morality of such counseling is also revealed in   questions about truth telling to the terminally ill (see entries 018, 027.

163   Frankel,   Yitzkaq Yedidya.   "The Sanctity of   Human Life."   In The Dying Human,   edited by Andre de Vries   and Amnon Carmi,   195-199.   Tel Aviv: Turtledove Publishing Company, 1979.

The   modern   controversy over the exact criteria   for   death raises important moral issues for the Jew.   How can a   mere human   being decide when death has occurred?   How do   human beings make decisions in organ transplantations.   Frankel in this   anthology (190) notes that Judaism rejects brain death as a valid criteria for death.   He emphasizes the primacy of life   in Jewish thinking and warns that seeking to   utilize the   dying as donors for organ transplantations can lead   to exploitation.   He   suggests that adherence to Jewish tradition   and   the   traditional guidelines of   Jewish   morality provide the best means of deciding these difficult issues. Compare entries 155 and 157 and the annotation there.

164 Freehof, Solomon B.   "Allowing a Terminal Patient to
Die." In his <u>Modern Reform Responsa</u>, 197-203. Cincinnati:
Hebrew Union College Press, 1971.

The question of when termination of life is a blessing and
when it is murder is approached cautiously, but in a liberal
spirit here.   Jewish law is acknowledged, but the physician
is given considerable power.   Freehof declares that the
attending physician must have complete autonomy.   Where
there is a chance for life, Judaism demands treatment.
Freehof notes the difference between healing a person and
merely prolonging a period of pain and dying.   See the
annotation at entry 156.

165 Freehof, Solomon B.   "Determination and Postponement of
Death."   In   his   <u>Modern   Reform   Responsa</u>,   188-197.
Cincinnati: Hebrew Union College Press, 1971.

Freehof discusses the classic problem of determining the
moment of death. He notes the prohibition against hastening
death as well as the permission to allow death to take its
course.   His approach is a cautious one; although he is a
liberal Jew, he acknowledges the risks taken when one tries
to determine how to act in such situations. See entry 155.

166   Freehof, Solomon B.   "Relieving Pain of a Dying Patient." In his <u>Reform Responsa for Our Time</u>, 84-89. Cincinnati: Hebrew Union College Press, 1971.

The problem of whether euthanasia is a possible remedy for
the pain of the terminally ill raises moral questions.   Is
consideration for personal pain a valid justification for
taking a life that is ultimately God's possession?   Freehof
looks at the question in the light of discussions of suicide
in Judaism. He contends that Jewish law recognizes the pain
that motivates both suicide and euthanasia even while rejecting them.   He distinguishes between methods of healing
and methods that merely prolong pain and dying.

167 Goldfarb, Daniel C. "The Definition of Death." <u>Conse-
rvative Judaism</u> 30 (1976): 10-22.

The dilemma of euthanasia has been deepened in modern life
through the use of medical instruments that keep a body
alive artificially.   Are these life-support systems merely
obstacles to death or are they tools for curing illness?
Goldfarb reviews various sources from the Bible to Golda
Meir as well as modern medical information to decide when if
ever, life-support systems should be withdrawn.   He emphasizes Judaism's concern with the primacy of life and takes
that as the guiding principle in making any decision.
Compare the annotation at entries 155, 156.

168   Greenberg, Hayyim.   "The Right to Kill?" In <u>Jewish
Reflections on Death</u>, edited by Jack Reimer, 107-116. New
York: Schocken, 1974.

This study by a Conservative Jewish leader in a useful
anthology (see entry 550) emphasizes the primacy of life.
It suggests that euthanasia puts the selfish personal desires of the patient before the principle of divine control
over life and death. The essay is filled with case histories as well as study of the talmudic debate on the the
meaning of suffering integrated with a comparative study of
Jewish and non-Jewish approaches to death and suffering.
Compare entries 156 and 161.

169 Halevi, Chaim David. "Disconnecting a Terminal Patient
From an Artificial Respirator" [Hebrew]. Tehumin 2 (1981):
297-305.

The author reviews relevant data on euthanasia including the
stages of dying, the prohibition on hastening death and the
permissibility of removing of obstacles. He examines whether such actions can be understood as murder or not and
emphasizes the primacy of life in any decision making. See
the annotation at entry 156.

170 Halibard, G. B. "Euthanasia." The Jewish Law Annual 1
(1978): 196-199.

Halibard asks whether pain is the sole or only one of the
criteria used in deciding to end life? Motivation and the
definition of taking one's own life is discussed as relevant
to this question. See the annotation at 156 and the theological arguments noted in entry 162.

171 Herring, Basil F. "Euthanasia." In his Jewish Ethics
and Halakhah For Our Time: Sources and Commentary, 67-90.
The Library Jewish Law and Ethics, 11. New York: Ktav
Publishing House, 1984.

Herring summarizes the major traditional arguments against
euthanasia including an emphasis on the primacy of life, the
differences between active hastening of death and passive
removing of obstacles to dying, and the question of suicide.
The chapter includes source material from the Bible and
rabbinic writers. See the annotation at entry 156.

172 Klein, Isaac. "Euthanasia: A Jewish View." In Perspectives On Jews and Judaism: Essays in Honor of Wolfe Kelman,
edited by Arthur A. Chiel, 249-255. New York: Rabbinical
Assembly, 1978.

Klein studies the various views on euthanasia in Judaism
(see entries 161 and 156) emphaszing life and God as the
sole arbiter of that life. He notes both the obligation to
heal and the permission to allow nature to take its course
rather than prolong pain as well as the exact definition of
death and the time of death; compare entry 155.

173 Maman, Claud. "Comment etablir le Moment de la Mort."
Revue D'Historie De La Medecine Hebraique 33 (1980): 9-12,
27-56.

Maman surveys the talmudic views, the codes of Judaism, and modern medicine seeking the define the time of death. He questions when the Sabbath may be violated for the sake of a dying person and also the status of the fetus. See the annotation at entry 155.

174 Novak, David. "Euthanasia in Jewish Law." In his Law and Theology in Judaism 2nd Series, 98-117. New York: Ktav Publishing House, 1976.

Novak reviews the major concerns Jewish tradition has with euthanasia (compare the annotation to entry 156). While Jewish compassion recognizes the need to deal with a patient's suffering, compassion never involves a direct attack on the patient's life. Contrast the theological liberalism of Bardfeld (157).

175 Novak, David. "Suicide in Jewish Perspective." In his Law and Theology in Judaism, 80-93. New York: Ktav Publishing House, 1974.

Novak recognizes Judaism's opposition to the taking of life, even one's own life, but also its confrontation with the human condition that induces such an action. Novak contrasts suicide and martyrdom, considering the former a type of illness. He notes Jewish compassion for the suicide and discusses the biblical and rabbinic precedents for understanding it. See also entries 157, 178, 180, 183, 187.

176 Rosner, Fred. "The Definition of Death." Tradition 10 (1968/1969): 33-39.

Rosner reviews medical and legal arguments defining death. He realizes that science and religion may differ but does not consider the legal system to be the appropriate forum in which those differences should to be resolved. He looks at Jewish evidence from the rabbis up through the present day. entry 025, pp. 124-131. Compare the references given in the annotation to entry 155.

177 Rosner, Fred. "The Jewish Attitude Toward Euthanasia." In Jewish Bioethics, edited by Fred Rosner and J. David Bleich, 255-265. New York: Sanhedrin Press, 1979.

This general review of Jewish thinking about death and the termination of life (see the annotation to entry 156), notes the various traditional concerns towards euthanasia as well as the difficulty of drawing a line to determine when care is no longer useful. The essay is reprinted in entry 022, 107-123 and appears in French in Revue D'Historie De La Medecine Hebraique 22 (1969): 53-67; 23(1970): 45-51.

178 Rosner, Fred. "Suicide in Jewish Law." In Jewish Bioethics, edited by Fred Rosner and J. David Bleich, 317-330. The York: Sanhedrin Press, 1979.

Rosner explains that while Judaism opposes suicide and considers it a sin, it is understandable because of physical or
mental duress. He notes the difficulties the rabbis established for a self-conscious and voluntary suicide since any
hint of mental or physical coercion makes the act no longer
a sin. See also entries 157, 167, 183, 187.

179 Rosner, Fred. "The Use and Abuse of Heroic Measures to
Prolong Dying." Journal of Religion and Health 17 (1978):
8-18.

Here again the question of what is the mere prolongation of
dying and pain and what is a physician's task is raised (see
also the annotation at 156).   Rosner notes recent cases and
deplores the slogans that cloud the real question.   He
suggests the Jewish and Christian values are dramatically
different towards this issue.   He also claims that once
heroic measures are begun Judaism refuses to have them
interfered with.

180 Shapira, Amos. "The Right to Die-Some Israeli and
Jewish Legal Perspectives." In The Dying Human, edited by
Andre de Vries and Amnon Carmi, 359-371. Tel Aviv: Turtle-
dove Publishing Company, 1979.

The question of euthanasia (see the discussion in the annotation to entry 156) and of suicide (see entries 157, 175,
183, 187) have particular poignancy in the state of Israel.
There, Jewish morality attempts to shape civil legislation.
This moral activism is present in laws that prohibit both
suicide and euthanasia.   Despite this legal prescription,
however, personal moral decisions have often gone against
the law.   Shapira, for this anthology, (190) reviews cases
in Israel regarding euthanasia and suicide and shows that
the legal force of the prohibition on suicide is extremely
weak.

181 Sherwin, Byron L.   "Jewish Views on Euthanasia." The
Humanist 34 (1974): 19-21.

Sherwin declares that the Jewish view is not as straightforward as usually thought.   He gives a careful study that
shows how even active euthanasia may at times be acceptable
in Jewish thinking.   The approach taken in this article is
more detailed and reveals more of the complexity of the
problem than his work in the following entry or in many
other current studies as well; compare this work with the
entries listed in the annotation to entry 156.

182 Sherwin, Byron. L. "To Be Or...A Jewish View of Euthanasia." United Synagogue Review 25,1 (1972): 4-5.

This essay summarizes traditional Jewish law and suggests
three basic principles: self-destruction is also murder, no
human being is an obstacle to be removed, all life is in-
trinsically valuable.   The primacy of life is explained

clearly and theologically in Sherwin's writing. While the
complexity he notes in the previous entry is not present
here in this one, he shows how Jewish principles can guide
behavior for a modern human being.

183 Siegel, Seymour. "Suicide in the Jewish View." Conservative Judaism 32 (1978): 67-74.

While focused on the difference between martyrdom and suicide, this essay looks at the various legal concerns in
Jewish thinking about taking one's own life. Siegel determines that the primacy of life may be set aside in the face
of ideals that transcend life. Life gains its meaning from
such ideals, but they do not negate life's importance. He
concludes with an epilogue looking at the mass suicide at
Jonestown. Compare entries 157, 175, 187.

184 Siegel, Seymour. "Updating the Criteria of Death."
Conservative Judaism 30 (1976): 23-30.

Siegel reviews the controversy concerning the definition of
death and the time of death; see the annotation at 155.

185 Silver, Daniel Jeremy. "The Right to Die." In Jewish
Reflections on Death, edited by Jack Reimer, 117-125. New
York: Schocken, 1975.

It may be possible to argue that authors like Silver in this
anthology (entry 550) and Solomon Freehof (see entries 153-
155) represent a more liberal position than do traditionalists. Certainly this essay represents a distinctly minority view which gives permission for euthanasia in more
cases than would normally be allowed. Thus, as Silver
reviews the differing attitudes of the Jewish tradition on
the appropriateness of interfering with the natural process, he concludes that such interference is justified. He
feels that life is more than mere biological functioning.
Compare the items mentioned in entry 156.

186 Smolar, Leivy. "The Right to Die, the Bioethical Fron-
tier: Creating an Agenda." Journal of Jewish Communal Service 53 (1977): 320-329.

Smoler investigates the modern controversy concerning the
right to die, the civil legislation discussed and the ethical and moral questions that must be raised. See the annotation at entry 155.

187 Spero, Moshe Halevi. "Violating the Shabbat for
Suicide Emergency: A Halakhic Explication." Journal of
Halacha and Contemporary Society 3 (1982): 72-83.

Spero raises the question of whether a Jew can transgress a
commandment to another from transgressing and concludes that
an attempt at suicide is really a cry for help and not an
intentional violation of Jewish law and so the Sabbath may

be violated to prevent such an act. Spero's sense of psychology leads him to a sympathetic view that is consistent with the Jewish tradition in its compassion for the suicide victim. What is of interest here is that Spero explicitly speaks of a case where two Jewish values conflict and in which the primacy of life is clearly enunciated. Compare entries 157, 175, 183.

188   Tendler, Moshe D. "Addendum." In his Medical Ethics: A Compendium of Jewish Moral, Ethical, and Religious Principles in Medical Practice, 5th ed. New York: Federation of Jewish Philanthropies of New York, 1981.

This final section of Tendler's anthology deals with problems of euthanasia, treating the dying, and the question of triage or priorities of treatment. While earlier essays in the volume dealt with similar issues (see entry *** this special section gives extended discussion to questions of withholding or providing treatment in the light of modern discoveries and technology. See the annotation for the volume as a whole in 037.

189   Tendler, Moshe D. "Care of the Critically Ill." In his Medical Ethics: Compendium of Jewish Moral, Ethical, and Religious Principles in Medical Practice, 5th ed., 53-84. New York: Federation of Jewish Philanthropies of New York, 1981.

This essay investigates truth telling to the patient, autopsies, treatment of the terminally ill and euthanasia, and the question of organ transplantations. The detailed consideration of various aspects of Jewish law make this a valuable survey of how Judaism takes practical measures to insure respect for the individual and for personal dignity even in the most extreme of human situations. Compare the discussions in 011, 027, 162 and the items there.

190   Vries, Andre, (de) and Carmi, Amon. The Dying Human. Tel Aviv: Turtledove Publishing Company, 1979.

This publication of a symposium held in Tel Aviv in 1978 includes a variety of views on death from philosophers, theologians, and physicians. The fact that both traditionalists and liberals are represented makes this a valuable collection. It looks at ethical issues such as euthanasia and also at psychological questions such as rituals and forms of mourning. Both traditional Jewish views and secular Jewish approaches are included to make the variety of responses truly representative of Jewish thinking about these crucial issues. This anthology is a good starting place for an investigation of the entire spectrum of contemporary Jewish moral reflection on the meaning of death and the modern dilemmas posed by it. Entries from this anthology include 163, 180, 544, 572, 573, 701.

191   Weinberger, Yaakov. "Euthanasia in Jewish Religious Law" [Hebrew]. Dine Israel (1976): 99-127.

Modern life has allowed people to consider both the extraordinary measures taken to continue life and the possibility
of removing them to allow death (note the discussion and
annotation in entry 156 and the references found there).
Some people face the problem of an unwanted continuation of
their life by writing a "living will" to insure that if they
are in a desperate situation they can be assured that no
extraordinary methods will be used to keep them alive.
Weinberger notes that Judaism obligates treatment and rejects the idea of a living will for the termination of
treatment. The duties of the physician are also studied.
He notes that Judaism takes account of the patient's condition in its decisions.

192 Weisbard, Alan J. "On the Bioethics of Jewish Law: The
Case of Karen Quinlan." Israel Law Review 14 (1979): 337-
368.

This essay raises the question of the determination of
death, particularly in relationship to the possibility of
euthanasia (see entry 155 and the references there). Weisbard summarizes the case of Karen Ann Quinlan and Jewish
contributions to the debate, relying heavily on the work of
J. David Bleich (see entry 160). Beyond giving a survey of
Jewish thinking, however, he discusses how such decisions
should be made. He agrees that an impartial judicial trial
would be helpful and contends that a jury rather than a
judge should decide cases of such moral weight.

2
Sexual Morality

GENERAL SEXUALITY

193 Bleich, J. David. "Transsexual Surgery." In his Contemporary Halakhic Problems, 100-105. The Library of Jewish Law and Ethics, 2. New York: Ktav Publishing House, 1977.

Sexuality defines role and destiny in Judaism, and Jewish morality therefore looks with disfavor at any attempt to change one's sexuality. This essay reviews the prohibition against mutilating the body, the prohibition against transsexual behavior, and the Jewish principle that marriage is the most complete expression of human sexuality. For Judaism sexual identity depends on the genital organs so that such surgery makes no essential change in a person's sexual status from the standpoint of Jewish law or liturgy. This essay can also be found in entry 025, pp. 191-196 and in Tradition 14: (1974): 94-98.

194 Borowitz, Eugene B. Choosing a Sex Ethic: A Jewish Inquiry. New York: Schocken Books, 1969.

This helpful book reviews a variety of secular and religious ethical principles for making sexual decisions. Borowitz provides an informed survey of Jewish sources and the implications of those sources for contemporary Jewish behavior. He clarifies both the rational approach of Judaism and its theological basis. The book demonstrates a sense of the contemporary dilemma of sexuality together with firm rooting in Judaic thought. Borowitz surveys a variety of possible guidelines for sexual behavior, including a useful reference to traditional Jewish law. His approach should be contrasted to the traditional views in entries 203-207, 210, 213, 214, to the Conservative Jewish thinkers in entries 195, 197, 198, 201, 202, 208, 212, and views of other liberal analysts in entries 200 and 209.

195 Dresner, Samuel H., and Sherwin, Byron L. "Pre-Marital Sex--Yes or No." United Synagogue Review 30,2 (1977): 6-7, 23-26.

Jewish leaders try a variety of strategies to convey their
views on sexual responsibility to Jewish youth. This fic-
tionalized correspondence between two sisters suggests a
Jewish approach to sexual decision-making. The main moral
admonitions are that one should not make sex a mechanical
act and that Jews are non-conformists with a tradition of
standing outside of popular trends. The essay touches upon
possible psychological and physical damage from incautious
sexual activity. In sum it concludes that waiting and
choices are hard but often worthwhile. Compare these views
with those in the items in the previous entry; contrast
especially Green (202), a conservative Jew with a more
liberal perspective on the question of pre-marital sexual
experience.

196 Elkins, Dov Peretz. Humanizing Jewish Life. New
Brunswick: A.S.Barnes, 1976.

Many Jewish thinkers confront the modern period in radically
new ways, finding new approaches to sexuality and the family. While such innovation is usually found in the liberal
forms of Judaism, Conservative Jewish leaders like Dov
Peretz make a distinctive contribution. Peretz suggests a
humanistic, albeit Jewishly informed, approach to family
life. Some essays are focused exclusively on family concerns (see pages 17-80) and redefine Jewish education and
the Jewish community according to the model of the mishpacha
for community. The family is understood as providing an environment for exchange and transactions.

197 Feldman, David M. Marital Relations, Birth Control and
Abortion in Jewish Law. New York: Schocken Books, 1974.

This valuable book (see entry 088) opens with an excellent
discussion of marriage, its relationship to procreation, the
stress on enjoyment, and the Jewish view of sexuality as
part of human well being. Feldman suggests that this
approach demonstrates a point of contrast between Judaism
and Christianity.

198 Feldman, David M. "Sexuality: The Scope of Tradition
and its Application." In The Second Jewish Catalogue,
compiled and edited by Sharon Strassfeld and Michael
Strassfeld, 94-96. Philadelphia: Jewish Publication Society
of America, 1976.

The Second Jewish Catalogue provides a panorama of Jewish
views on sexuality, including traditional and non-traditional approaches alike (see entries 202, 208, 344). Feldman, a
Conservative Rabbi but a traditionalist within his movement,
provides a lucid explanation of Jewish moral principles
concerning sexuality notes that sexual pleasure and sexual
development can be separated. Feldman contends that sexual
discipline within family bounds provides the basis for
holiness, that is for civilized restraints on the pursuit of
personal pleasure. Compare entry 194.

199 Freehof, Solomon B.   "Surgery for Trans-sexuals."   In
his Modern Reform Responsa, 128-133. Cincinnati: Hebrew
Union College Press, 1971.

Note how this response corresponds to that of a traditionalist such as J. David Bleich (in entry 193) indicating
a common repugnance to altering biological nature.   Freehof
advocates following the traditional Jewish moral code with
its emphasis on avoiding danger and on the duty of procreation.   He notes that both men and women are under the commandment not to endanger life and that men are under obligation to procreate.   Judaism, his view, opposes sex changes
in general because of its orientation towards life and
health.   On the basis of the same two principles, however,
life-saving surgery, even if it wounds the genital organs,
is to be approved.   Compare his views on the marriage of a
transsexual (entry 323).

200 Friedman, Maurice. "Love and Sex." In his The Hidden
Human Image, 165-184. New York: Delta Publishing Company,
1974.

Friedman contends that love requires existential courage.
He reviews modern literature, existential psychology and the
views of Martin Buber to criticize those whose false need
for intimacy comes from their confusion of eros and love.
His existentialist approach advocates mutuality and reci-
procity rather than detailed rules or elaborate theoriza-
tion.   Contrast this view with the Orthodox approaches of
Harris (203), Jung (204) or Lamm (205) on the one hand or
the more liberal views of Borowitz (194), Gordis (201) or
Matt (208) on the other.

201 Gordis, Robert.   Love and Sex: A Modern Jewish Perspective. New York: Farrar, Straus, and Giroux, 1978.

Gordis is a major representative of Conservative Judaism and
his confrontation with the problems of sexuality demonstrate
a perceptive blend of response to the modern world and
steadfast advocacy of the values of tradition. His response
should be compared to that found in the other items noted in
entry 194.   This is a wide-ranging book bringing together
many of the concerns Gordis expresses in regard to Jewish
morality in other essays.   He looks at sexuality, marriage,
intermarriage, divorce, the place of omen in Judaism, birth
control and abortion, adultery, illegitimacy, and homosexuality.   His approach shows how the tradition developed
and its application in modern times as it responds sensi-
tively to the needs of Jews today. See his essays on particular subjects in entries 238, 280, 291.

202 Green, Arthur. "A Contemporary Approach to Jewish
Sexuality."   In The Second Jewish Catalogue, compiled and
edited by Sharon Strassfeld and Michael Strassfeld, 96-99.
Philadelphia: Jewish Publication Society of America, 1976.

The modern world has presented young Jews with a bewildering
array of possibilities for sexual exploration. Jews need to
consult the tradition, but to feel comfortable with it; they
need to be assured that it recognizes their perplexities.
This sensitive and creative article analyzes the tradition
of Judaism with its emphasis on marriage and the family in
the light of modern Jewish problems. Compare his views with
the guidance offered by Borowitz (194), Gordis (201), Matt
(208) and Porter (209).   In a more traditional vein, Green
urges single Jews to think of the violation of the trust
generations have placed in them caused by the decision not
to propogate.

203   Harris, Monford.   "Pre-Marital Sexual Experience: A
Covenantal Critique." Judaism 19 (1970): 134-144.

This theological investigation contrasts with the detailed
studies of Jewish sexuality found in many of the essays
mentioned in entry 194.   It should be compared specifically
to the essay of Friedman (200).   Harris explains Jewish
sexual morality by contrasting love understood by the covenant and romantic love.   In Judaism marriage is neither
secular nor sacramental but a covenantal bond linking
partners in love and obligation to each other.

204 Jung, Leo. Love and Life. New York: Philosophical
Library, 1979.

In contrast to the above entry Orthodox Jewish moral thought
can be presented lyrically as well as polemically.   Jung
offers such a rendering.   His work should be compared with
the other items mentioned in entry 194.   This book develops
the idea of love in marriage, in women's sexual satisfac-
tion, and in the knowledge and love of God.   It provides a
guide through the moral decisions that arise when sexuality,
love, and human existence are understood through the concept
of obedience to a divine law that animates what is best in
every human being. See also entries 247, 248, 339.

205 Lamm, Maurice. The Jewish Way in Love and Marriage.
New York: Harper and Row, 1980.

This detailed study from a traditional Orthodox Jew bears
comparison with the equally specific and broadly conceived
works of Feldman (197) and Gordis (201) as well as with the
studies by Silverstein (213) and Tendler (201). Lamm offers
a traditional summary of Jewish concerns in marriage and
sexuality, reviews basic rules for finding a marriage partner, sexual conduct, prohibited and preferred partners,
homosexuality, bigamy, and birth control. The moral thrust
of this work goes beyond summarizing the legal material,
however.   Questions of ritual observances, interfaith marriages, divorces, and sexual dysfunction show the author's
concern for establishing basic principles of Jewish sexual
behavior. Lamm suggests that Jewish morality considers
sexuality a means by which human beings are bound to one
another and to God.

206   Lamm,   Norman.   "The   New   Morality   Under   Religious
Auspices."   Tradition 10 (1968): 17-30.

This essay is an example of Orthodox polemic against modernity with a particular emphasis on modern sexual mores.   Lamm
understands Jewish sexuality from a practical and moral
standpoint.   He claims that Judaism is more realistic in its
positive approach to sexuality combined with a rejection of
the pleasure mentality than either a restrictive religious
outlook or a promiscuous one.   He repeats Judaism's call for
moral responsibility in the face of a "new morality" which
he feels institutionalizes immorality.   The essay can also
be found in his Faith and Doubt, Studies in Traditional
Jewish Thought (New York: Ktav Publishing House, 1971), pp.
247-269.

207   Lamm,   Norman.   "The   Role of the   Synagogue   in   Sex
Education."   The Jewish Family in a Changing World,   edited
by Gilbert S. Rosenthal,   156-176. New York: Thomas
Yoseloff, 1970.

Traditional Judaism is not prudish, and the same author may
present a different appearance in a different   context.   In
this contribution to a collection of essays generally representing a sensitive Orthodox response (entry 358) Norman
Lamm affirms a positive approach to sexuality . He finds
that Judaism teaches sanctification through sexuality and
includes sex education as part of Torah learning.   An understanding of Jewish law, he declares, requires a knowledge of
sexual practices.   The synagogue, in his view, is the best
place for learning sexual morality because religion can
teach the meaning of shame without inculcating a stultifying
guilt.   This process of learning is therapeutic since
healing begins with the objectification of the subjective.
This fascinating essay demonstrates that sexuality is crucial in Jewish law and lore and is sanctified through the
process of Torah study.   Sexual education and counseling in
Judaism also merits attention in Tendler (215).

208 Matt, Hershel J. "Sex and Sexuality." In The Second
Jewish Catalogue, compiled and edited by Sharon Strassfeld
and Michael Strassfeld, 91-94. Philadelphia: Jewish Publication Society of America, 1976.

Matt, a Conservative rabbi, declares that sexuality is a
benefit and boon to humanity. Developing a sexual identity
is part of the formation of human personality.   Sexual
morality, however, is required since modesty is a way of
nurturing the self rather than allowing exploitation.   This
modernistic approach to sexuality has its roots in the
double moral approach of Judaism--a positive view of
sexuality combined with an insistence that the sexual be
controlled by obedience to divine commandments.   This view
should be compared to a more traditional view suggested by
another Conservative rabbi, Feldman (198), to Orthodox
thinkers like Jung (204) or Steinberg (214), and to liberals
such as Borowitz (194) or Porter (209).

209   Porter, Jack Nusan.   "Sexuality and Judaism."
The Reconstructionist 44,10 (1979): 11-17.

Jewish tradition finds it difficult to accept the modern
style of sexual experimentation, just as modern Jews find
traditional norms inapplicable to their lives. Jewish theologians struggle to find ways in which modernity and tradition can communicate and Porter reviews the attempts of some
of these Jewish thinkers like Eugene Borowitz (see entry
194) and Arthur Waskow (see entry 371) to present traditional Jewish sexual morality in a contemporary way.   He claims
that the task is impossible because of the general restric-
tiveness in Jewish sexual ethics and because of its anti-
feminist bias. His views are difficult to accept especially
in the light of the very perceptive and imaginative use of
traditional ideas and categories that modern theologians are
able to discover.

210   Rackman, Emmanuel.   "Privacy in Judaism." Midstream
28,7 (1982): 31-33.

Judaism's approach to sexuality can be understood as
symptomatic of its general concerns.   Thus Rackman points to
Judaism's careful protection of the right to privacy in all
areas, and especially in sexual purification. He draws the
general conclusion that religious practice should be
voluntary.   From this perspective he contends that coercive
legislation, particularly in the realm of family law, in the
State of Israel misunderstands Judaism.   This sensitive
Orthodox viewpoint should be compared to Harris (203) and to
the other entries noted in entry 194.

211 Shapiro, David S. "Be Fruitful and Multiply." In his
Studies in Jewish Thought, 375-399.   New York: Yeshiva
University Press, 1978.

While some authors use the commandment to be fruitful and
multiply as an incentive for producing larger Jewish families, Shapiro takes a more theological approach to the
question. He seeks to know what ontological presuppositions
about being male and female, about being a biological human
being, lie beneath this commandment.   He notes that the
command to propagate the species is both a blessing and an
obligation.   He rationalizes that the man is commanded rather than the woman because the man's sexual drive is stronger and the woman suffers more in childbirth.   He explains
the depth-significance Jewish mysticism invests in the act
of procreation and the inherent importance of this natural
process for Jewish religious life and belief.   This essay
can also be found in Tradition 13/14 (1973): 42-67 and in
entry 025, 59-79.   Contrast his view of this commandment
with that of Frank (098), Gordis (100). and Rackman (102).

212   Siegel, Seymour.   "Some Aspects of the Jewish Tradition's View of Sex." In Jews and Divorce, edited by Jacob
Fried, 158-185. New York: Ktav Publishing House, 1968.

Siegel's useful bibliography provides this volume (entry 423) with a sketch of Jewish views on sexuality and sexual morality from the biblical period and the Talmudic sources. He suggests that the moral foundation of Jewish views of sexuality is the realization that the Yetzer Ha-Ra or evil inclination is important for life but must be contained and channeled constructively. He reviews the positive aspects of Jewish sexual morality, the theories of the mystics, and some less well known aspects of Jewish moral teachings about concubines, homosexuality, contraception and abortion. Siegel's views should be compared with the items in entry 194 and in particular with other Conservative Jewish thinkers such as Feldman (198), Green (202), and Matt (208).

213 Silverstein, Shraga. The Antidote: Human Sexuality in a Torah Perspective. New York: Feldheim, 1979.

This traditional presentation defends Jewish sexual mores on marriage, family purity, and various types of sexual behavior in the context of homiletical and sermonic admonition. The interested reader will find traditional laws and lore as well as ethics in this volume. A more balanced view will be found in the following entry as well as in Lamm (205). Compare the items mentioned in entry 194.

214 Steinberg, Avrahom. "The Jewish Attitude to Sexual Life" [Hebrew]. Assia 4 (1983): 190-206.

An advantage to this study lies in its comparative perspective. Its traditionalism compares with that of other authors (such as Harris in entry 203, Lamm in entry 205, and Shraga in the previous entry). Steinberg contrasts Judaism to Christianity on the basis of its positive view of sexuality. He focuses on the Jewish command for propagation and sexuality as a means to assuage the body and to conquer passion. Idolatry, he suggests, can be abolished by utilizing the Yetzer Ha-Ra (the evil impulse) rather than attempting to destroy it. He contends that sexuality is a special type of knowledge and because of that rejects sexual intercourse outside of marriage. He finds the Jewish way the way of the "golden mean" which recognizes legitimate pleasure while rejecting such perversions as homosexuality or adultery.

215 Tendler, Moshe. "Sex Counseling", in Medical Ethics: A Compendium of Jewish Moral, Ethical and Religious Principles in Medical Practice, 5th ed., 44-47. New York: Federation of Jewish Philanthropies of New York, 1975.

Tendler includes in his compendium (entry 030) a survey of sexual dilemmas including homosexuality, sex reversal surgery, the status of a newborn with ambiguous genitalia, and cases of sex dysfunction. While primarily a compilation of decisions from Jewish law this chapter responds to human needs and notes that Judaism considers sexual development important to human life. Compare Lamm (297).

FEMINISM AND JUDAISM

216 Adler, Rachel. "The Jew Who Wasn't There: Halacha and the Jewish Woman." In Contemporary Jewish Ethics, edited by Menahem Marc Kellner, 347-399. Sanhedrin Jewish Studies. New York: Sanhedrin Press, 1978.

Jewish feminists claim that they have been overlooked in Judaism and treated as if they were not really Jews (see the poignant description given in entry 239 and the classic indictment of the male establishment in 260). Adler presents an articulate exposition of this position. Her critical argument declares that when tradition associates of women, slaves, and children it reveals a negative view of the feminine. Indeed it concludes there is no continuous tradition of learned women in Judaism. This lack needs rectification in the modern period. Adler joins with a vocal group of feminists in calling for Judaism to change its approach to women. In addition to the two works cited above compare her views to entries 224, 226, 228, 230 239-243, 245, 252-253, 260, 264, 275. Contrast the critique of Jewish feminism given by Friedfertig (232), Johnson (246) and Pelcovitz (248). The essay is reprinted in Heschel (244), pp. 12-18.

217 Baron, Sheryl. "National Liberation and the Jewish Woman." In Jewish Radicalism, edited by Jack Nusan Porter and Peter Dreier, 255-260. New York: Random House, 1973.

Radical Jewish women are torn in three directions. They have sympathy and concern for Jews, Judaism, and communal solidarity. They fight for their own liberation and that of other women both in Jewish life and in modern society as a whole. They are often equally concerned with the improvement of the world as a whole and with general human liberation on all fronts. How are they to balance these concerns? Baron argues that best way for a woman to fight for her own liberation is side by side with those fighting for national liberation--that is in Israel. For many feminists, however, Israel has been a disappointment; it promised important changes and then reverted to a male dominated reality (see entries 270 and 278).

218 Berkovits, Eliezer. "The Status of Woman within Judaism." In Contemporary Jewish Ethics, edited by Menahem Marc Kellner, 355-374. Sanhedrin Jewish Studies. New York: Sanhedrin Press 1978.

Berkovits offers a traditional Jewish perspective with, nonetheless, a sympathy and recognition of the problems faced by modern women. Some statements in the tradition, Berkovits admits, to being objectionable. He perceives a gap between the concrete expression of Jewish law and its essential ethic. He feels it possible to make changes in the first in order to bring it into harmony with the second without disturbing the essence of tradition. The moral essence of the halakhic procedure is, therefore in his view, characterized as being responsive to personal need.   This very sensitive traditional response should be compared to entries 219, an equally sensitive viewpoint and contrasted to the rather dogmatic presentations by Orthodox Jews in Ellinson (215), Friedfertig (232), Johnson (246), and Pelcovitz (248); the thorough study of the place of women in Judaism by Meiselman (243) falls into this category but should be seriously considered as a full and detailed explanation of the Orthodox standpoint.   The lyrical approach of Jung (247-249) is somewhat unrealistic despite a valiant attempt to confront relevant issues.

219   Berman,   Saul J.   "The Status of Women in Halakhic Judaism." Tradition 14 (1973): 5-18.

This classic review of women's status in Judaism is both supportive of tradition and critical of its expression in the contemporary period.   This remarkable statement of an Orthodox Jewish leader recognizes contemporary questions even as it reaffirms the authority of halakha. Berman looks at three basic issues: women have been deprived of positive commands, have been given a disadvantaged legal rights, and have played a subservient role.   He suggests that the goals of society should not bar a woman from seeking her personal religious and spiritual development. He also claims that Jewish law, particularly in regard to divorce, needs to be more responsive to women's needs. The quest of Jewish women for equality has not been limited to traditional Jews, but has met obstacles in all branches of Judaism as entries 227, 228, 257, and 280 demonstrate. The essay is reprinted in Koltun (251), pp. 114-118.

220 Bleich, J. David.   "Slacks."   Tradition 16 (1976): 155-158.

The traditional approach to women is based upon a keen sense of morality and the limitations on behavior that must be invoked to maintain it;note this approach in Kahana   (250). One such limitation declares that women should not dress in male apparel nor men in women's clothing.   In the modern world women wear slacks that are clearly not the same in style or appearance as those worn by mean. Is such clothing moral or immoral to wear?   Bleich seeks to set priorities in immoral dress.   He concludes that while the wearing of slacks might not violate the prohibition against donning male attire they are tightfitting and immodest.   Torah scholars, he insists, must not wear unbecoming garments.

221 Blumenthal, Aaron.   "The Status of Women in Jewish Law." Conservative Judaism 31 (1977): 45-55.

This is a courageous and fascinating blend of traditionalism and openness to modern questions.   The ancient rabbis, Blumenthal contends, were proud of their women at home and of their men in the outside community. In its original context that was understandable, but today he finds no reason to be proud of how Jewish women are treated. He notes that the so-called principle that women have freedom from command- ments tied to time has been applied inconsistently. Given that history he calls for changes in Jewish law concerning women. The debate within Conservative Judaism on the place of women has split traditionalists such as Feldman (230), Ostrow (259) and Shapiro (275) from those advocating more dramatic changes such as Blumenthal here, Gordis (238), Hauptman (292), Hyman (245), Ofseyer (258), Pearl (261) and Strauss (279). Siegel's review of the entire question (276) provides a valuable summary of the major lines of argument.

222 Brayer, Menachem M. The Jewish Woman in Rabbinic Literature, 2 volumes. New York: Ktav Publishing House, 1985.

In two volumes, one dedicated to "a psycho-social perspec- tive" and one to a "psycho-historical perspective" Brayer gives a comprehensive analysis of the status, attributes, and accomplishments of the Jewish woman. The two volumes, which can be read independently, form a complement to one another through complementary perspectives on the status and contribution of women in Judaism. Brayer takes a tradition- al position and documents it with details from Jewish history and literature and with portraits of great Jewish women. Brayer compares the Judaic perspective with that of feminism and psychology. His work investigates the basic rationale for Judaism's separation of men and women, and he defends that separation as one that appreciates the variety of women's contribution to Judaism.

223 Breslauer, S. Daniel. "Women, Religious Rejuvenation and Judaism." Judaism 32 (1983): 466-476.

Many Jews claim that the halakha is responsive to human need. The author suggests that this principle must be tested by its responsiveness to women. The way Jewish law reacts to the demands of women is taken as an indication of its ability to rejuvenate itself. The article juxtaposes classical texts and modern problems. Other essays seeking to use the problem of women in Judaism as a means of under- standing the halakhic process as such include entries 231, 245, 254, 260, 273, 281.

224 Brin, Ruth F. "Can a Woman Be a Jew?" In A Coat of Many Colors: Jewish Subcommunities in the United States, edited by Abraham D. Lavender, 243-251. Westport: Greenwood Press, 1977.

It may come as a shock to think of women as a "subcommunity" in American Jewry. The particular self-interests and growing self-awareness of women and their recent experiments in rituals and cultural expressions uniquely their own makes them such a subgroup. Brin claims that women have been seen as vicarious Jews who participate through their husbands.

In her view the tradition looks at them as expressions of
the demonic which must be contained.   She laments this
situation and demands that it be altered.   This view should
be compared with the items in entry 216.

225   Bulka,   Reuven P.   "Woman's Role: Some Ultimate
Concerns."   Tradition 17 (1979): 27-40.

Traditional Jews often idealize their view of women and the
place of women in Judaism (see the items in entry 218 and
especially Jung, entries 247-249).   Men and women are assigned different roles according to an assumed different nature established by a divine design.   Bulka defends traditional halakha and its view of women.   He contends that it is
necessary to establish the radical otherness of male and
female, a radicality obscured by the feminist movement.   He
suggests that the willingness to recognize this unalterable
distinction between male and female is a test of civilization itself.   By obliterating the divinely given difference
between men and women modernity testifies to its lack of understanding of reality.

226   Clamar, Aphrodite.   "Torah True and Feminist Too."
Journal of Jewish Communal Services 56 (1980): 297-300.

Sociological studies show the problems contemporary Jewish
women face, whether traditional or non-traditional, in solving the double dilemma of being female in the modern world
and being faithful to Judaism (see entries 252, 253, 256,
268, 277).   This essay studies the way traditional Jewish
women reconcile their roles as professionals and their acceptance of secular values with their self-image as observant Jews.

227   Cohn, Haim H.   "Discriminations of Women," in Human
Rights in Jewish Law, 167-177.   New York: Ktav Publishing
House, 1984.

This perceptive article recognizes the problematic morality
motivating much of Jewish legislation concerning women (compare entries 219, 224, and 231).   Cohn points to talmudic
laws restricting female participation in Jewish legal procedures, particularly those involving husbands and wives, to
demonstrate discrimination against women in Judaism.   He
notes the stereotypes of feminine character which have pre-
vailed in traditional Judaism and their negative effect on
Jewish women.

228   Elazar, Daniel J. and Monson, Rela Geffen.   "Women in
the Synagogue Today."   Midstream 27 (1981): 25-30.

While the Jewish community has spoken at length about the
strides women have made, little actual data has been
collected to authenticate that claim (against it see the
arguments in the items mentioned in entries 216 and 221).
The two authors here seek to remedy that situation and this

article gathers data concerning the progress of American Jewish women comes to a disappointing conclusion. The two authors recognize that while much progress has been made it has been too slow and not enough. The issue has split the Jewish community (not necessarily along gender lines) and has made the distinction between American Jewry and other Jewish communities more obvious than ever before.

229 Ellinson, Getzel [Elikim]. Woman and the Mitzvot: An Anthology of Rabbinic Teaching [Hebrew]. 3 Volumes. Jerusalem: World Zionist Organization, 1974, 1981.

This fascinating anthology summarizes basic approaches to women in Jewish law, questions of the rationale of such laws, the separation of men and women, and the ways of modesty (comparison should be made with entries 219 and 249). The three volumes are compendiums reducing massive legal literature to basic principles and their illustrations. The approach is traditional but, for the Hebrew reader, exceedingly illuminating and helpful. The first volume is a textbook, complete with review questions. The next two volumes illustrate modern concerns including covering questions of modesty and procreation. Compare Ellinson's other writings (entries 077, 103, 104).

230 Feldman, David M. "Woman's Role and Jewish Law." In Conservative Judaism and Jewish Law, edited by Seymour Siegel with Elliot Gertel, 294-305. New York: Rabbinical Assembly, 1977.

Conservatism is deeply divided on the question of what role women should play in Jewish life (note the discussion found in entry 221) Here Feldman offers a traditionalist summary of Jewish views on why women are allowed to assume commandments for themselves but not as part of a male quorum. He discusses the problem of sexual distraction and of those commandments which women are indeed obligated to perform. His restatement of traditional Jewish views demonstrates the morality associated with a particular view of both male and female sexuality. The essay first appeared in Conservative Judaism 26 (1972): 29-39.

231 Fields, Rona M. "In God's Image: The Liberation of the Jewish Woman." United Synagogue Review 25 (1972): 4-5, 29-31.

Fields surveys the concerns of Jewish women, including a review of biblical women prototypes, of controversial divorce laws, and the various roles that women could play. She insists that women are not merely to act as wife, mother, or sex object but also as politicians and educators. She suggests that the inherited sexual taboos and handicaps are distortions borrowed from the Philistines and not from Jewish law. Compare this rationale for the place of women in Judaism with that given by Levinas (255) and Segal (273).

232 Friedfertig, Raizel Schnall and Schapiro, Freyda, eds.
The Modern Jewish Woman: A Unique Perspective.   Boston:
Lubavitch Education Foundation, 1981.

The editors demonstrate through their selection of material
a dedication to the traditional view of the place of women
and the legitimacy of the Orthodox understanding of woman's
nature.   This collection of testimonial essays is more important as data than for the analysis it offers.   Most of
the essays are apologetics for marriage, for the traditional
place of women, for the protection of privacy.   An interesting viewpoint suggests that population control is God's
task,   not that of the Jewish family (one wonders why the
same could not be said for increasing the Jewish population?).   The critique of feminism implied in this anthology
should be compared to the voices of the movement noted in
entry 216 as well as to the critical approach of even Orthodox thinkers as evidenced in entry 219.

233 Friedman, Maurice. "Women's Liberation." In his
The Hidden Human Image, 183–223. New York: Delta Publishing
Company, 1974.

Friedman draws on contemporary world literature to find
categories by which to understand both male domination of
women and the feminist struggle against it.   He charts his
own experiences with feminism and his recognition of the
limitations in its ideology.   He calls upon women to move
from consciousness raising, from a "promethean" protest
against men, to an exploration of alternative social forms
that can solve the problem of exploitation by altering
communal structures.

234 Friedman, Maurice. "Women's Liberation."   In his The
Confirmation of Otherness in Family, Community and Society,
197–205. New York: Pilgrim Press, 1983.

This essay restates Friedman's basic theme of respect for
the human image.   He is concerned not with women as adver-
saries of men but as one image of human selfhood.   He seeks
a liberation from all stereotypes and from a mechanistic
society.   His concrete examples and sense of compassion for
all participants in the conflict between men and women make
this a valuable study.   He draws upon modern literature,
psychology, and feminist excesses to demonstrate the danger
of being too strident in one's attempt at liberation.

235 Gantz, Paula.   "Our Golden Years--You Should Live So
Long." Lilith 9 (1982): 6–9.

Gantz points out that as women grow older their options
decrease; they have a fear of dependence in old age.   She
notes that daughters cannot care for their mothers.   She
calls for some provision by the Jewish community and gives
as an example some programs in New York City.   Old age, she
suggests, is a feminist issue.

236 Gendler, Mary. "Woman and Judaism--Time for a Change."
In Jewish Radicalism, edited by Jack Nusan Porter and Peter
Dreier, 261-270. New York: Random House, 1973.

This essay represents a radical demand that women be given
equal rights in Judaism.   Jewish religion has divided women
from men too long and kept women separate from religious
experience. Gendler demands that women participate in every
element of Jewish life. She claims that a woman has a right
to be Jewish, to be a woman, and to find a way of uniting
those two identities. Her recognition that a struggle for
power between men and women is being waged finds confirmation and explanation in the other works noted at entry 221.

237 Gittelsohn, Roland B.   "Women's Liberation and
Judaism." Midstream 17 (1971): 51-48.

The rhetoric and record of Reform Judaism on the question of
the place of women is as mixed as is that of either Orthodoxy or Conservatism (see entries 266 and 267).   Reform has
liberals calling for complete equality (see Lipman, entry
255) and women rabbis (see Priesand, 269).   Some Reform
leaders, such as Gittlesohn here, however, reiterate the
traditional apologetic statement of Jewish high regard for
women.   He provides a rationale for the lack of feminine
Jewish scholars, and holds out marriage as protection of the
woman, and remarks upon the many advances women have made in
modern times.

238 Gordis, Robert.   "Women's Rights in Jewish Life and
Law." United Synagogue Review 29,3 (1977): 4-5, 29-31.

Gordis represents a liberal approach within Conservative
Judaism towards women (see entry 221).   In this essay he
provides a historical perspective on women in Jewish life
(compare his historical review with that of Lacks, entry
252, Lerner,   253, Mann, 256, Preisand, 269, and Schneider,
271).   Gordis recalls the history of struggle of women in
modern Judaism.   He reviews the problem of the aguna, the
controversy of the inclusion of women in the minyan and
finally the acceptance of certain commandments as appropriate for women.   He calls for the evolution of new rituals
for women and a union of both orthodox and conservative
rabbis to deal with the problem.

239 Greenberg, Blu. On Women and Judaism: A View from
Tradition. Philadelphia: Jewish Publication Society, 1981.

This book provides a variety of essays focused on feminism
and Judaism including issues of whether feminism is good for
Jews, of Torah study for women, of the theoretical religious
basis for women's equality, of reforming the liturgy, of
using the ritual bath, the mikveh, of the problematic laws
of divorce, of the controversy surrounding abortion.   She
offers a balancing position between tradition and feminism.
Her views should be compared with the others noted in entry

216. Essays from this book are found in entries 119, 240, 241, 509, 510.

240 Greenberg, Blu. "Feminism: Is it Good for the Jews?" In A Coat of Many Colors: Jewish Subcommunities in the United States, edited by Abraham D. Lavender, 263-271. Westport: Greenwood Press, 1977.

The question of integrating women into Jewish life has been raised by most feminist writers; see entry 216 and the items there, especially Brin (224), Hyman (245), and Ozick (260). This essay looks at the Jewish woman who practices her religion by proxy, who must face questions of abortion and the the traditions command to revere life. Greenberg sees the need for dialogue between both traditionalists and feminists. The essay is reprinted in entry 239, pp. 3-20.

241 Greenberg, Blu. "Jewish Women: Coming of Age." Tradition 16 (1977): 79-94.

When feminist Jews sketch the history of their development they do more than merely describe the past; they make a statement about the present and the future as well (see for example Mann, 256, and Schneider, 271). Here Greenberg traces evolution of the position of women in Judaism from their being men's property in the ten commandment through a variety of talmudic views of women that nevertheless resulted in inequality in the law and continued in the medieval persistence of that basic inequality. She concludes that the modern feminist movement wants not only change but participation in the halakhic process. The essay is reprinted in entry 239, pp. 57-73.

242 Hauptman, Judith. "Women and Change in Jewish Law: A Symposium." Conservative Judaism 29 (1974): 20-21.

Conservative Judaism's debate about the place of women (see entry 221) is remarkable because of the vigor with which many women participate in it. Hauptman offers a woman's perspective on the subject. She points to the clearly sexist quality in much of traditional Judaism. At the same time she notes the positive religious motivations felt by many Jewish women. She urges that Judaism become more inclusive, not just for the sake of women but for the sake of religious life itself.

243 Hauptman, Judith. "Women's Liberation in the Talmudic Period: An Assessment." Conservative Judaism 26 (1972): 22-28.

The study of women in the Bible and early rabbinic period sheds light upon contemporary problems faced by Jewish women (compare Swidler, entry 280). Hauptman asks whether talmudic legislation was an advancement for women. While slaves were given legal equality, women were not. In the historical context there were examples of independent women, but these examples were not chosen by the rabbinical leadership. Hauptman doubts the truth of the apologetic claim that talmudic Judaism was an advance for its times.

244 Heschel, Susannah.   On Being a Jewish Feminist.   New York: Schocken, 1983.

This useful anthology includes various essays from a variety of sources.   It includes personal reflections, intellectual studies, and examples of Jewish feminist rituals.   The moral perspectives involved are illuminated by Heschel's insightful comments.   She provides a helpful introduction that touches upon the major moral issues in the various religious movements in contemporary Judaism.   See entries 214, 260, 336, 508, 511.

245 Hyman, Paula E.   "The Other Half: Women in the Jewish Tradition."   Conservative Judaism 26 (1972): 14-21.

Hyman, a perceptive sociologist who has focused on Jewish women and the Jewish family, describes the condition of women in traditional Jewish life.   While she acknowledges the traditional justifications for distinguishing between men and women, she rejects them as basically apologetic. Hyman notes that women have been given tokenism, placed on a pedestal or handed apologetical poetry.   Yet it was the needs of women that helped stimulate the growth of non-orthodox Judaism.   Today change and not apologetics is needed. The essay is reprinted in 251, pp. 105-113.

246 Johnson, George E.   "Halakha and Woman's Liberation." Midstream 20 (1974): 58-61.

Traditional Jews often argue that feminists are destroying the basis of Judaism.   When feminists ask that Jewish law be changed they fail to realize the radicality of their demand. Johnson is aware of that radicality and suggests that the feminist call for changes in the halakha shows their distance from traditional Jewish life.   He analyzes why change of halakha is the central focus for Jewish feminists.   In his view feminism represents a rejection of role models and institutions of tradition.   He asks what role models will eventually replace them?

247 Jung, Leo.   "Problems of Our Women in Our Own Times." In his Love and Life, 19-30.   New York: Philosophical Library, 1979.

Traditional Jews often attempt to meet the criticism women raise against them.   Jung, for example, offers a compromise solution to the problems of Jewish women.   Unfortunately his compromise will only attract those already securely lodged within traditional life.   He does not disputes the validity of having women liberated.   He delimits that liberation as including the rights of Jewish day school education, of entrance into religious and educational movements and of equality in the business world. He suggests that if the duties of a husband to his wife were fulfilled there would be less unhappy women. He also suggests celebrating birth of a daughter and the creation of ceremony of maturation at the age of 18.

248 Jung, Leo. "Woman's Threefold Role." In his Love and Life, 31-34. New York: Philosophical Library, 1979.

Jung builds his essay on the premise that love is the basis of marriage. The woman's role springs from this. Her work is irreplaceable in the home; she is her husband's lover, her home's esthetic engineer, and her children's example of goodness, truth, and grace. This traditionalist view of a woman's nature will not satisfy feminists but demonstrates good will on the part of a traditional rabbi.

249 Jung, Leo "Women." In his Between Man and Man, 3rd enlarged ed., 20-27. New York: Board of Jewish Education, 1976.

This is basically an apologetic statement of Jewish recognition of woman's distinctiveness. Jung defends the institution of niddah or feminine purity as prevention of rape and abuse within marriage. Note the detailed examination of this commandment in entry 250 as well as the personal experience that Blu Greenberg reports in 239.

250 Kahana, Kalman. Daughter of Israel: Laws of Family Purity, trans. by Leonard Oschry. New York: Feldheim Publishers, 1977.

While primarily a compendium listing the laws of purity and the relationships between husband and wife, the rules regarding sexual intercourse, childbirth, modest behavior, and the prohibition against birth control this traditional tract demonstrates an Orthodox view of femininity is both morally correct and best for a woman's nature.

251 Koltun, Elizabeth. The Jewish Woman: New Perspectives. New York: Schocken Books, 1978.

This challenging anthology includes a number of articles exploring the resources Jewish possesses for feminist symbols, stories, and rituals. A description of the status of women in Judaism joins with a feminist critique of that status. Articles from this work can be found in entries 219, 245, and 264.

252 Lacks, Rosyn. Women and Judaism: Myth, History and Struggle. Garden City: Doubleday, 1980.

This book employs a journalistic approach which surveys women in Judaism from the modern woman rabbi to the myths of the Ancient Near East. It provides interesting highlights of the problems facing women when rabbis refuse but laity allow the ordaining of women. Compare entry 271.

253 Lerner, Anne Lapidus.   "Who has not made me a Woman:
The Movement for Equal Rights For Women in American Jewry."
American Jewish Yearbook 1977. (1977): 3-38.

This essay sees Jewish feminism as a response to secularity.
It surveys the 1973 United Synagogue resolution on the
ordination of women and concludes that Judaism has survived
by an evolution which has never been painless.

254 Levinas, Emmanuel.   "Judaism and the Feminine Element,"
trans. by Edith Wyschograd. Judaism 18 (1969): 30-35.

This essay is translated from Difficile Liberte Essais Sur
Le Judaism, 2nd edition. Paris: Albin Michel, 1976, 50-60.
In it Levinas declares that woman completes man and that
Judaism includes an affirmation of the feminine element in
the world.

255 Lipman, Eugene J.   "Women's Liberation and Jewish
Tradition." In A Coat of Many Colors: Jewish Subcommunities
in the United States, edited by Abraham D. Lavender, 239-
242. Westport: Greenwood Press, 1977.

Lipman represents a liberal Judaism that understands the
needs of Jewish women and the importance of religious
change. He contends that Jewish tradition stimulates a
concern for women's rights. He claims that the Jewish
community supports and is a foundation of the woman's
movement.

256 Mann, Denese Berg. The Woman in Judaism.
Hartford: Jonathan Publications, 1979.

This little volume summarizes the history, role and status
of women in Jewish law and liturgy, offering brief discussions of Jewish sexual laws, the controversy about abortion,
women's laws of purity, and of future change.
The view of the history of feminism and the Jewish woman
expressed here should be compared with the other items
mentioned in entry 238.

257 Meiselman, Moshe. Jewish Woman in Jewish Law.
Library of Jewish Law and Ethics, 6. New York: Ktav
Publishing House, 1978.

Meiselman presents a comprehensive and exhaustive case for
the Orthodox view of the status of woman in Judaism (see the
annotation at entry 218). His approach is to collect the
massive date found in Jewish law and lore concerning women
and suggest that the Jewish views presented are the most
natural and satisfying. This extensive treatment of an
important subject represents a major Orthodox contribution
to the discussion of women in Judaism.

258 Ofseyer, Jordan S.   "Toward the Equality of Jewish
Women." United Synagogue Review 26,2 (1973): 8-9, 31.

Ofseyer contends that Jewish apologetics do not change the problems of the status of Jewish women. He asserts that the conditions of rabbinic times were backward, and so the discrimination involved then was understandable. Today, however, he thinks that new legal approaches are possible. He notes that equality is not sameness but does entail similar dignity and responsibilities. His call for active change in Conservative Judaism should be compared with the other views expressed as found in entry 221 and below.

259 Ostrow, Mortimer. "Women and Change in Jewish Law: A Symposium." Conservative Judaism 29 (1974): 3-12.

Among the various views found in Conservative Judaism about women (see entry 221) are those espousing the traditional separation of male and female not on religious grounds but on psychological ones. Ostrow's rather Freudian psychology emphasizes the value of the traditional Jewish views of men and women. He claims that women represent the dark, temptress side of the subconscious and so are symbolically relegated to a place of their own in Jewish worship.

260 Ozick, Cynthia. "Women: Notes Toward Finding the Right Questions." Forum 35 (1979): 37-60.

This often reprinted and influential article should be read in conjunction with the other feminist works noted in entry 216. Ozick begins by looking at the theology of Eve and the problem of women being distinct but equal. She finds that in Judaism such a principle has meant exclusion from Torah and history. A look at the sources reveals the unequal treatment and unequal seriousness given to women. She concludes that Judaism cheats itself by using only half its resources. This essay is reprinted in entry 244, 120-151; see also Lilith 6 (1979): 19-29.

261 Pearl, Chaim H. "The Woman's Role: A Continuing Discussion." Conservative Judaism 32 (1978): 67-70.

This contribution to the debate within Conservative Judaism (see entry 221) suggests that women should be encouraged to obey all the mitzvot since the idea of exemption to be a mother is untenable. Pearl defends the traditional view of marriage as a safeguard for the women in which the traditional ketuba provides the best protection against the pornography of the age which exploits woman's sexuality.

262 Pelcovitz, Ralph. "'Women's Lib' in Torah Perspective." Danger and Opportunity, 111-122. New York: Shengold Publishers, 1976.

This defense of Jewish traditional views of womanhood contends that it is not the anatomical differences that mark the nature of men and women but rather the ideal purposes that God has in mind. Pelcovitz derives these ideals from a reading of Genesis and describes the putative personality traits of women as established by Jewish tradition. The sexual morality that Judaism demands is, on this account, not based on prejudice but on the will of God. He concludes that the modern woman's problems stem from a neglect of traditional Jewish law. Pelcovitz represents an extreme Orthodoxy as can be seen by comparing his views with that of others noted in entry 219.

263   Plaskow, Judith.   "Blaming the Jews for the Birth of Patriarchy."Lilith 7 (1980): 11-12.

This article laments the anti-semitism of the feminist movement and stresses the need for dialogue among all women. Plaskow's call is followed by Annette Daum's study on Blaming the Jews for the Death of the Goddess' and an open discussion of the problem, pp. 12-17. See now Nice Jewish Girls: A Lesbian Anthology, edited by Evelyn Torton Beck. Trumansburg: Crossing Press, 1982. The theme of anti-semitism in the feminist movement can also be found in entries 265 and 272.

264   Plaskow, Judith.   "The Jewish Feminist: Conflict in Identities." In The Jewish Woman: New Perspectives, Edited by Elizabeth Koltun, 105-113. New York: Schocken Books, 1978.

Feminist Judaism is constructive as well as critical (note the variety of approaches evidenced in entry 216). Plaskow offers a positive contribution to Jewish thinking. Her theological exploration of the Lilith myth seeks a positive understanding of woman from the sources of Jewish folklore. Plaskow asserts that reconstructing a feminine experience of God will enrich both women and Jewish theology.

265   Pogrebin, Letty Cotten.   "Anti-Semitism in the Woman's Movement." Moment 7,7 (1982): 28-34, 49-53.

Pogrebin describes disillusionment with the Feminist movement as it becomes a forum of anti-semitism. She insists that Jewish patriarchalism is not worse than others. She draws an interesting parallel between the tensions and similarities separating Jews and Blacks and those involved in the woman's movement. Compare her views on feminist anti-semitism with those of Plaskow (264) and Schreiber (272).

266   Prell, Riv-Ellen.   "The Dilemma of Women's Equality in the History of Reform Judaism." Judaism 30 (1981): 418-426.

This study provides historical perspective on the double message Reform Judaism gave concerning equality of women. Prell shows how an ideology of equality led in fact to an even greater dilemma: that of implementing an impossible ideal in a male-oriented tradition. The importance attached to the gaining of power and its infrequency of attainment can be found in the items noted in entry 218 and in the following, companion entry, here.

267   Prell,   Riv-Ellen.   "The Vision of Woman in Classical
Reform Judaism." Journal of American Academy of Religion 50
(1982): 575-589.

The   framers of Reform Judaism considered the   treatment   of
women in the synagogue as a residue of orientalism. Their
approach   promised equality to Jewish women.   However this
promise   was unrealized since there was no realistic   opportunity in society for utilizing the new equality.

268   Pressma, Donna C.   "The Changing Role of Jewish Women:
Implications for Family,   Social Work Agency and Social Work
Practice." Journal of Jewish Communal Service 58 (1981): 67-
75.

This   study provides a historical perspective on   the
sacrifices made by Jewish mothers.   It surveys the emerging
roles   of Jewish women in the 1950s and the 1980s   including
the disillusionment of becoming part of the new poor through
divorce.

269   Priesand, Sally.   Judaism and the New Woman.   New York:
Behrman House Publishers, 1975.

Priesand, the first female Rabbi in the Hebrew Union
College, provides a survey of the history of women in
Judaism, of changes in Jewish law affecting women, of the
status of Jewish women in Israel, of women's roles in Jewish
ritual, and of the contribution by women to Jewish life.
She points to future ethical development in Jewish views of
marriage, divorce, and education as essential for the
further evolution of Jewish women.   Compare her construction
of the history of Jewish women with that found in the   other
items mentioned in entry 252.

270   Rosenberg, Bernard.   "Woman's Place in Israel." Dissent
24 (1977): 408-417.

Rosenberg notes the contradictions between Israel's stated
egalitarianism and its discrimination against women by
employing traditional Jewish family law.   He notes the
inequality brought about by restrictive laws on abortion and
birth control.   In noting the relationship between formal
education and careers, he shows how laws on equal pay are
circumvented so that women are paid less.   He suggests that
parliamentary politics works against the welfare of women.
Compare his findings with those in entries 217 and 278.

271   Schneider, Susan Weidman.   Jewish and Female: Choices
and Changes in Our Lives.   New York: Simon and Schuster,
1984

This extensive and fascinating book looks at both the
history of women in American Jewish life and at the way
women today are now refashioning this life (compare this
view of the American Jewish women with that of Priesand,

269, or of Gordis, 238). Filled with her experiences as editor of Lilith, the foremost journal of American Jewish feminism, this book explores the religious and cultural possibilities for American Jewish women today.

272 Schreiber, Regina (Pseudonym). "Copenhagen: One Year Later." Lilith 8 (1981): 30-35.

The author discusses feminist anti-semitism and laments the situation in which women attack other women. Statements by other women attendees confirm the problem. She declares that the Jewish woman is led to the slaughter by her Christian sisters, is harassed by women from the Palestine Liberation Organization, and must therefore declare the importance of Israel for any Jewish feminism. See also entries 263 and 265 on feminist anti-semitism.

273 Segal, J. B. "The Jewish Attitude Towards Women." Journal of Jewish Studies 30 (1979): 121-137.

Perspectives on Jewish feminism often draw strength from historical analysis of the roots of the Jewish position (see entries 217, 255, 263). Here Segal reviews Jewish ambivalence towards women in religious life because of the Ishtar cult and because of the biblical omission of the sacred marriage from Jewish liturgy. Judaism looked at women suspiciously because they held high status in intertestamental times in cults associated with paganism. This contextual background explains why the rabbis give little status to women so as to offer no concession to paganism.

274 Segal, Sheila F.. "Feminists for Judaism." Midstream 21 (1975): 59-65.

The varieties of feminism (see entry 216) suggest that Jewish feminists represent a spectrum of concerns. These personal reflections on Jewish feminism describe Jewish feminists as education vultures. The practical response, she reviews, centers not on the debate over female participation in Jewish life but on the formation of women's minyanim. She discusses the alienation of women in Jewish Orthodoxy in contrast to the the celebration of femaleness in the feminist movement.

275 Shapiro, Miriam. "The Woman's Role: A Continuing Discussion." Conservative Judaism 32 (1978): 63-66.

This is a response to the musings of Aaron Blumenthal (entry 221) from a traditional perspective. Ms. Shapiro argues that women do not need to imitate men but instead need to strengthen what possibilities and images they have been provided in the tradition.

276 Siegel, Seymour. "Women and Change in Jewish Law: A Symposium." Conservative Judaism 29 (1974): 13-15.

Siegel calls for using traditional methods to change the clearly unethical results of practical halakhic tradition concerning women. He notes that Conservative Judaism works through the mechanism of the halakha so that the ideals of Judaism become expressed through the concrete reality of Jewish law. The debate found in the various entries by Conservative thinkers on the place of women in Judaism, however, denotes as much disagreement on the ethics of the Jewish view of women as on the specific halakhic injunctions or suggestions being discussed. See the variety of Conservative Jewish positions noted in entry 221.

277 Singer, Shalom. "The Jewish Woman and her Heritage." The Reconstructionist 40,7 (1974): 10-17.

Not only traditionalists like Jung (247-249) become enthusiastic when evoking the past glories of Jewish women. The Reconstructionist movement is liberal, but Singer expresses a nostalgia for the tradition. He contrasts the rich Jewish heritage of concern for woman's welfare with contemporary problems and disappointments for modern women.

278 Stiller, Nikki. "Peace Without Honor: The Battle of the Sexes in Israel." Midstream 22 (1976): 33-41.

Feminist disappointment in the State of Israel occasions a variety of responses (see entries 217 and 270). Singer explodes the myth of women's equality in Israel. In fact, she claims, Israel is rife with male chauvinism and pornographic advertising. She criticizes the religious establishment as well because halakhic disabilities combine with the cultural climate to keep the Israeli woman a sex symbol not a person.

279 Strauss, Ruby G. "In the Door of the Tent." United Synagogue Review 28,2 (1975): 12-13, 28-29.

A Conservative Jewish women gives vent in this essay to her desire for a new approach to feminine status in Judaism. She notes how Sarah had to use subterfuge and stand at the door of the tent in order to overhear God speaking to Abraham. Her eavesdropping, according to Strauss, begins her life of active participation. So too Jewish women today, she insists, must seize the opportunity to come from the door of the tent into active Jewish life.

280 Swidler, Leonard. Women in Judaism. Metuchen: The Scarecrow Press, 1976.

This study reviews the biblical and talmudic views of women in the cult and in sexual life with an eye towards the contemporary issues involved. Compare Hauptman (243).

281 Timberg, Judy. "Are Jewish Women Oppressed." In Jewish Radicalism, edited by Jack Nusan Porter and Peter Dreier, 247-254. New York: Random House, 1973.

Sociological data and traditional Jewish law provide an example of how Jewish women have fared in the past. The present, however, appears to be more hopeful. Timberg calls upon modern Jewish women to move beyond oppression in the past, make use of a legacy of strength and ability to cope to gain a rightful place in modern Judaism.

282 Tyron-Montalembert, Renee De. "Le Judaism, est-il Misogyne?" Les Nouveaux Chaiers 18:68 (1982): 26-32.

The view of women in Judaism has often been criticized, but it has also been glorified (see entry 255). This essay reviews the biblical view of women, taking note of the liberal tendency in Judaism and rabbinic concern for the rights of women. The place of women in the creation story is explored as a positive view of femininity.

283 Yellin, Richard M. "A Philosophy of Jewish Masculinity: One Interpretation." Conservative Judaism 32 (1978): 89-94.

Although ostensibly focused on a view of masculinity this is merely a thinly disguised polemic against allowing women to be rabbis. The author asserts that the rabbi represents the ideal male and therefore a woman cannot serve as an appropriate symbol. He argues for the male-oriented view of women as the ideal mother and men as the ideal scholar. Compare this view with some of the more staunchly feminist opinions noted in entry 221.

HOMOSEXUALITY

284 Bar Zev, Asher. "Homosexuality and the Jewish Tradition." The Reconstructionist 42,4 (1976): 20-24.

Bar Zev notes the growing call for acceptance of Gays in Jewish life. He contends that while Judaism cannot view homosexuality as licit Jews must still show compassion for the condition as either sickness or sin. Compare his view with other Reconstructionists in entries 285 and 300, with Conservative Jewish thinkers in entries 272, 290, 291, 297, 298, 302, Reform thinkers in 287, 289, and contrast his view with Orthodox writers in 292-295 and 304-305.

285 Eisenstein, Ira. "Discrimination is Wrong." Judaism 32 (1983): 415-416.

While Eisenstein admits that homosexuality contradicts current social mores, he claims that discrimination dehumanizes both its victims and its perpetrators.

286 Feldman, David M. "Homosexuality and Jewish Law." Judaism 32 (1983): 426-429.

Feldman takes a compassionate, if traditional view. He cites Rav Abraham Isaac Kook who suggests that a Gay

shochet, or ritual slaughterer, who had been removed from
his position may have repented and should be trusted in
matters of kashrut. Feldman contends that a sin not a
disease is involved.

287 Freehof, Solomon B.   "Homosexuality." In his Current
Reform Response, 236-238. Cincinnati: Hebrew Union College
Press, 1969.

Homosexuality is a challenge for Reform Jewish liberalism
(compare the following entry, entry 289, and entry 289).
Freehof comments that the prohibition against homosexuality
is only part of a general discussion of sexual offenses in
Judaism.   He contends that since the Talmud refuses to
suspect this evil of Jews and because of a paucity of information about Jewish homosexuality one can believe in the
purity of Jewish youth!

288 Freehof, Solomon B.   "Judaism and Homosexuality."
Central Conference of American Rabbis Journal 20 (1970): 30-
32.

Freehof reiterates the traditional Jewish stand against
homosexuality.   Nevertheless, he concludes that even the
worst sinners are included as fullfledged Jews and so there
should be integration of Gays into a synagogue.   He objects
to the formation of Gay synagogues since he feels they might
entice bewildered youth to transgression.   For the positive
view expressed by Gays, see Lester (296), Mehler (299) and
Rabinowitz (287).

289 Friedman, Norman.   "Boundary Issues for Liberal
Judaism." Midstream 19 (1973): 47-52.

Homosexuality is taken as a case in which Jews must choose
between liberalism and Judaism. See entries ***, ***, ***.

290 Gordis, Robert.   "Homosexuality and the Homosexual."
In Homosexuality and Ethics, edited by Edward Batchelor, 52-
60. New York: Pilgrim Press, 1980.

This excerpt of his book, Love and Sex (entry 201), suggests
compassion for the homosexual but recognition of the
immorality of the act in Jewish thought.

291 Gordis, Robert.   "Homosexuality and Traditional
Religion." Judaism 32 (1983): 390-391.

Gordis provides an introduction to a number of essays that
represent the range of opinion in the current debate among
Jewish thinkers as to whether homosexuality is a sin or a
disease.   While the essays are short, they demonstrate the
variety of responses by leading Jews to the problem of Gays
and Jewish religious life.

292   Herring, Basil F.   "Homosexuality," in Jewish Ethics
and Halakhah For Our Time: Sources and Commentary, 175-196.
Library of Jewish Law and Ethics, 11.   New York: Ktav
Publishing House, 1984.

Herring declares Judaism's unequivocal rejection of
homosexuality.   He contends that the context of Gays asking
to be part of the Jewish world is the modern sexual
revolution and charges that Reform Judaism is more lenient
in this regard than Orthodoxy. He shows that the biblical
rabbinic, and medieval sources are unanimous in declaring
homosexuality anathema to Jewish morality. He discusses the
distinction between male and female homosexuality in the
context of the commandment to propagate the species.   In
this light he concludes that even a non-practicing Gay
commits a sin.   Compare this view with other Orthodox
opinions in entries 292-293 and 304-305.

293 Lamm, Norman.   "Judaism and the Modern Attitude To
Homosexuality."   In Contemporary Jewish Ethics, edited by
Menahem Marc Kellner, 375-399.   Sanhedrin Jewish Studies.
New York: Sanhedrin Press, 1979.

Lamm sets forth a categorical rejection of homosexuality.
He considers it a sin even if it can be said to be a
psychological condition.   Even non-practicing homosexuals
can be said to contradict God's intention for the propagation of humanity.   He considers the condition a psychological pathology, and, as a mental illness, the victim requires
compassion and treatment but not toleration for the
aberration.

294 Lamm, Norman.   "The New Dispensation on Homosexuality."
Jewish Life 35,3 (1968): 11-16.

This popular summary of Lamm's views takes a clear stand not
only against homosexuality but against the sexual revolution.   Lamm reiterates the traditional view of homosexuality
as an abomination. He concludes that a Jew's loyalty should
be to halacha and not to the newest canons of liberalism.
The case of homosexuality, in his view, shows why religion
must reject current practices and must teach society true
morality rather than taking its morals from society.

295 Lehrman, Nathaniel S.   "Homosexuality and Judaism: Are
They Compatible?" Judaism 32 (1983): 392-404.

Lehrman insists that Judaism and homosexuality are incom-
patible on biological, psychological and traditional
grounds.   He finds that certain myths impede the curing of
homosexuals;   the   idea   that Judaism   could   tolerate
homosexuality is, in his view, such a myth.

296 Lester, Eleanor.   "Gays in the Synagogue." Present
Tense 2 (1974): 13-15.

This is an anecdotal report on a visit to a Gay synagogue.
The author is clearly sympathetic to the moral dilemma of
Jewish Gays. She suggests that the challenge and contribution of such groups to Jewish life is their ability to
infuse Judaism with renewed inspiration and insight.
Compare her views with those of Mehler (299) and Rabinowitz
(301) and contrast them with Freehof (288)

297 Matt, Hershel J. "A Call for Compassion." Judaism 32
(1983):430-432.

Matt urges that the Jewish response should not be condemnation for Gays but compassion.   Theologically he suggests
that God can create exceptions to the biological rule.   His
compassion does not represent the consensus of Conservative
Jewish thinkers;compare his views with that of Feldman (286)
and Gordis (291) and Schwartz (302).

298 Matt, Hershel J. "Sin, Crime, Sickness or Alternative
Life-Style: A Jewish Approach to Homosexuality." Judaism 27
(1978): 13-24.

Matt seeks the integration of Gays into existing congregations.   He affirms their humanity but sees them as in need
of help and in a psychological sickness.   In the context of
American Jewish moral thinking this is a moderate   viewpoint
and is reprinted in Edward Batchelor, ed., Homosexuality and
Ethics (New York: Pilgrim Press, 1980), pp. 114-124.

299 Mehler, Barry Alan. "Gay Jews: One Man's Journey from
Closet to Community." Moment (1977): 22-56.

This is an intimate description of an awakening realization
of homosexuality on the part of someone immersed in a traditional Jewish context.   The moral quest includes an attempt
to find a community that is suited to both Judaism and his
sexuality.   The author recognizes the variety of Gay Jewish
expression and the need to legitimate the Jewishness of the
struggle by the Gay community.   Contrast his views with
those of Freehof (288) and compare them with Schwartz (302)
who shows greater appreciation of the particular needs of
Jewish homosexuals.

300 Miller, Judea B.   "The Closet: Another Religious View
of Gay Liberation." The Reconstructionist 44,10 (1979): 18-
25.

The liberalism of Jewish Reconstructionism (see entries 284
and 285) is illustrated by its positive view of liberation
movements, including Gay Liberation.   The author contends
that the liberation of women or Gays can only liberate all
minority groups. While admitting that Judaism requires dis-
ciplined sexuality the author contends that the wholesome
consequences of the Gay liberation movement should not be
overlooked.

301   Rabinowitz, Henry.   "Talmud Class in a Gay Synagogue."
Judaism 32 (1983): 433-443

Here is an example of the quest to find religious expression
in the midst of the tensions of being Gay and Jewish (compare entries 296 and 299). Rabinowitz notes the traditional
response to homosexuality but declares that Judaism allows
sinners their rights.   He urges Jews to realize that Gays
are not a threat to Judaism and need help expressing their
Judaism.

302   Schwartz, Barry Dov.   "Homosexuality--a Jewish Perspective."   United Synagogue Review (1977): 4-5, 23-28.

Schwartz summarizes the rise of Jewish Gay activists and
their special needs.   He notes the reluctance of the Jewish
community to cope with these questions.   He does not condone
homosexuality but he does castigate established Jewry for
its insensitivity.   The desire of Gays for a Jewishness that
will express their own sense of identity is clearly established in his article.   Contrast the compassion shown here
with Matt (297).

289   Soloff, Rav.   "Is There a Reform Response to Homosexuality."   Judaism 32 (1983): 415-424.

Soloff declares that law and morality are different.   He
abhors a legal system that would penalize Gays, but does not
advocate condoning their moral choices.   He suggests a shift
from a punitive response to Gays to compassion for them.   He
offers a review of the biblical outlook and the traditional
Jewish stance as evidence for continued moral disapproval
while being legally compassionate.

304   Spero, Moshe Halevi.   "Homosexuality: Clinical and
Ethical Challenges."   Tradition 17 (1979): 53-73.

Spero argues that homosexuality is contrary to the halakhic
ideal of family structure and of ideal male-female relationships.   He also claims that it destroys the idea of complete
human being.   In his view the task is to reveal the ethical
roots of a homosexual's tension and to move from that tension to its cure.   The essay is also found in his Judaism
and Psychology: Halakhic Perspectives (New York: Ktav Publishing House, 1980), pp. 153-167.

305   Wurzburger, Walter S.   "Preferences are not practices."
Judaism 32 (1983): 425.

Wurzburger provides a sharp rejection of the plea to accept
Gays as one normative Jewish expression.   He reiterates
traditional Jewish objections to such behavior.   His brief
comment summarizes the point of view represented in such
entries as 292-293 and the previous entry.

3
Morality and the Family

MARRIAGE, CHILDREN AND THE FAMILY

306   Bernstein, Philip.   "The Jewish Family." In his To
Dwell in Unity: The Jewish Federation Movement in America
Since 1960, 161-171.   Philadelphia: Jewish Publication So-
ciety of America, 1983.

The moral crisis facing the Jewish family has aroused concern from public Jewish institutions.   The federations and
philanthropic organizations feel morally obligated to help
reestablish the family as the central structure of Jewish
life.   Bernstein notes the crisis that has arisen in the
changing contemporary situation. He surveys the problems of
drug usage, adoption, child care, and finances that plague
the contemporary Jewish family.   He suggests that the centrality of the family and children in Judaism demands that
priority be given to solving these problems.

307   Bleich, J. David.   "Mamzerut." In his Contemporary
Halakhic Problems, 159-176.   The Library of Jewish Law and
Ethics, 4.   New York: Ktav Publishing House, 1977.

Marriage and divorce in Judaism have consequences that go
beyond the couple involved in sexual relationships (see the
discussion, particularly focused on civil marriages and
divorce found in entries 318,   319, 338, 363, 370, 393, 418,
439.   While Judaism has a rigorous definition of bastardy
(only the offspring of a married woman sired by someone not
her husband is so designated) the stigma is a burdensome
one.   Bleich deals with the increase in such children in
recent years as Jews remarry after merely having a civil
divorce.   Technically the first marriage continues in force
and the children are considered mamzerim or bastards.
Bleich explores the various contemporary cases in which no
divorce has been given and concludes that some solutions are
false ones and more misleading than helpful.   See also his
essays in Tradition 12,2/3 (1972): 125-128;   13,4/14,1
(1973): 192-200; 14,2 (1973): 127-131.

308 Blidstein, Gerald. Honor Thy Father and Mother: Filial Responsibility in Jewish Law and Ethics. New York: Ktav Publishing House 1976.

Blidstein focuses on the theological statement that parents are co-creators with God. The duty of children to parents comes from the ethics of gratitude and while there is no natural filial concern, the Noahide covenant made such concern part of natural law. He discusses the relationship of filial duties and parental obligations, particularly that of the father to the son, declaring that the master-student relationship is both the highest model and fulfillment of filial duty. Compare entries 329, 334, 335, 346, 347, 349, 253, 362.

309 Bluestone, Naomi. "Sunset, Sunset: The Life of Jewish Singles." Moment 2 (1976): 22-42.

This witty and sensitive article chronicles Bluestone's trials and tribulations as an observant single Jewish woman. She rejects the liberal ploy of lumping all "deviant" (singles, gays, etc.) into one general category and notes the special problems confronting traditional Jews who remain single. Compare Porter (354) and Zelizer (372).

310 Borowitz, Eugene B.   "Reading the Jewish Tradition on Marital Sexuality." Journal of Reform Judaism 29 (1982): 1-15.

Borowitz notes that his thought has matured, although not changed, since his early study of Judaism and sexuality (entry 194). In the present essay he provides a sharp investigation of Jewish sexual morality and its modern implications. He claims that traditionally sexuality is affirmed in a very limited sphere with procreation as its major justification. In his view such an approach procured stability at the cost of subordination of the wife. He recognizes the roots of this approach in the fact of Jewish communal control over private sexuality. The modern Jewish woman, in his view, must create a more positive view of her sexuality.

311 Bubis, Gerald B. Serving the Jewish Family. New York: Ktav Publishing House, 1977.

This anthology(including entries 343, 360 and 362) reviews findings in social science, ethical concerns, and the responses of Jewish institutions, both specifically religious such as the synagogue and non-religious as family service agencies, to the contemporary crisis of family life. It includes both traditional and innovative viewpoints.

312 Bubis, Gerald B.   "The Modern Jewish Family." Journal of Jewish Communal Service 47 (1971): 238-247.

Bubis points to pressures from within and without placed
upon the family: strained relationships, the evolving role
of women, the decline of the nuclear family, the rise of new
values, and intergenerational conflict (compare entries 306,
309, 342-344, 348, 354, 366, 368, 369, 371). He calls for
increased Jewish innovation so that Judaism can continue to
contribute an ethical inspiration to the family and provide
relevant help through its rituals and values.

313 Bulka, Reuven P. Jewish Marriage: A Halakhic Ethic.
The Library of Jewish Law and Ethics, 12. New York: Ktav
Publishing Company, 1985.

Bulka provides a compendium of Jewish thinking about
marriage, its goals, its purposes, and its psychology. He
offers a traditional guide to Jews seeking marital peace and
a survey of the literature concerning divorce. Compare his
work to entries 317, 339, 340, 346, 349, and 351.

314 Cohen, Steven Martin. "Singlehood, Childlessness,
Divorce, and Intermarriage: The Meaning of Recent Family
Trend for Jewish Identification." In his American Modernity
and Jewish Identity, 113-133. New York: Tavistock Publications 1983.

This study of new trends in Jewish family life points out
the conflict between modern life and the moral ideals
inculcated by Judaism. He suggests a new approach to Jewish
family service. The moral implications of this new reality
can be found in the studies mentioned in the entry 312.

315 Cohn, Haim H. "The Right to Marry and Found a Family."
In his Human Rights in Jewish Law, 90-86. New York: Ktav
Publishing House, 1984.

Judaism sees marriage as both a commandment and a right.
The legal aspects of familial organization and the moral
impetus for founding a family are central to Jewish
tradition. Cohn summarizes the basic talmudic discussions
concerning marriage, touches on importance of children, the
role of women in Jewish life, the prohibition on intermarriage and other modern problems a Jew faces when seeking to
marry and found a family.

316 Dashevsky, Arnold and Levine, Irving M. "The Jewish
Family: Continuity and Change." In Families and Religions:
Continuity and Change in Modern Society, edited by William
V. D'Antonio and Joan Aldous, 163-190. Beverley Hills: Sage
Publications, 1983.

This is an intriguing addition to an anthology of social
scientific investigation. The Jewishness of the authors
will not permit them to remain distant from the subject they
are studying. In a historical prologue they describe
Jewish family life from biblical times through the American
experience (1654-1984). The modern period is characterized,

they claim, by an emphasis on mobility, transmission of identity and child orientation. Their moral message is that intermarriage erodes family and communal life. Compare the discussion in entries 306 and 312.

317   Eisenberg, Yehuda. Adam Uveito: The Foundations of Family Law in Judaism [Hebrew]. Brooklyn: Haskel Publications, 1968.

This is a popular presentation in Hebrew that expresses the basic moral precepts of Judaism's view of the family, emphasizing holiness through appropriate sexuality, modesty, and purity. The sanctification of life through fulfilling the commandments of sexual behavior is stressed. Various specific problems are raised including those of immorality, of the Levirate marriage, of divorce, and of a father's duties to his children. The moral rationale for family purity is that restraint breeds love. The problem caused by civil marriages and civil divorces which lead to the creation of mamzerim is also discussed. Compare the following entry as well as the discussion in entry 313.

318   Ellinson, Getsel [Elikim]. Non-Halachic Marriages: A Study of the Rabbinic Sources [Hebrew]. Jerusalem: Devir Publishing House, 1975.

The question of civil marriages raises many problems for Israel Jews (see the following entry and the annotation at 307). This scholarly study of how Jews have dealt with the problem of non-halakhic marriages, and of course more importantly non-halakhic divorces begins with a preface in which the moral issue of the unity of the Jewish people is raised. Will a rigorous approach to the laws of marriage and divorce divide the Jewish people? Ellinson thinks that the absolute separation of religion and state is impossible in Israel and so some reconciliation of secularists to traditional marriage law must be made. He provides useful chapters on the concubine, marriage by intention, Reform Jewish and civil marriages and divorces.

319   Ellinson, Getsel [Elikim]. "Civil Marriage in Israel: Halakhic and Social Implications." Tradition 13:2 (1972): 24-34.

This essay repeats the major ideas of the previous one. Halakhically the problem of civil rather than Jewish marriage and divorce laws comes with divorce and remarriage. In Israel Ellinson notes that the possibility of mamzerut is real and offers a distinct challenge since social dissension caused by allowing non-halakhic marriages could threaten Jewish unity. Civil divorce, he thinks, will jeopardize the unity of Jews for generations.

320   Elon, Menachem. "The Special Trend in Legislation in Part of Family and Succession in Law" [Hebrew]. In his Jewish Law: History, Sources, Principles, Part II, 676-712. Jerusalem: Hebrew University Magnes Press, 1973.

Not only is this chapter a detailed history of pecuniary aspects of family law, marriage, divorce, and annulment. A short concluding section on Israeli laws of marriage and the family shows sensitivity to the double moral question of the unity of the Jewish people and sensitivity to human suffering.

321 Freehof, Solomon B. "Adoption of Children of Mixed Race." In his Current Reform Responsa, 196-205. Cincinnati: Hebrew Union College Press, 1969.

Freehof rejects a racist argument against adoption of children of mixed race. He notes that the Bible records such inter-racial unions and that such marriages do not violate the command to keep separate species apart. In a controversial move he claims that a Jewish child may in these days, when essential, be given for adoption to a non-Jewish home. Compare entry 341.

322 Freehof, Solomon B. "The Impotent Bridegroom to Be." In his Modern Reform Responsa, 121-127. Cincinnati: Hebrew Union College Press, 1971.

The question of whether marriage is only for the sake of procreation is raised by an impotent bridegroom. Freehof avers that marriage is for the sake of intercourse and children. Only if there is prospect of the bridegroom's cure should the rabbi participate, and then with trepidation knowing the marriage is at best a problematic one.

323 Freehof, Solomon B. "Marrying a Trans-sexual." In his Reform Responsa For Our Time, 196-200. Cincinnati: Hebrew Union College Press, 1971.

Freehof offers a brief summary of medieval and talmudic sources which considered trans-sexuals to be mutilated. He admits that if a trans-sexual is legally a woman, the marriage would be permitted. Since such sexual changes are not legally binding, however, he cannot see that a marriage with one would be legitimate. See Freehof (199).

324 Freehof, Solomon B. "Reform and Mamzerus." In his New Reform Responsa, 256-261. Cincinnati: Hebrew Union College Press, 1980.

He notes that Judaism is lenient and places may restrictions on the definition of who is a mamzer. He remarks that Reform Judaism accepts civil marriage as valid Jewish marriage and civil divorce as a valid Jewish divorce. He opines, although many traditional Jews would disagree, that even in tradition the stigma of mamzerut can be removed. Compare the discussion in entry 307.

325 Freehof, Solomon B. "Reform Marriage Formula." In his Reform Responsa For Our Time, 191-195. Cincinnati: Hebrew Union College Press, 1971.

In token of marital equality Freehof seeks a formula for the
bride to say. He notes that there is no legal validity in
any formula in a Reform wedding ceremony and suggests that
since such marriages are clearly non-halahkic, a halakhic
sounding formula should not be used.

326   Freehof,   Solomon B.   "Unmarried Couples and Temple
Membership." Reform Responsa For Our Time,   238-244.
Cincinnati: Hebrew Union College Press, 1971.

Freehof seeks to define the status of unmarried couples
within the Jewish community. The moral issue is more than
just Jewishly relevant, he claims, since the laws of the
state must be taken seriously. While some authorities would
accept such relationships, giving them the status of concubinage, Freehof affirms the medieval Jewish prohibitions on
having concubines. Children, he declares, deserve a Jewish
education despite their parents' status.

327 Friedman, Daniel. "The Unmarried Wife in Israeli War."
Israel Yearbook on Human Rights 2 (1972): 287-316.

In Israel the question of non-halakhic marriages has a
pecuniary dimension. May the reputed wife who has not had a
religious marriage seek pensions when "widowed" by war? The
problem of civil marriages for those who reject religion has
economic as well as moral consequences.

328 Friedman, Maurice. "Can Otherness be Confirmed in the
Family?" In his The Confirmation of Otherness in Family
Community and Society, 119-130. New York: Pilgrim Press,
1983.

Friedman's thinking about the modern family is sensitive and
insightful. In this essay he notes that marriage involves
individuals but also extends through a multigenerational
family. In such circumstances genuine dialogue is called
for. The family is a web of responsibilities, but Friedman
points out the limits of both responsibility and guilt.

329 Friedman, Maurice. "Problems of Confirmation in the
Family." In his The Confirmation of Otherness in Family
Community and Society, 107-117. New York: Pilgrim Press,
1983.

Friedman considers the relationships between children and
parents and the balance between domination and self-expression that must be reached within every family. He analyzes
the problems faced by a family through divorce, adoption,
and reconstituted families and suggests that one important
lesson parents teach children is that of learning not to
repeat the suffering of the parents.

330 Friedman, Maurice. "The Role of the Father in the
Family." In his The Confirmation of Otherness in Family,
Community and Society, 77-83. New York: Pilgrim Press,
1983.

Friedman remarks upon the role of the father in providing a
child a relationship out of which to find a direction of the
self. Fathers need to provide images of successful cooperation with others, he suggests, instead of images of competition and struggle. In this way the human and the masculine
can be united.

331 Friedman, Maurice. "Sex and Love in Marriage and the
Family." In his The Confirmation of Otherness in Family,
Community and Society, 85-106. New York: Pilgrim Press,
1983.

Friedman indicts modern society for its emphasis upon technique and mechanistic love making. He traces the problems
in modern sexuality such as incest and homosexuality to the
difficulties involved in balancing distancing with relationship, with uniting warmth of concern with the alienation
currently found in sexuality.

332 Frimer, Norman E. and Frimer, Dov I. "Reform Marriages
in Contemporary Halakhic Responsa." Tradition 21 (1984): 7-
39.

The authors review the controversy that divides Reform and
Orthodox Judaism over marriage. The various elements that
make a Reform marriage invalid are discussed together with
the problematic elements that suggest a religious divorce or
get may still be needed before remarriage. Looking at the
way in which Reform leaders regard the Orthodox the authors
hold out some hope for reconciliation, particularly as Reform rabbis become more concerned with following traditional
Jewish guidelines. Compare entry 307.

333 Goldstein, Harriet. "What's Jewish About Jewish Child
Care." Journal of Jewish Communal Service 49 (1974): 309-
317.

Goldstein suggests the Jewish child care ministers to the
entire spectrum of Jewish life. It provides subsidies for
Jewish family events: Bar Mitzvah, Hebrew School, Shabbat,
and festivals. In this way Jewish child care agencies
create the Judaic atmosphere which families require.

334 Green, Kathy. "Honoring Parents." In The Second Jewish
Catalogue, compiled and edited by Sharon Strassfeld and
Michael Strassfeld, 84-87. Philadelphia: Jewish Publication
Society of America, 1976.

Green notes the theological view that parents are the link
between God and humanity. The place of the command to honor
parents in the ten commandments suggests this view. She
studies the way honor has been bestowed traditionally, in
contemporary life, and in psychology to find a moral approach for the modern child. Compare the items noted in
entry 308 and especially the following entry.

335   Herring,   Basil F.   "Parents and Children."   In his
<u>Jewish</u> <u>Ethics</u> <u>and</u> <u>Halakhah</u> <u>For</u> <u>Our</u> <u>Time</u>: <u>Sources</u> <u>and</u> <u>Commen-</u>
<u>tary</u>,   197-219.   The Library of Jewish Law and Ethics,   11.
New York: Ktav Publishing House, 1984.

Herring   notes the conflict over values occurring in contemporary Jewish families.   As an antidote he cites the Jewish
sources on honoring parents and its integration of fear with
honor.   Facing the problem directly he asks what should   be
done if a parental directive is injurious to parent, son, or
another   person   or if it is in conflict   with   Torah.   The
basic   principle of the primacy of life and of Torah as   the
guide to life provides an answer to this dilemma.   Obedience
to parental guidelines for marriage is discussed.

336   Hyman,   Paula E.   "The Jewish Family: Looking for   a
Usable Past."   In <u>The</u> <u>Sociology</u> <u>of</u> <u>American</u> <u>Jews</u>, Jack Nusan
Porter,   126-131.   Washington: University Press of America,
1978.

Hyman   notes that while family life is central   for   Jewish
survival its structure is socio-cultural not religious.   The
role of the woman, for example, is not traditionally that of
house-cleaner but rather as economic provider for the household.   Family morality in Judaism is, thus, not necessarily
tied   to   any one socio-economic model of the   family.   The
essay   is   reprinted in   entry   244, pp.   19-26;   it   first
appeared in <u>Congress</u> <u>Monthly</u> 42 (1979): 10-15.

337   Indig,   Yizhak.   "The Problems of Support of a   Child
Born of Artificial Insemination." <u>Dine</u> <u>Israel</u> 1 (1970):   83-
115.

Indig notes the modernity of the problem he faces,   but uses
traditional   sources to determine that the child is that   of
the   husband   if the semen is of the father and   all   duties
follow from that.   If the semen is from a foreign male then
the husband must practice the <u>zedakah</u> or charity of   support
for wife's relations.   In the case of divorce he notes that
exact stipulations are needed.

338   Jacobs, Louis. "The Problems of the Mamzer." In his <u>A</u>
<u>Tree</u> <u>of</u> <u>Life</u>: <u>Diversity</u>, <u>Flexibility</u>, <u>and</u> <u>Creativity</u> <u>in</u>
<u>Jewish</u> <u>Law</u>, 257-275.   Oxford: Oxford University Press,
1984.

Jacobs   studies the problem of the <u>mamzer</u> (see also   entries
in the annotation at 307) using the tradition of leniency in
the   Bible   and Talmud as his guide.   His historical   review
includes reference to magic and absentee pregnancies. Jacobs
reviews four proposals for dealing with the problem: that of
calling   the   first relationship only that   of   concubinage,
that of annulling the first marriage,   that of   purification
of the taint of <u>mamzerut</u>, and that of losing oneself through
a process of hiding ones status.

339 Jung, Leo.   "Guidelines to a Happy Marriage."   In his
Love and Life, 1-18. New York: Philosophical Library, 1979.

Jung celebrates the joy of obedience to the commandments.
Judaism, he claims, shows one how to care for a wife.   The
laws of family purity, in his view, protect the woman from
unwanted sexual intercourse, but he calls upon American Jews
to build clean and attractive ritual baths.   Compare entry
313 and entry 145 in which this essay occurs.

340 Jung, Moses. "Some Challenges to Jewish Marriage." In
Judaism in a Changing World, 205-216.   The Jewish Library,
4. London: Soncino Press, 1971.

This essay from an early twentieth century Jewish leader has
relevance even now.   After a brief historical review of
Jewish views about marriage, he notes the modern problems of
mobility, instability, birth control, mixed marriages, and
the fragmentation of the family.

341 Keech, Florence.   "Adoption and the Jewish Community."
in The Jewish Family in a Changing World, edited by
Gilbert S. Rosenthal, 52-62.   New York: Thomas Yoseloff,
1970.

Keech, contributing to a useful anthology (entry 358), like
Freehof (see entry 172), emphasizes the need to serve the
best interests of the child.   She argues that religion
should not deprive a child of the chance for adoption.

342 Kranzler, Gershon.   "The Changing Orthodox Jewish
Family."   In Dimensions in Orthodox Judaism, edited by
Reuven Bulka, 359-372. New York: Ktav publishing House,
1981.

Kranzler notes that the family has evolved from an organic
to a contractual association.   Women have joined the job
market and disrupted family ties.   He traces the decline in
Jewish values to this change together with the disappearance
of grandparents within the family structure.   He claims that
even Orthodox Jewish families are affected and calls for a
new moral fervor, a new type of rebbe who will guide Jewish
families. Compare the following entry and entry 312.

343 Lamm, Norman. "Family Values and Family Breakdown: An
Analysis and Prescription." In Serving the Jewish Family,
edited by Gerald Bubis, 35-52. New York: Ktav Publishing
House, 1977.

Lamm, in this addition to Bubis' anthology (see entry 343)
points to the reciprocal relationship between family solidarity and Jewish survival to argue for stronger Jewish family
life.   This traditionalist approach is both a criticism of
contemporary life and a panegyric to Jewish morality.   Lamm
thinks that the modern family has transferred responsibility
to the school but needs to reclaim it.   Compare annotation
at entry 312.

344   Lang,   Judith.   "The   Changing Jewish Family and the
Crisis of Values." Journal of Jewish Communal Services 56
(1980): 301-305.

Lang studies traditional Jewish women and finds conflicts in
their lives. The variety of influences on the lives of even
traditional Jewish women has undermined the stability of the
family.   She discovers that the family is in crisis because
traditional values have lost their force in family life.

345 Liebman,   Charles S. "Student Activists and the Jewish
Family." Bar Ilan Annual 10 (1972): 9-20.

Liebman traces Jewish student activism to a particular type
of Jewish family life.   Activists are usually successful
youth who never felt deprivation.   They perceive the school
authorities as an extension of their permissive parents.

346   Linzer,   Norman.   The Jewish Family: Authority and
Tradition in Modern Perspective.   New York: Human Sciences
Press, 1984.

Linzer looks at traditional views of rebellious children and
notes that parents are both symbols and real people.   They
are models of authority and also of independence.   He studies adolescence in modernity through the prism of Jewish
family values and concludes that modern narcissism can be
overcome through the type of self-transcendence cultivated
in Jewish religious life.   He notes the impact of the Holocaust on survivors and their children. Compare entry 313.

347   Linzer,   Norman.   "The Jewish Family." In his The
Nature of Man in Judaism and Social Work, 162-182.   New
York: Commission on Synagogue Relations, 1978.

Linzer reiterates the need for extended institutions of
social life and finds that need exacerbated by the breakdown
of family roles.   He sees the family as a moral center of
society that cultivates responsibility and duty.

348 Maller, Allen S.   "The Jewish Family Today."   The
Reconstructionist 46,8 (1980): 7-12.

Maller complains that the level of family life, of
Jewishness, of involvement in Jewish activities, and of
spiritual life has declined. He suggests that the average
level of involvement in each of these needs to be raised.

349 Mann, Morris N. "Mothers and Fathers: A Conceptualiza-
tion of Parental Roles." Tradition 21 (1983): 52-65.

The study demonstrates how Joseph Soloveitchik's theological
views of human development can be applied to the psychology
of growth.   Traditional Judaism is said to provide the
parental models, security, trust, and framework for creative
interaction needed in a child's personal development.
Compare entry 313.

350 Matzner-Bokerman, Shoshana. The Jewish Child: Halakhic
Perspectives. New York: Ktav Publishing House 1984.

This comprehensive if superficial survey of Jewish views on
the development of children, child care and child rearing,
discipline, health, socialization, confronting birthdays,
personality development, and the rites of passage is often
rooted in traditional morality and is unreflective on its
own basic principles. Compare the discussion at entry 308.

351 Mills, Robert.   "Family and Synagogue: Partners in
Search for the Holy." Journal of Religion and Health 17
(1978): 130-135.

This essay examines the theological basis for family life.
According to Mills religion enables the family to develop
quality of life in a society in which driftlessness pre-
vails, it is therefore the moral hub of contemporary life.
Compare the annotation at entries 313 and 346.

352 Monson, Rela Geffen.   "The Jewish Family in America
Today: Is it Jewish?" In Perspectives on Jews and Judaism:
Essays in Honor of Wolfe Kelman, edited by Arthur A. Chiel,
275-282. New York: Rabbinical Assembly, 1978.

This essay looks at contemporary Jewish family life in
contrast to the traditional Jewish family that, according to
Geffen, fosters the wholeness of life.   She laments the
fragmentation of the American Jewish family and the tension
between humanistic concerns and the needs of individuals.
She suggests that traditional Jewish communal virtues helped
place these various needs into proper perspective.

353 Novak, David. "Parents and Children in Jewish Ethics."
In his Law and Theology in Judaism, 2nd Series, 47-97.
New York: Ktav Publishing House, 1976.

This challenging article reviews halakhic sources, history,
psychology, and theology to outline the reciprocal responsibilities and obligations that fall on family members.   Sexual roles are looked at in detail, with particular references to the distinctiveness between the roles of the mother
and the father. In this regard he remarks on women students
of the Torah as a sexual distraction. His insight into
problems of parental sadism, of adoption, and of a child's
obligation to parents is helpful.

354 Porter, Jack Nusan. "Jewish Singles." Midstream 21,10
(1975): 35-43.

Porter contends that a new Jewish group, that of the Jewish
singles, exists needing special attention from the Jewish
community. He traces a spectrum of Jewish involvement
covering four basic types. He suggests that new types of
Jewish involvement be created, particularly of non-synagogue
centered activities. Compare the annotation in entry 309.

355 Roberts, Hyman J. "Endogamous Jewish Genocide." The Reconstructionist 40,8 (1974): 8-17.

Roberts laments the reduced Jewish fertility and notes that Jewish tradition affirms birth. He also traces the declining Jewish population to the problems of divorce and religious escapism. He bolsters his argument by commenting on the hazards of contraception and abortion.

356 Rosen, Gladys. "The Impact of the Women's Movement on the Jewish Family." Judaism 28 (1979): 160-168.

Contemporary Jewish family life must compete with new styles of Jewish living (compare the annotation at entry 312). that something is wrong with the way Jewish women are treated and that the Jewish community is suffering. There need to be more inventive and supportive ways in which to help parents cope with children and to bring unity to a dispersed and fragmented suburban environment.

357 Rosen, Gladys. "The Jewish Family: An Endangered Species." Journal of Jewish Communal Services 53 (1979): 345-352.

Rosen notes the problems threatening to destroy the Jewish family. She brings the sensitivities of social service training to bear on the problems. Her recognition of the moral as well as social and economic aspects of the threat to the Jewish family make this entry valuable reading.

358 Rosenthal, Gilbert S. The Jewish Family in a Changing World. New York: Thomas Yoseloff, 1970.

This anthology (see entries 074, 075, 081, 207, 341, 369, 384, 401, 403), focused on a Jewish response to adoption, drugs, sex education, aging, and other issues faced by the contemporary family includes a number of traditionalist Jewish views spiced with a modernist perspective.

359 Rubenstein, Amnon. "The Right to Marriage." Israel Yearbook on Human Rights 3 (1973): 233-255.

Rubenstein points to a modern Israeli paradox. Because of the religious element and the one hand and the secularist on the other hand who rejects a rigid definition of marriage, many Israeli Jews are finding it better to go unmarried than married. He claims that since untraditional couples exist the right to marriage should not be denied to them. Compare entries listed in the annotation at entry 307.

360 Sanua, Victor D. "The Contemporary Jewish Family: A Review of the Social Science Literature." In Serving the Jewish Family, edited by Gerald Bubis, 11-34. New York: Ktav Publishing House, 1977.

Sanua contributes (to entry 311) an emphasis on the importance of feminism in shaping contemporary Jewish family life in a non-traditional world. Compare the annotation in entry 312. This essay appeared in Journal of Jewish Communal Service 50 (1974) :297-312.

361 Schlesinger, Benjamin. The Jewish Family: A Survey and Annotated Bibliography, Florence Strakhovsky, editorial Consultant. Toronto: University of Toronto Press, 1971.

This survey includes three articles from the 1960s that define modern problems in Jewish family morality: Jewish ethics and family, intermarriage, and life on the kibbutz as well as a bibliography from the 1940s through 1970.

362 Shapiro, Menachem. "In My Footsteps: Some Dilemmas of Jewish Parents." In Serving the Jewish Family, edited by Gerald Bubis, 53-60. New York: Ktav Publishing House, 1977.

Shapiro's contribution to this anthology (see entry 311) reviews the problems of being a role model. While focused on the problems of being a parent it deals almost exclusively with the father-son relationships in the modern world. The essay was originally published in 1963.

363 Shiloh, Isaac S. "Marriage and Divorce in Israel." Israel Law Review 5 (1970): 479-498

This essay dealing with the moral problem of non-halakhic marriages and divorces in Israel charts the history of Jewish legal decisions, the concern of the religious authorities, and the needs of the general secular Jew. The moral dilemma of living in a Jewish State and having respect for Judaism but also for personal liberty is clearly illustrated in the situation of those who choose a civil and secular marriage and divorce only to find that their children are branded with the stigma of bastardy. See also entries listed in the annotation to entry 307.

364 Siegel, Seymour. "Religion and Family Policy: A Jewish Perspective." In Formation of Social Policy in the Catholic and Jewish Traditions, edited by Eugene J. Fisher and Daniel F. Polish, 43-62. Notre Dame: University of Notre Dame Press, 1980.

This essay is unusual since it advocates that Jews play a significant role in shaping the moral and legal environment in which they live. Siegel summarizes Jewish thinking about the sexual encounter and the command for procreation. He emphasizes that sexuality implies responsibility. He also claims that government policies should be informed by and responsive to Jewish morality.

365 Sklare, Marshall. "The Greening of Judaism." Commentary 58,6 (1974): 51-57.

This delightful review essay shows an understanding of the problem of American Jewish family life and of a morality focused on the individual rather than the group. The Jewish Catalogue represents the flowering of the Jewish youth culture in America and Sklare shows a lack of basis in family weakens sensitivity to moral obligations and ethics.

366   Teplitz, Saul I.   "The Threatened Jewish Family." United Synagogue Review 28:1 (1975): 12-13.

A Conservative Jew joins in the chorus of those who lament the decline of the Jewish family (see the annotation to entry 192).   Compare his view to that of both traditional Jews and Reform Jews who agree with his sense of a problem in the Jewish family.

367   Unna, Isaac.   "Marriage in Judaism."   In Women, edited by Leo Jung, 84-100.   The Jewish Library, 3.   London: Soncino Press, 1970.

In the realm of sexual practices traditional Jews find Judaism to be far more rigorous in its demands than contemporary youth is willing to accept.   Traditional Jews defend the morality of their stance and the value of following its precepts.   This article discusses the customs, laws, and values of Jewish marriage and divorce, contending that the Torah law is purer and clearer than modern authors.

368   Vorspan, Albert.   "The Jewish Family in Transition."   In his Great Jewish Debates and Dilemmas: Jewish Perspectives in Conflict in the Eighties, 53-78.   New York: Union of American Hebrew Congregations, 1980.

Vorspan points to the danger of individualism in the modern world.   The family has been torn apart through feminism, Gay liberation, and other causes such as the demand for zero-growth, abortion, and the growing toleration of intermarriage.   In each case he claims that what is needed on both sides is sympathy and recognition of the mutual obligations shared by the institution and the individual.   This essay should be compared to other attempts at coming to grips with the challenge of modernity and the new organization of family life that it requires.   Compare the annotation at entry 312.

369   Warach, Bernard.   "Leisure Time and the Jewish Family." In The Jewish Family in a Changing World, edited by Gilbert S. Rosenthal, 63-86.   New York: Thomas Yoseloff, 1970.

In this contribution to a valuable collection (see entry 358).   Warach raises the challenge of leisure in the modern world.   He finds the concept to be rooted in both religious belief and social practice.   With the decline of the Sabbath and acculturation Jews lost their insight into leisure as a religious and familial pursuit.   He hopes for a possible recovery of earlier models.

370 Warhaftig, Zerah. "Should Civil Marriage be Instituted in the State of Israel?" [Hebrew]. Dine Israel 7 (1976): 215-220.

The problem of civil marriages leads to a division among Israel Jews (see entries listed in the annotation to entry 307) and demands the attention of Jews seeking unified community. The dilemma of Israeli Orthodox Jews who seek to impose their values and ideals upon a largely secular con- stituency is illustrated by the problems Warhaftig must face. He argues that halakhic marriages and divorces are central for Jewish life.

371 Waskow, Arthur. "Mishpacha: New Jews, New Families." In his These Holy Sparks: The Rebirth of the Jewish People, 98-117. New York: Harper and Row, 1983.

Waskow seeks to discover new ways of organizing Jewish kinship groups. The symbolism of the family, of the mishpa- cha is powerful, but it need not be reserved only for those social constellations that tradition designated by it. Was- kow is sensitive to the needs of singles, to the crisis of marriages, and to feminism in contemporary Jewish life.

372 Zeff, David. "The Jewish Family Agency: Individual and Group Casework Services that Build Jewish Identity." Journal of Jewish Communal Service 49 (1974): 303-308.

Zeff reviews the crisis of identity within Jewish family services. He notes the new needs of the aged and of adoles- cents. He finds the root of the crisis to lie in the disto- rtion of Jewish family life and its role models that has occurred with modernity.

373 Zelizer, Viviana A. "The Unmarried Jew: Problems and Prospects." Conservative Judaism 32 (1978): 15-21.

Zelizer contends that Jewish singles can contribute to the synagogue of new values of survival and Jewish life are es- tablished. She claims that the centrality of the nuclear family to halakha is a myth that has led to social, reli- gious, economic and psychological exploitation. Compare entries 309, 310, 354, 356.

INTERMARRIAGE

374 Abrams, William. "Intermarriage: Catastrophe or Challenge." United Synagogue Review 26 (1973): 12-13, 27- 29.

The Conservative movement in Judaism has sought to come to terms with intermarriage and understand its implications. Abrams points to the need to counsel both partners in an in- termarriage and to provide for the Jewish education of the children. He also seeks increased Jewish education and a change in the Jewish community's policies on mixed marriages to find ways of integrating the non-Jewish partner into the community so as to make the Jewish life of children of mixed marriages more viable. Abrams represents one response given by Conservative Jewish thinkers to the problem of intermarriage. The movement is diverse and encompasses a variety of responses; see entries 396, 397, 399.

375 Berman, Louis. Jews and Intermarriage: A Study in Personality and Culture. New York: Thomas Yoseloff, 1968.

This detailed, case-oriented, study of viewpoints on intermarriage and sex norms in Judaism surveys intermarriage in contemporary Jewry. It points to the strain intermarriage places on Jewish life, on the difficulties of conversion to Judaism, and of the need to study the successful intermarriage. The author claims to be neither a survivalist nor an assimilationist but a scholar who thinks that analysis of a problematic situation can lead to a greater ability to cope with it. Examples of the approaches he analyzes as well as more recent attempts to study intermarriage academically can be found in entries 378, 379, 382, 387, 391, 401, 403, 408.

376 Blank, William. "Zentermarriage." Moment 4 (1978): 9-10.

This personal report of a rabbi who does not perform intermarriages but did perform such a service for followers of Zen who claimed that their meditation had no religious significance demonstrates the problematic nature of the modern situation. The rabbi is worried that there is a conflict here and tries to come to terms with it.

377 Bleich, J. David. "The Prohibition Against Intermarriage." In his Contemporary Halakhic Problems 2, 268-282. Library of Jewish Law and Ethics 10. New York: Ktav Publishing House, 1983.

Bleich represents a traditional denunciation of mixed marriage (see entries 378, 384, 386, 398, 400, 408). He reviews the biblical and post-biblical sources for the prohibition against intermarriage and the detailed laws concerning those to whom it applies.

378 Bubis, Gerald B. "Intermarriage, the Rabbi, and the Jewish Communal Worker." Journal of Jewish Communal Service 50 (1974): 85-97.

Bubis in this article defines a variety of types of marriages--from that in which the Jewish partner converts out of Judaism to that in which the non-Jewish partner converts into Judaism. He describes the moral dilemma of the rabbi such a situation as that of counselor rather than teacher. He suggests that teaching about intermarriage needs to bring ideals and reality into closer harmony with each other. Compare this article with those alluded to in entry 375.

379 Fein, Leonard J.   "Some Consequences of Jewish Intermarriage." Jewish Social Studies 33 (1971): 44-57.

Fein distinguishes between various types of intermarriages:
mixed marriage in which neither partner converts and intermarriage in which the non-Jewish partner converts to
Judaism.   He contends that far from being a moral problem,
this latter can strengthen Jewish life.   Compare this
analysis to entry 375 and the other entries listed there.

380 Freehof, Solomon B.   "Mixed Marriages on Temple
Premises," in Modern Reform Response, 108-115. Cincinnati:
Hebrew Union College Press, 1971.

The problem of intermarriage takes on a particular resonance
in Reform Judaism (see entry 381 and the other entries
listed there).   Here, Freehof claims that both Reform and
traditional Jews are saddened by intermarriage but that the
former seek to strengthen the Jewishness of the intermarried
family.   Despite this leniency, however, he declares that
using a synagogue to sanctify such a marriage is condoning
what the synagogue cannot condone.

381 Friedman, Norman.   "Boundary Issues for Liberal
Judaism." Midstream 19 (1973): 47-52.

Reform Judaism has struggled to find a consistent way of
dealing with intermarriages between Jews and non-Jews.   The
rabbinical leadership is split with some officiating at such
marriages and others refusing to do so.   The integration of
Gentile partners of Jewish members of a synagogue is also a
problem for Reform Judaism.   The opinions range from
extremely tolerant to extremely rigorous (see particularly
entries 380, 385, 388-390, 394, 405).   The dilemma is that,
as a liberal faith, Reform encourages and accepts differences, but, as a Jewish movement, it desires to retain a distinctive identity. Friedman contends that the commitment of
liberal Judaism to liberalism and to Judaism is tested by
certain issues: which takes precedence, Judaism or liberalism.   The three issues he examines are Gay synagogues,
Mixed Marriages, Jews for Jesus.   See entries 289, 806 and
830.

382 Hochbaum, Jerry.   "Towards the Development of a Planned
Communal Response to Jewish Intermarriage." Journal of
Jewish Communal Service 51 (1974): 131-138.

Hochbaum declares that Jewish morality places an emphasis on
peoplehood of Israel as well as on personal happiness.   He
sees intermarriage as a result of neglecting the moral
dimension of loyalty to Judaism, especially among children
during their high school years.   He notes that American
Jewry, as a voluntary community, must depend upon moral sensitivity to the importance of remaining Jewish rather than
on social coercion to survive.   Compare entry 375 and
references there.

383 Kahane, Meir. Why Be Jewish: Intermarriage, Assimilation and Alienation. New York: Stein and Day, 1977.

This often angry and vehement condemnation of American
Jewish leaders seeks to explain the rise of intermarriage
among American Jewish youth. Kahane suggests that the
problem lies in the alienation from Judaism created by
hypocritical leaders that makes being Jewish dispensable for
Jewish youth. He advocates, as the only legitimate
response, the creation of a militant and exclusive Jewish
Orthodoxy to counteract the present situation. This
vitriolic denunciation of intermarriage is characteristic of
Orthodox Judaism as a look at entry 377 and the other
entries listed there will show.

384 Kogan, Henry Enoch. "Reflections on Intermarriage."
In The Jewish Family in a Changing World, edited by Gilbert
S. Rosenthal, 284-294. New York: Thomas Yoseloff, 1970.

Kogan reflects on the psychology of intermarriage and
concludes that Jews must develop an ego identity in which
self is not subordinate to sexuality. Jewish moral values,
he contends, will enable sexuality to be sanctified without
rebelling against Judaism itself. This article represents
both trends within Rosenthal's anthology (358). It is both
sensitive to Jewish moral questions and religious issues
while utilizing sophisticated social scientific theories and
techniques.

385 Kominsky, Neil. "Rabbinic Ethics and Mixed Marriage:
An Exercise in Catch 22.'" Central Conference of American
Rabbis Journal 23 (1976): 64-66.

In the midst of Reform Judaism's perplexity concerning intermarriage (see entry 381 and the comment there) Kominsky
laments that a lack of rabbinic veto power, the power of
congregational decisions on rabbinical candidates, and the
vehement response of congregants to a rabbi's position often
make a moral consistency on the question of mixed marriages
almost impossible.

386 Lamm, Maurice, "Interfaith Marriage," in The Jewish
Way in Love and Marriage, 48-65. New York: Harper and Row,
1980.

This extraordinary section of Lamm's excellent work (entry
148) is a welcome alternative to the often uncharitable
harshness with which Orthodox Jews face intermarriage (see
entry 377 and the annotation given at the entry). Lamm
writes patiently, explaining the various reasons for Jewish
communal concern, he notes with charity the concern of the
Jewish community for the Jewish children of an interfaith
marriage, and discusses the various rights of both the intermarried and their children. His note of caution and care
to those contemplating intermarriage is a model of sensitivity. This is a worthy essay expressing the deepest
commitments and humanitarianism of Orthodox Judaism.

387   Lazerwitz, Bernard.   "Jewish-Christian Marriages and
Conversion." Jewish Social Studies 43 (1981): 31-46.

This serious attempt at social scientific study is an
example of survivalism combined with realism (see entry 375
and the comment there). In the face of growing intermarriage, Lazerwitz suggests that such marriages are not necessarily morally wrong. They may help Judaism. Conversions,
he thinks, can strengthen religious separatism in the face
of declining social separatism.

388   Maller, Allen S.   "Jewish-Gentile Marriage: Another
Look at the Problem." Central Conference of American Rabbis
Journal 23 (1976): 65-74.

Maller's contribution to Reform Judaism's debate on mixed
marriages (see the annotation at entry 381) is a suggestion
that opposition to intermarriage is self-defeating.
Instead, he advocates a mitzva' marriage, in which the
synagogue leads the non-Jewish partner to wish to convert.
He uses as his proof results of a 1972-1973 survey.

389 Maller, Allen S. "Mixed Marriage and Reform Judaism."
Judaism 24 (1975): 39-48.

This essay should be read in conjunction with the preceding
one. Contrast this positive approach to mixed marriage with
the views in entry 428 and in the reference found in the
comment on entry 381. Maller argues that mixed marriages
can be saved for Judaism through a course of study which
will bring seriousness to the family.

390 Martin, Bernard.   "Contra Mixed Marriages: Some
Historical and Theological Reflections." Central Conference
of American Rabbis Journal 24 (1977): 75-85.

Martin distinguishes between intermarriage (with conversion
to Judaism) and mixed marriage (with no conversion) and
contends that the latter is a danger to Judaism and that the
survival of the Jewish family is morally essential in post-
Holocaust world. See the comment on entry 381.

391 Massarik, Fred. "Rethinking the Intermarriage Crisis."
Moment 3 (1978): 29-33.

Massarik suggests that intermarriage may not be a tragedy
but an opportunity to be used to maximize the chances of
Jewish survival. He suggests that both the intermarried Jew
and the non-Jewish partner be offered educational opportunities so that Judaism is strengthened even in the midst
of an intermarriage.

392 Mayer, Egon. Love and Tradition: Marriage Between Jews
and Christians. New York: Plenum Press, 1985.

Mayer offers a study of how marriage has changed from a moral obligation with social responsibilities to an individualistic practice. He also notes, however, that in Jewish-Christian marriages the non-Jewish partner converts more often than does the Jewish one. He suggests that Judaism has a social hold over its members as an explanation.

393 Minkowitz, M. Aaron. "Religious and Civil Marriages and Intermarriage" [Hebrew]. Bitzaron 60 (1969): 11-14.

This study investigates the problem in Israel of secular Jews and civil marriages, intermarriages, and the Israeli rabbinate contending that marriages violating Jewish law have divided Jews and that civil marriage will not solve the problem, and claiming that legalization of marriages condemned by Jewish tradition will only lead to greater tragedy for the children of such marriages.

394 Mirsky, Norman. "Mixed Marriage and the Reform Rabbinate." Midstream 16 (1970): 40-46.

Mirsky notes the controversy in Reform Judaism over mixed marriages (see entry 381 and the references there). He condemns the hypocrisy of supplying a list of rabbis who will perform such marriages. He discerns a need to cope with the social reality and to come to terms with it. He also claims, like Friedman (381) that the ideological commitment of Reform to both liberalism and Judaism needs careful scrutiny in the light of this reality.

395 Moskowitz, Mark A. "Intermarriage and the Proselyte: A Jewish View." Judaism 28 (1979): 423-433.

American culture has fostered a type of popularized view of intermarriage. The television comedy of "Bridget Loves Bernie" demonstrated this. Novels like Bernard Malamud's The Assistant show non-Jews and Jews emotionally involved with one another. This essay takes a look at the process by which the hero of Malamud's book, Frank Alpine, becomes Jewish. The author finds the view of intermarriage unrealistic and the writing unpersuasive. The use of Christian images and the facile conversion in the book, according to Moskowitz, desecrates the history of Judaism.

396 Ofseyer, Jordan S. "No Sanction For Intermarriage." United Synagogue Review 24,2 (1971): 14-15, 29-30.

A Conservative Jew, Ofseyer writes out against the practice of rabbinic officiation at mixed marriages. Unlike other Conservative Jewish thinkers (compare entries 374 and 399) he is unwilling to accept the American dilemma of intermarriage and calls for the creation of meaningful alternatives for strengthening American Judaism. Among the various plans he suggests are those calling on American Jews to redouble efforts to live full Jewish lives at home, encouraging the Jewish partner to remain a Jew and reminding intermarried couples that the children of a Jewish woman are Jewish.

397   Ofseyer, Jordan S.   "Where We Have Failed."   United
Synagogue Review 25,2 (1972): 8-9, 28-29.

In this article Ofseyer continues investigating the causes
of intermarriages and suggesting solutions to the problem.
Intermarriage according to him, grows out of Jewish minim-
alism and demonstrates where Jewish education has failed.
He considers the bar mitzvah ceremony of most American
Jewish youth a travesty of the tradition, examines the
leftist social causes that animate young Jews, and concludes
that Judaism has failed by requiring only a minimal commitment and by not demonstrating the worthiness of its ethics
and moral seriousness.

398 Pelcovitz, Ralph. "The Intermarriage Issue: Crisis and
Challenge," in Danger and Opportunity, 123-134. New York:
Shengold Publishers, 1976.

This trenchant piece represents militant Orthodox (compare
entry 377 and the other entries mentioned in the annotation
there) Pelcovitz condemns both civil marriages and those
performed by non-Orthodox Rabbis. He claims that the inner
strength of Judaism lies in its separatism and exclusivism.
Reform, according to Pelcovitz, makes Judaism like Christianity and thereby reduces the barrier to intermarriage.
He scorns rituals that mix Jewish and Christian elements for
an "ecumenical" marriage as absurd.

399 Routtenberg, Max J. "The Jew Who Has Intermarried," in
Decades of Decision, 76-82. New York: Bloch, 1973.

Routtenberg ponders the question of whether the Jewish
partner of a mixed marriage may join a Conservative Jewish
synagogue. He declares that standards not halakha is at
stake. Jewish Standards allow Sabbath breakers to be
counted in a minyan since they are considered like a
captive child' to the ignorance of this generation. He
applies this standard to those who intermarry and suggests
that synagogues cultivate the family's Jewishness and
encourage conversion of the non-Jewish partner. The pathos
and sympathetic view found here together with a respect for
Jewish law and tradition typifies the approach of Conservative Judaism to the dilemma of intermarriage (see entry 374
and the annotation there).

400   Rozwaski, Chaim Z.   "Jewish Law and Intermarriage."
Jewish Life 36,6 (1969): 18-23.

Rozwaski argues, in a typical Orthodox manner (see entry 377
and the comment given there) that the problem of intermarriage requires not a pragmatic answer but a halakhic
dimension since it is obedience to divine decree that is at
issue. Rejecting divine law, in his view, removes one from
the presence of God. The act of intermarriage is considered
equal to idolatry and far from being a new phenomenon goes

back to biblical apostasy and must be treated now as it was then.

401 Sanua, Victor D.   "The Attitude of Jewish Students to Intermarriage."   In The Jewish Family in a Changing World, edited by Gilbert S. Rosenthal, 240-261. New York: Thomas Yoseloff, 1970.

This study of representative Jewish students offers an appropriate response of a social scientist to the problem of intermarriage demonstrating both factual data and insightful analysis (see entry 375 and its annotation). Sanua provides insight in his contribution to this anthology (entry 358). This survey shows that most Jewish college students do not regard such a marriage as unethical and have integrated it into their understanding of Judaism.

402 Seltzer, Sanford.   "The Psychological Implications of Mixed Marriage." Journal of Reform Judaism 32 (1985): 21-37.

The reaction of Jews to the Nazi Holocaust parallels the response to mixed marriages. The full danger becomes clear only through creating a sense of distance from the event. Only when American Jews have this distance can they appreciate the real threat that mixed marriages have for Jewish survival in the modern world.

403 Shapiro, Manaheim S.   "Intermarriage and the Jewish Community."   In The Jewish Family in a Changing World, edited by Gilbert S. Rosenthal, 262-271. New York: Thomas Yoseloff, 1970.

Rosenthal's anthology (entry 358) includes traditionalist arguments such as this article as well as social scientific data. Shapiro takes a traditional look at intermarriage and its moral dimension. He declares that the ethical concern that prevents intermarriage should not be with personal happiness, but with the good of the community. In that regard he concludes that strong identification with the community will prevent intermarriage.

404 Silberman, Lou H.   "Reprobation, Prohibition, Invalidity: An Examination of the Halakhic Development Concerning Intermarriage." In Judaism and Ethics, edited by Daniel Jeremy Silver, 177-198. New York: Ktav Publishing House, 1970.

Silberman reviews the biblical and rabbinic background of hostility to intermarriage. He examines the experience of Jews in the middle ages in contrast to their experience with Napoleon, noting Napoleon's pointed question to the Jews of his time about intermarriage. He suggests that the peculiarly modern dilemma is that of the religious status of civil marriages.

405   Silver,   Samuel.   Mixed Marriage Between Jew and
Christian. New York: Arco Publishing Company, 1977.

While this book begins with a defense of Jewish endogamy it
soon turns toward a positive response to intermarriage.
Silver suggests the possibilities for a ceremony in which
Jews and Christians could participate as equals.   He offers
advice on ways of coping in an intermarriage.   Many Reform
Jewish leaders disagree with his rather positive approach
and have demanded that rabbis such as he cease from their
actions (see the debate and its analysis as represented in
entry 381 and the other entries given in the annotation to
that entry).

406 Singer, David. "Living with Intermarriage." Commentary
68:1 (1979): 4-13.

Singer suggests that the twin goals of integration and
survival may not be compatible.   If that is the case then
the choice for intermarriage is a choice for integration.
While integration may at times lead to survival it does not
in this case.   Instead it raises the question about the
limits of accommodation to the general society.

407 Sklare, Marshall.   "Intermarriage and Jewish Survival."
Commentary 49,3 (1970): 51-58.

Sklare is clearly a survivalist in his approach to intermarriage (see the typology established in entry 377 and the
other entries mentioned in the annotation to that entry).
In this essay he sets forth the ethics of survival in an environment of accommodation.   He notes the decline of the
pragmatic argument that mixed marriages do not succeed and
finds that the contemporary situation presents Jews with   a
choice between liberal toleration or Jewish exclusiveness, a
choice which is really that between survival and the disappearance of the Jewish people.

408   Weinberg, Alezah F.   "The Response of Jewish Family
Service To the Issue of Conversion and Intermarriage."
Journal of Jewish Communal Service 50 (1974): 340-348.

Weinberg suggests that the best response to conversion and
intermarriage is education for family living. She advocates
content education and the creation of a sense of Jewish
community.   She considers the task of the social worker to
be that of helping the non-Jewish partner reach self-
understanding and better integration with community.

DIVORCE

409 Arussi, Razon.   "The Ethnic Factor in Rabbinic
Decision-Making (enforcement of Divorce on the Grounds of
Revulsion in the Yemenite Community" [Hebrew]. Dine Israel
10-11 (1981-1983): 125-126.

This sensitive study of a modern Israeli problem includes a sketch of the halakhic background and the modern cultural conflicts that make a halakhic compromise on the question of rationale for divorce imperative today.

410 Bleich, J. David. "The Aguna Problem." In his Contemporary Halakhic Problems, 150-159. The Library of Jewish Law and Ethics, 4. New York: Ktav Publishing House, 1977.

Bleich notes the continual anguish which rabbis felt about the deserted wife. He remarks on rabbinic views of conditional divorces given before going to battle, of problems of men home on furlough, and of problems from the refusal to grant a religious divorce, and problems with the Conservative Jewish strategies for solving the problems. On the problem of the aguna see entries 411, 413, 414, 419, 420, 421, 430, 433, 434, 438, 445. The article first appeared in Tradition 11 (1970): 96-99.

411 Bleich, J. David. "Modern-Day Agunot: A Proposed Remedy." The Jewish Law Annual 4 (1981): 167-187.

Bleich surveys the way in which modern Jews (he calls them "post-Enlightenment") have sought to alleviate the problem of the aguna. He notes how the secular courts have left the Jewish bet din without power to enforce its enactments and the problems this has upon women stranded by husbands refusing to deliver a religious divorce. After reviewing traditional authorities he offers a solution of his own, a document to suggest the obligations in case of a civil divorce.

412 Bleich, J. David. "Impotence as Grounds for Divorce." In his Contemporary Halakhic Problems 2, 100-103. The Library of Jewish Law and Ethics, 10. New York: Ktav Publishing House, 1983.

A Jewish woman has some leverage of her own in a marriage and can have the Jewish court compel a divorce. On the grounds of divorce generally see entries 409, 415, 444. Here Bleich agrees that divorce is permissible on the grounds of a husband's impotence, but emphasizes that preference is given to psychological counseling to solve the problem. The essay can also be found in The Jewish Law Annual 1 (1978): 84-86 and Tradition 16 (1977): 117-119.

413 Bleich, J. David. "Indirect Coercion in Compelling a Get." In his Contemporary Halakhic Problems 2, 93-100. The Library of Jewish Law and Ethics, 10. New York: Ktav Publishing House, 1983.

Bleich explains the halakhic requirement for divorce to be given voluntarily and the problems arising from this requirement. He suggests that offering criminals an inducement to divorce through reduction of sentence is not direct compulsion and is permissible from the standpoint of traditional Jewish law. Compare entries 414, 419, 420.

414   Bleich, J. David.   "Refusal to Grant a Religious Divorce." The Jewish Law Annual 1 (1979), 179-183.

Bleich discusses the problems with the abandoned wife and with civil divorces. He reviews the various practical suggestions that have been made in recent times and the drawbacks of each of them (on this issue see entry 410 and the other references given in the annotation there). This essay appeared first in Tradition 13 (1972): 129-133.

415 Brayer, Menachem M. "The Role of Jewish Law Pertaining to the Jewish Family, Jewish Marriage, and Divorce." In Jews and Divorce, edited by Jacob Fried, 1-34. New York: Ktav Publishing House, 1968.

This essay in Fried's anthology (see 423) analyzes four kinds of divorce: by mutual agreement, by the husband's petition, by compulsion of the court on the instigation of the wife, and by compulsion of the court alone, a discussion on pp. 34-43; compare the detailed discussion by Haut (429).

416 Bulka, Reuven P. "Divorce: The Problem and the Challenge." Tradition 16 (1976): 127-133.

Bulka emphasizes the importance of sharing the self in marriage, a requirement that demands a mature self. He suggests that human values must be taught and that the public school is not the right context for such education. Compare his views to entries 417, 423, 426, 432, 435, 447.

417 Cottle, Thomas J. Divorce and the Jewish Child. New York: American Jewish Committee, 1981.

This detailed examination of case studies shows how religion can sometimes function as substitute for the family and sometimes as a focus of anger. The moral question of family life, the effect of divorce upon children, and the relevance of religious life as a means of coping with the trauma is considered. Compare items mentioned in the previous entry.

418 Dichovsky, Shlomo. "Civil Marriage." [Hebrew] Tehumin 2 (1981): 252-235.

Dichovsky points out the traditions of leniency and rigor in Jewish marriage law, including an analysis of the difficulty of a woman obtaining a religious divorce as a cause for civil marriages. See entry 307.

419 Dichovsky, Shlomo. "Forcing the delivery of a Bill of Divorce by Means of Reducing a Jail Sentence" [Hebrew]. Tehumin 1 (1980): 248-254.

The necessity for a freely given divorce presents a peculiar problem for Jewish Orthodoxy (see the discussion at entry 413). Dichovsky's contribution is to distinguish between the prevention of a benefit and the threat of harm with only the latter being truly compulsion.

420 Ellinson, Getsel [Elikim]. "The Refusal to Deliver a
Get." Sinai 69 (1972): 135-158.

Ellinson reviews the means by which a woman can coerce her
husband through the court so as not to remain an aguna.
Rabbinic Judaism, he shows, has responded to women left
vulnerable to a husband's vindictiveness.

421 Falk, Zeev W. The Divorce Action by the Wife in Jewish
Law. Jerusalem: Institute for Legislative Research and Comparative Law, 1973.

Falk offers a comprehensive survey of halakha concerning the
woman's right to initiate a divorce and provides suggestions
of his own for future halakhic action.

422 Falk, Zeev W. "Forensic Medicine in Jewish Law." Dine
Israel 1 (1969): xx-xxx.

See entry 014.

423 Fried, Jacob. "Introduction." In his Jews and
Divorce, vii-x. New York: Ktav Publishing House, 1968.

Fried provides a useful introduction to his anthology. See
entries 212, 415, 426, 432.

424 Friedman, Edwin H. "Bar Mitzvah When the Parents are
No Longer Partners." Journal of Reform Judaism 28 (1981):
53-66.

Friedman discusses the trauma of divorce for Jewish children
and the role Judaism can play in reducing it.

425 Fubini, G. "Gli Ebrei e il Divorzio." La Rassegna
Mensile di Israel 36 (1970): 355-365.

Fubini studies how Jewish divorce law developed in Italy and
how it affected and was affected by the development of
Italian divorce codes.

426 Goldberg, Nathan. "The Jewish Attitude Toward
Divorce." Jews and Divorce, edited by Jacob Fried, 44-76.
New York: Ktav Publishing House, 1968.

Goldberg summarizes the Jewish assumptions about human
nature that underlie its emphasis on marriage. Marriage is
both a private and a communal act. Persecutions made
marriage important for Jewish survival. This background
makes Jewish marriage law comprehensible. See the discussion
on pages 76-90 of entry 378.

427 Greenberg, Blu. "Jewish Attitudes toward Divorce," in
On Women and Judaism: A View from Tradition, 125-145.
Philadelphia: Jewish Publication Society of America, 1981.

Greenberg studies the traditional problem of the aguna and declares that, while much has changed, rabbinic authorities need to use a takanah, or decree, to give women a right to initiate divorce.

428 Harris, Monford. "Toward a Theology of Divorce" Conservative Judaism 23 (1969): 33-44.

Harris celebrates the realism of Judaism which is family centered and which sees divorce not as a concession to the evil inclination but as an outgrowth of concern for the growth of all members in the family. Compare entry 437.

429 Haut, Irwin H. Divorce in Jewish Law and Life. New York: Sepher-Hermon Press, 1983.

Haut's comprehensive look at marriage, the ketuba, takanot, woman's right to a divorce requirements for a get, the procedure itself and its legal consequences, the equality of women and the giving of the get together with modern responses in Israel and America provides evidence on rabbinic sensitivity to the problem of the aguna.

430 Haut, Irwin H. "A Problem in Jewish Divorce Law: An Analysis and Some Suggestions." Tradition 16 (1977): 29-49.

Haut asks whether the ketuba can afford the basis for a civil court to compel the giving of a get. He notes the problems in instituting a new takanah but avers that they can be overcome so that halakha can regain its moral force.

431 Jakobovits, Immanuel. "Marriage and Divorce." In Women, edited by Leo Jung, 101-112. The Jewish Library 3. London: Soncino Press, 1970.

Jakobovits summarizes the legal regulations, the rights and responsibilities, and the procedures for Jewish divorce.

432 Kravitz, Julius. "Judaism as it Confronts The New Morality In Regard to Divorce." In Jews and Divorce, edited by Jacob Fried, 149-157. New York: Ktav Publishing House, 1968.

Kravitz outlines the history of Jewish divorce from the Bible through Talmud, summarizing the halakha including the grounds of divorce, its enforcement, the legal procedure, and the moral problem of the aguna. See entry 423.

433 Kreitman, Benjamin. "Updating Jewish Laws of Marriage and Divorce." United Synagogue Review 21,3 (1968): 8-9, 28-30.

Kreitman discusses the problems of the aguna, of civil marriage, and divorce. He provides a history of attempted remedies for these problems and their lack of success. He suggests that the Conservative movement holds the key to solving this problem for modern Jews.

434 Landes, Aaron. "The Antenuptial Agreement." Conservative Judaism 26 (1972): 61-63.

Landes reviews the success of Conservative Judaism's creation of a Ketuba agreement that provides at marriage for the
possibility of a Jewish divorce in the case of a civil
divorce. He provides helpful case histories to show the
advantages of this approach. Compare the previous entry.

435 Lang, Judith. "Divorce and the Jewish Woman." Journal
of Jewish Communal Service 54 (1978): 220-280.

This field study of traditional Jewish women studies how
they cope with their experience of divorce. The trauma
affects them particularly harshly since it undermines their
preconceptions of value, personal worth, and worldview.

436 Lipman, Eugene F. "The Rabbi and Divorce." Central
Conference of American Rabbis Journal (1977): 29-34.

Lipman cautions rabbis to be wary of being drawn into a
divisive battle and urges them to provide support and help.

437 Maller, Allen S. "A Religious Perspective on Divorce."
Journal of Jewish Communal Service 55 (1978): 192-194.

This theological argument contends that divorce can be a
part of personal development and growth. Maller contends
that the traditional writ of divorce, the Get symbolizes
this achievement and calls for a Reform Jewish writ of
divorce. Compare entry 428.

438 Novak, David. "The Aguna or the Case of the Uncoopera-
tive Husband." In his Law and Theology in Judaism, 31-54.
New York: Ktav Publishing House, 1974.

Novak defines how a woman becomes an aguna and suggests
solutions through such mechanisms as obligatory divorce,
abrogation, defacto annulment and declaring the marriage
erroneous. He compares the various solutions offered by
both Orthodox and Conservative Jewish leaders. Be sure to
compare this essay with the following entry.

439 Novak, David. "Annulment in Lieu of Divorce in Jewish
Law." The Jewish Law Annual 4 (1981): 188-206

This article argues for rabbinic power to annul marriages as
a means of eliminating the immoral religious blackmail and
vengeance that husbands practice on their former wives. made
in the previous entry. Novak reviews the Jewish divorce
crisis in modern times and the views concerning divorce and
annulment by earlier authorities. He concludes that annulment is the only appropriate rabbinic response to a situation that is unacceptable on the internal Jewish criteria of
morality.

440 Rabinowitz, Stanley. "The Megillah and the Get." Conservative Judaism 26 (1972): 64-69.

Rabinowitz claims that Judaism has shown in the past an
ability to circumvent a law or even to negate it as history
demands. Today, he declares, a takanah, avoiding the radical solutions of liberal Jews, can solve the problem of the
modern tragedies of women who are stranded because of civil
divorce without a Jewish get.

441   Rakeffet-Rothkoff,   Aaron.   "Annulment of Marriage
Within the Context of Cancellation of the Get." Tradition
15 (1975): 173-185.

The author examines cases in which Orthodox authorities have
annulled marriages and questions whether leniency is really
a key to solving the problem He remarks on the traditional
limitations on such annulments and argues that this strategy
must be used warily despite humanitarian concerns for
suffering women.

442   Schaffer, Sylvan.   "Child Custody: Halacha and the
Secular Approach." Journal of Halacha and Contemporary
Society 5 (1983): 32-45.

The burden of support, according to Schaffer, is on father,
although children of either sex stay with the mother until
six years of age. Thereafter the sexes are separated. The
welfare of the children, he argues, is always primary, and
parents have no "rights of visitation." See Halacha and
Contemporary Society, edited by Alfred S. Cohen, 70-82. New
York: Ktav Publishing House, 1983.

443   Schapira, Moshe.   "Divorce on Grounds of Revulsion"
[Hebrew]. Dine Israel 1 (1970): 117-153.

Summarizing the evolution of Jewish views toward divorce and
both traditional restrictions and exceptions to them,   the
author discusses the moral rationale for divorce and for its
limitation in Jewish life.

444   Schwartz, Sidney. "Conservative Judaism and the
Agunah." Conservative Judaism 36 (1983): 37-44.

This summary of the debate on how to cope with the problem
of the aguna from the 1930s through the present disputes
that Orthodox Jewish approval provides the only legitimation
for religious change.

445 Seligman, Ruth. "Divorce." Midstream 28 (1982): 35-
37.

Seligman focus attention on a mitzva group organized in
Israel to help women seeking a religious divorce. While
this self-help has been useful, she contends, changes in the
halakha are still needed.

446   Shilo, Shmuel.   "Impotence as a Ground for Divorce."
The Jewish Law Annual 4 (1981): 127-143.

While specifically a historical study this essay shows the
moral aims of Jewish divorce law.   It insists upon giving a
women full financial support.   The presumption that a woman
giving such evidence tells the truth suggests the moral
principles of rabbinic Judaism.

447   Siegel, Seymour.   "Divorce."   In The Second Jewish
Catalogue, compiled and edited by Sharon Strassfeld and
Michael Strassfeld, 108-121.   Philadelphia: Jewish Publica-
tion Society of America, 1976.

This article summarizes Jewish procedure, describes the get
and explains why it is needed in addition to civil divorce.
Siegel explains the Lieberman ketuba (marriage certificate)
and the problem of the aguna.

448   Warhaftig, Zerah.   "Sources of Obligation for Child
Support" [Hebrew].   Tehumin 1 (1980): 255-272.

Warhaftig notes that a husband's obligations are dependent
on the mother's status as his wife.   He does have some
direct duties to children, which is a specifically Judaic
view.   Warhaftig distinguishes between charity and
obligation in these duties as well as discussing until what
age the support must last.

4
The Morality of Jewish Images

JEWISH EDUCATION

449 Ackerman, Walter I. "Jewish Education Today." American Jewish Year Book 80 (1980): 139-148

Ackerman insists the Jewish education needs to create imaginative approaches so that a child experiences a total education. He claims that Jewish education needs to convey the culture of Judaism and that this is best done in an inclusive setting such as the day school. This essay surveys the major questions debated in contemporary Jewish thinking about education and learning. Not only is this an excellent introductory essay (compare other such essays in 450, 451, 456,464, 467, and 468), but it touches on the major themes concerning Jewish education in general. It focuses on the need to teach values as well as skills (see entries 452, 453, 457, 459, 465, 472, 476, 480, 486, 487), on the challenge of the Jewish day school and its interaction with the public schools (see entries 454, 459, 462, 463, 471, 473, 479, 483, 485, 488-494, 496, 497) and on the need for experiential as well as intellectual stimulation (see entries 469, 482, 484, 493).

450 Ackerman, Walter I. "Jewish Education--For What?" American Jewish Year Book 70 (1969): 3-6.

This influential essay, reproduced in David Sidorsky, ed., The Future of the Jewish Community in America (New York: Basic Books, 1973), pp. 176-210, argues that Jewish education must convey feeling as well as knowledge. He contends that one goal must be education for democracy and that the democratic ideal can be conveyed only through a democratically structured educational system.

451 Ackerman, Walter I. "The Present Moment in Jewish Education." Midstream 18 (1972): 3-24

Ackerman shows how Jewish education has been influenced by various tendencies in public schools such as student-orien

tation, a new curriculum, and new materials, but also how
it lacks an overall purpose. The crisis of moral values
evident in such an education points to the need of integrating goals and means in a philosophy of Jewish learning.

452 Ben Horin, Meir. "Education as Religion." The Reconstructionist 47,1 (1981): 15-23.

Ben Horin recognizes that education can help solve the
crisis of symbols and meaning in Jewish life. He suggests
that Jewish education become the training ground for students to learn the democratic process through association
with Jewish ideals and values in action. On the orientation
that sees Jewish learning as a form of worship compare entry
455.

453 Berkovits, Eliezer. "Jewish Education in a World Ad-
rift." Tradition 11 (1970): 5-12.

Liberals argue that Jewish education should not threaten the
public schools and that parochial Jewish day schools are
such a threat. Orthodox thinkers reverse the argument and
claim that Jewish private education benefits the public
system (see entries 459, 479, 489). The moral question of
public or private education is, according to Berkovits, no
longer valid. The public schools show their inadequacy so
that Judaism is needed as an answer to the contemporary
moral dilemmas which public schools cannot handle.

454 Berman, Saul J., et al. "The Jewish Day School."
Tradition 13 (1972): 95-130.

The support for private day schools by traditional Jewish
educators (see the previous entry and annotation) is
expressed in this colloquium. Here Jewish educators reflect
on the possibilities and challenges of the Jewish Day School
as a response to secularity. The moral justification for
private education is thus found in the goals, ideology, and
program of social action these schools represent.

455 Bernstein, Marven H. "Learning as Worship: A Jewish
Perspective on Higher Education." In Go and Study, edited
by Raphael Jospe and Samuel Z. Fishman, 15-28. Washington,
D.C.: B'nai B'rith Hillel, 1980.

This fascinating study shows how Jewish study can be a
worship experience. Education involves more than intellectual or conceptual skills. Adult education, in particular
that on the college campus, requires that the entire life of
the individual be addressed.

456 Bernstein, Philip. "Jewish Education," in To Dwell in
Unity: The Jewish Federation Movement in America Since 1960,
107-123. Philadelphia: Jewish Publication Society of
America, 1983.

Bernstein notes the moral questions facing the American Jewish community in its decision as to priorities of spending. Different types of Jewish education need different types of funding, choosing which to support is a moral and ideological decision no less than a financial one. He reviews the value of formal and informal education, of the day school and its needs, and of the educational ethics.

457 Bleich, J. David. "Education." In his Contemporary Halakhic Problems 2, 108-119. The Library of Jewish Law and Ethics, 10. New York: Ktav Publishing House, 1983.

This compilation of articles originally appearing in Tradition 16 (1977), pp. 119-122 and 19 (1981), pp. 261-266, focuses on moral issues arising from Jewish education. Bleich examines the general importance of education, cheating on examinations, and damage to property. He investigates the rights of students to privacy and the appropriateness of different forms of punishment including expulsion. He demonstrates that in traditional Judaism learning conveys values by its very process as well as cognitively.

458 Bleich, J. David. "Torah Education of the Mentally Retarded." In his Contemporary Halakhic Problems 2, 300-310. The Library of Jewish Law and Ethics, 10. New York: Ktav Publishing House, 1983.

Bleich demonstrates Jewish concerns for both education and for the handicapped in this study. He shows that while there is no compulsion on the community to provide education to the retarded the tradition demands care for every human being. While a severely retarded child may not achieve even the minimal of education in Torah required by halakha, Bleich insists that communities find some way of ministering to such children. Compare entries 466, 475, 478.

459 Brickman, William W. "Ethical Values, Education, and the Morality Crisis." In Building Jewish Ethical Character, edited by Joseph Kaminetsky, and Murray I. Friedman, 118-121. New York: The Fryer Foundation, 1975.

This example of traditional Jewish support for the parochial school (see the annotation at entry 453) contends that the need for separation of church and state needs re-evaluation these are taught through religious training. The moral duty today, Brickman feels, entails supporting parochial education.

460 Brickman, William W. "The Jewish Day School's Contribution to American Public Education" Jewish Life 38,5 (1971): 10-21.

As background for the traditional Jewish support of the Jewish day school (see the annotation at entry 460), Brickman provides historical background on the interaction of Jewish private education and public learning from Colo-

nial times until the present.   He contends that the Jewish
school models curriculum and pedagogy for public schools.
In that light, he suggests a re-examination of the dises-
tablishment clause since with financial security Jewish Day
Schools can contribute more to American life.

461   Cohen, Jack Simcha.   "Halakhic Parameters of Truth."
Tradition 16 (1977): 83-97.

Cohen contends that the sanctity of truth is not inviolate.
At times truth wounds feelings or ruins reputations.   The
prohibition on telling falsehoods is subordinate to other
values. Compare entries 470, 474, 477, 481.

462   Cohen, Naomi Werner.   "Religion and Government: Recent
American Jewish Opinions." Michael: On History of Jewish
Life in the Diaspora 3 (1975): 340-392.

Cohen offers a summary of the contemporary debate over
parochial Jewish education (see the annotation at 449).   She
offers a historical perspective on the relation of Jews to
public education and the recent changes in that relationship.

463 Cohen, Naomi Werner. "Separation of Church and State."
In her Not Free to Desist: The American Jewish Committee,
1906-1966,   433-452.   Philadelphia: Jewish Publication Society of America, 1972.

Cohen examines the history of the Jewish emphasis on limiting state support of religious education.   As Jews became
more comfortable with pluralism and as new private options
developed, it moderation on its previous stance on parochial
education became more common.

464 Cohn, Haim H.   "The Right to Education and Participation in Culture." In his Human Rights in Jewish Law, 137-
145.   New York: Ktav Publishing House Publishing House,
1984.

The moral issue of public education consists of its enabling
citizens to participate in the general society.   Private
Jewish education also had this intention, with the cohesive
Jewish community as its goal.   Cohn notes the place of
public education in rabbinic Judaism and sees it as a means
of restricting the influence of foreign cultures on Judaism.

465 De Sola Pool, David.   "The Challenge to Jewish Educa-
tion--The Problem." In Judaism in a Changing World, edited
by Leo Jung, 217-227.   The Jewish Library, 4.   London:
Soncino Press, 1971):217 227

De Sola Pool sees the purpose of Jewish education to be that
of combating an essentially non-Jewish and even anti-Judaic
environment.   He calls for an extensive curriculum that
includes both the major skills and concepts needed for a

Jewish life.   He urges family and school to cooperate in
order to cultivate deep commitment to Judaism, a commitment
that can only be conveyed by the school with parental involvement.

466   Faigel,   Harris.   "Every Tenth Child."   Moment 4,1
(1978):60-62

Faigel examines the communal responsibility for education
the Jewish child who is learning disabled. Because the duty
of learning is central, he claims, religious schools should
make it possible for such a child to accomplish something.
The inclusion of such children in Jewish education will
strengthen Jewish life generally and not just for the child
involved.

467   Fein, Leonard J.   "Suggestions Toward the Reform of
Jewish Education in America." Midstream 18 (1972): 41-50.

Fein points to the conflicting ideologies of Judaism and
modernity.   The survival of Judaism depends upon transmit-
ting its values and view of life.   This can be done only by
educating children for Judaic competence.   That goal can be
accomplished when institutions provide better funding and
alternative systems to the congregational/afternoon schools.

468   Fisch, Dov, and Fisch, Linda Yellin." Problems of
Jewish Education." Midstream 26 (1980): 39-43.

Since the purpose of Jewish education must be to establish
the Jewish model of living in contrast to the secular one
the means and instruments of Jewish learning need to be
altered. In the view of the authors the current program and
its curriculum is too limited to cope with assimilation and
intermarriage.   They find the current system to produce a
low level of learning affecting both children and parents.

469   Friedman, Maurice.   "Education." In his The Hidden
Human Image, 239-260.   New York: Dell Publishing Company,
1974.

Friedman discovers that education implies a variety of social and psychological aims and goals.   The primary concern
is with the transmission of identity ot a new generation.
He suggests that education requires that students respond as
unique individuals rather than merely imitate what they are
being taught.   Education draws out and develops each student's unique self in a dialogue with ideas and values
transmitted from the past and through the teacher.

470   Frimer, Norman E.. "A Midrash on Morality or When is a
Lie Permissible." Tradition 13 (1973): 23-34.

Using the case of Jacob and Leban as an example, Frimer
argues that a falsehood can be utilized if the point is not
the manipulation of another person or to go against the

divine decree.   He adds a caution against self-deception as
to motivation when contemplating such an action.   Compare
entries 461, 467, 477, 481.

471 Frost, Shimon.   "The Needs of the Solomon Schechter Day
Schools: A Practitioner's View." Conservative Judaism 33,3
(1980): 74-79.

The Conservative Movement in Judaism is deeply divided on
the question of parochial education rather than supplemental
Jewish education in afternoon schools or weekend schools.
Frost indicts the supplementary Jewish school that, he says,
accepts ignorance as a given. He calls, instead, for track-
ing, guidance, and developed Jewish education within a day
school community.   Compare this outlook with that found in
entries 473, 483, 488, 489, 491

472 Gettinger, Emanuel.   "Education for Moral Behavior."
In Building Jewish Ethical Character, edited by Joseph
Kaminetsky and Murray I. Friedman, 86-91. New York: The
Fryer Foundations, 1975.

Gettinger notes that the individual is an image of God.
Through self-discipline that image can be actualized and a
personal can become self-taught.   He advocates that method
for teaching values to Jewish children in a day school.

473 Gilbert, Arthur.   "Teaching Religion in Public
Schools." Religious and Public School Curriculum: Proceed-
ing of the National Council on Religion and Public Education, edited by Richard Upsher Smith, 35-38.

This classical consideration of religion in public education
calls for a curriculum to sensitize students to non-theistic
religion, to anti-semitism, and to questions of cultural
pluralism.   While the context of this article is a general
discussion, it should be noted that Gilbert is part of the
Conservative Movement and his views should be contrasted
with those found in entry 471 and the cross references given
in the annotation there.

474 Gruenwald, Max.   "About Flattery (The Term Hanaf)."
In Rabbi Lookstein Memorial Volume, edited by Leo Landman,
163-173. New York: Ktav Publishing House, 1980.

The prohibition against flattery is taken to be directed
against lying either to other people or to God.   The ultra
pious need to recognize that God should not be flattered.
The Jewish tradition, on the contrary, cherishes a protest
or argument against the deity. Compare the concern with the
teaching of moral values and the morality of speech here
with that in entries 461, 470, 477, 481.

475 Hammer, Reuven.   "The Jewish School and the Special
Child." Conservative Judaism 36 (1983): 13-15.

Hammer insists that Jewish education should not seek to provide a remedial program, but rather an inspirational one. When understood in terms of the values meant to be transmitted rather than particular academic goals Jewish learning is fitting and suitable for the special child. Compare the similar treatment given in entries 458, 466, 478.

476 Hertzberg, Arthur. "Jewish Education and Brute Survival." Midstream 26 (1980): 32-36.

Hertzberg notes that Jewish education is often oriented towards Jewish survival. A more important goal is the survival of Judaism. He claims that Jewish educators should focus more on the teaching of the values and morals of Judaism in contrast to those of American life than on rudimentary skills or sentiments for survival. He notes in this context the problems of the congregational school, the need for alternatives, and the primacy of the Jewish day school.

477 Jung, Leo. "Tongue Control." In his Between Man and Man, 81-88. 3rd enlarged ed. New York: Board of Jewish Education Press, 1976.

Jung stresses the importance of restraint in speech and notes that slander is considered a major Jewish sin. Truth and words that are meant to hurt others cause division among people and should be avoided. This stress on teaching moral restraint should be compared with the emphasis in entries 461, 470, 474, 481.

478 Kelman, Joseph. "Jewish Education and the Disabled Child." Conservative Judaism 36 (1983): 5-12.

Kelman focuses on the the obligation of the community to provide a Jewish education for all its members. He claims that religious events must be open to all and that parents should be able to find enjoyment at their child's achievement without comparing it to that of other children. He agrees that the purpose of Jewish education for the disabled child is not remedial but inspirational and offers concrete proposals on how to teach and inspire the child. Compare the approach given here with that in entries 458, 466, 475.

479 Kreitman, Benjamin. "Crisis in Public Education." United Synagogue Review 22,2 (1969): 4-5.

Kreitman suggests that the public schools have failed to minister to the needs of many Americans. The private day schools fill the gap that has been created. He advocates Jewish day schools and claims that support for them does not violate the principle of separating church and state. He calls for a reassessment of the approach American Jews have historically taken to parochial education. Compare entry 449 and the items mentioned there.

480   Lipmann,   Eugene   J.   "The Uses of Jewish   VAlues   in
Counseling   Jewish   Students."   In Go and Study,   edited   by
Raphael Jospe and Samuel   Z.   Fishman,   57-74.   Washington,
D.C.: B'nai B'rith Hillel, 1980.

Lipman argues against a non-directive counseling or therapy,
noting   the type of student who comes for assistance desires
a Jewish response.   He shows how information and counseling
on various matters including sexuality and basic human   conduct can be carried out on a college campus.   Compare entry
455.

481   Reines,   Chaim   Zeev.   "Slander in the Bible and   the
Aggada" [Hebrew].   In his Essays and Investigations in Jewish Ethics and Law,   31-37.   Jerusalem: Rubin Mass Company,
1972.

This   example of Jewish moral education shows how truth   and
honest   are the constant themes (compare entries   461,   470,
474,   477).   Reines explains the social and ethical reasons
for   the   prohibition   against   slander   based   on   talmudic
sources with medieval citations and modern interpretations.

482 Reisman, Bernard.   The Jewish Experiential Book: The
Quest For Jewish Identity   New York: Ktav, 1979.

This valuable offering combines a critical analysis of   Jewish   identity   and the way it is strengthened by   experience
and activity with a catalogue of activities.   The   impetus
for   the   book   grows out of the new awareness   that   Jewish
learning is not merely cognitive but also   affective.   Compare the annotation at entry 449.

483   Routtenberg,   Max   J.   "Crisis in the Congregational
School."   In his Decades of Decision,   30-41.   New   York:
Bloch, 1973.

The Conservative Movement has long prided itself on its supplemental   educational institutions.   Routtenberg   disturbs
that complaisancy.   He declares in brutal honesty that only
a Jewish day school meets the needs of the American Jew.   He
feels   that only there can the aims of rabbis and   educators
be   met.   With   that in mind,   he calls for new and   higher
standards.   Compare this essay with that found in entry 471
and the references given in the annotation there.

484   Schiff, Alvin I.   "Programming Jewish Values for Jewish
Adolescents in Jewish Community Centers."   Journal of Jewish
Communal Service 48 (1971): 174-181.

Shiff   calls   for rededication to education as   a   means   of
instilling   values.   He   notes that Jewish values are   all-
embracing and need to supplement formal education.   He suggests   that all aspects of Jewish education create a   sense
of belonging to the Jewish people and are necessary both for
Jewish survival and in instilling Jewish values.

485 Schwartz, Shuly Rubin. "Ramah Philosophy and the Newman Revolution." In Studies in Jewish Education and Judaica
in Honor of Louis Newman, edited by Alexander M. Shapiro and
Burton I. Cohen, 7-21.   New York: Ktav Publishing House,
1984.

This tribute to the memory of a beloved pedagogue who transformed Jewish education demonstrates how a concern for experiential Judaism interacts with Jewish ethics.   The Judaica learning and the informal setting sponsored by Louis
Newman provided opportunities not only for affective Jewish
learning but also for putting into practice Jewish values.

486 Segal, Bernard. "Government Aid to Parochial Schools -
Why The Conservative Movement is Opposed." United Synagogue
Review 24,1 (1971): 6-7.

Again, the division within Conservative Judaism is clearly
apparent (see the previous entry and the annotation at entry
471).   This essay summarizes the wariness many Jews have
with federal support for religious education.   Segal suggests problems a religious group may encounter when dependent on government subsidies. He declares that Judaism cannot risk the integrity and freedom of its schools by accepting governmental aid.

487 Segal, Kenneth.   "Ethical Values of Jewish Youth: The
Implication for Our Schools." Central Conference of American Rabbis Journal 24 (1977): 29-34

Segal argues that Jewish education must be for the sake of
instilling belief and commitment to ethics and values.   To
do this he calls upon a curriculum that includes more than
factual material and for a system of education that relies
upon the informal setting of the religious camp as an important ingredient.

488 Siegel, Morton. "In Defense of the Afternoon School."
United Synagogue Review 24,1 (1971)10-11, 30-31.

The advocacy of the parochial school as the only alternative
to Jewish ignorance disturbs as many Conservative Jews as it
persuades (see the previous entry and the discussion and
annotation in entry 471).   Here Siegel defends the Jewish
afternoon school, contending that the parochial day school
is not the only answer to Jewish educational needs.   He
feels that the afternoon school has not failed but has not
used all its opportunities. He seeks to move beyond the
isolated congregational school to utilize all facets of the
Jewish environment.

489 Siegel, Seymour. "Tuition Tax Credits for Non-Public
Schools? Yes." Face to Face (1978): 7-8.

Siegel argues for supporting parochial education on the
grounds of the good of the nation as a whole. This essay by

a Conservative Jewish leader should be seen in the context
of the division within Conservative Judaism (see the previous entries and the annotation at entry 471). Siegel
defends giving individuals tax credits for expenditures for
parochial as not establishing any one religious group.
Since such private education helps public education by challenging it with a model of excellence, he feels support is
salutary. He enunciates a public need for pluralistic models of learning and for values education.

490 Singer, David. "The Growth of the Day School Movement"
Commentary 56,2 (1973): 53-57.

Singer places the growth of the day school movement in the
context of a tension between integration and isolation in
Jewish life in America. He suggests that American Jewish
preoccupation with Jewish survival and Jewish identity will
lead to the continuation of the day school movement in the
United States.

491 Singer, Howard. "Crash Program for Day Schools."
United Synagogue Review 23,1 (1970): 6-7, 29-30.

This view of a Conservative Jew demonstrates the support
that flourishes, not without opposition, for parochial Jewish schools in that movement (see the annotation to entry
471). Singer voices the need to establish a means of coping
with decline in public schools and of re-assessing the
Jewish relationship to them. He suggests retraining a staff
and personnel for a quality day school in every community.

492 Vorspan, Albert. "Religious Liberty, Public Educa-
tion." In his Great Jewish Debates and Dilemmas: Jewish
Perspectives in Conflict in the Eighties, 152-167. New York:
Union of American Hebrew Congregations, 1980.

Vorspan presents a Reform Jewish defense of public education
as a means for developing American culture. He reviews and
affirms the compromise of separating church and state and
suggests that priorities demand a choice between the welfare
of public institutions or of parochial ones. He clearly
favors public institutions as the basis of American life.

493 Waskow, Arthur. "The Fusion of Learning and Loving."
In his These Holy Sparks: The Rebirth of the Jewish People,
22-41. New York: Harper and Row, 1983.

Waskow notes the development of Jewish education in the
United States. He suggests that struggle and experience are
the basis means for Jewish learning and advocates the experiential technique is education.

494 Wurzberger, Walter. "Separation of Church and State
Revisited." Face to Face (1981): 7-8.

This essay reaffirms Orthodox Judaism commitment to parochial education (see entry 492). Wurzberger suggests that America has a history of benevolent neutrality toward religion. Today, he finds, religious pluralism includes atheism and non-theistic options which challenge the adequacy of the public school as a carrier of morals. With this problem as a challenge, he calls for change in tactics needed so that parochial schools receive equal rights. Such equality, he contends, is not establishment of religion but simple parity. He stands against secularism and the Moral Majority.

495 Yapko, Benjamin L. "Jewish Social Service Agencies and the Jewish School." Journal of Jewish Communal Service 45 (1968): 165-172.

Yapko finds modernity a challenge to Jewish educators. The survival of Judaism depends on the transmission of values and the public school does not fulfill this task. He also suggests that Jewish schools must serve the special student as well as do public schools. He suggests that the curriculum must change to retain the students who now leave.

496 Yosef, Ovadiah. "Is It Preferable to Study in a Yeshiva High School or in a Yeshiva Without Secular Education?" [Hebrew]. Tehumin 1 (1980): 299-301.

Even in Israel the question of parochial or public education is a pressing one. The Israeli sponsored schools are not known for their hospitable attitude towards religious practice. They may, however, be necessary for learning a trade and economic success. Yosef considers whether learning a trade is morally consistent with learning Torah. He notes that some rabbinic authorities advocate such a move, but also that some say only Torah should be studied. He concludes that the choice depends upon the quality of the student. Compare this entry with the following one.

497 Yosef, Ovadiah. "Parental Privilege to Require Children to Pursue Secular Education." [Hebrew]. Tehumin 3 (1983): 235-237.

The moral question of whether children may seek Torah even against parental wishes is discussed. Ovadiah permits this but suggests that a student try to combine both to fulfill the command of honoring parents.

FEMINISM AND JEWISH IMAGES

498 Berman, Saul J. "Kol Isha". In Rabbi Joseph H. Lookstein Memorial Volume, edited by Leo Landman, 45-55. New York: Ktav Publishing House, 1980.

Traditional Jewish law relegates women to a spectator status in Jewish worship because of a desire to prevent the interruption of worship by the kol isha, a woman's voice. Is this law a remnant of male chauvinism or does it represent a realistic appraisal of human intersexual relationships? This scholarly review of the rabbinic concern about women joining men in prayer seeks to discover whether the fear is of sexual stimulation or merely of distraction. To answer this question historically Berman traces the growing rabbinic concern from focused on distractions while reciting the Shema to concern for all prayers to equating a woman's voice with a form of nudity. Modern Orthodoxy leniency, however, is said to have barred floodgates to further severity. Compare entries 505, 527.

499 Bleich, J. David. "Bat Mitzvah Celebrations." In his Contemporary Halakhic Problems, 77-78. The Library of Jewish Law and Ethics, 4. New York: Ktav Publishing House, 1977.

The Bat Mitzvah is a modern invention with no rooting in tradition. While some traditional Jews favor creating a celebration for women, Bleich considers the Bat Mitzvah an imitation of the non-Jew and a violation of the sanctity of the synagogue. He allows a modest home celebration and feast. This essay originally appeared in Tradition 14 (1973): 126-127.

500 Bleich, J. David. "Women in a Minyan." In his Contemporary Halakhic Problems, 78-83. The Library of Jewish Law and Ethics, 4. New York: Ktav Publishing House, 1977.

The question of whether women are permitted to count for a quorum of Jews at prayers has caused bitter controversy among contemporary Jews. Modern Jewish women do not want to be second class Jews, but the halakha on the subject is at best ambiguous, and is probably clearly against counting women in such a quorum (see entries 502, 503, 513, 524, 527). Bleich admits that public prayer is indeed allowed to women but is not mandatory for them. He suggests that a woman might serve as the tenth for a religious prayer quorum, just as a minor might in order to represent the divine presence. He notes that there is controversy on even those areas where women are counted and suggests that feminists are following the way of modernity rather than the way of Judaism. The essay first appeared in Tradition 14 (1973): 113-117.

501 Bleich, J. David. "Women on Synagogue Boards." In his Contemporary Halakhic Problems 2, 254-267. The Library of Jewish Law and Ethics, 10. New York: Ktav Publishing House, 1983.

Women demand rights not only in ritual matters but also as leaders in the synagogue and the community. Are women allowed to assume such roles in determining Jewish religious life? Bleich reviews medieval literature and sources concerning the placing of women in positions of religious responsibility. He notes that women can be elected by women to serve in particular functions.

502 Blumenthal, Aaron. "An Aliya For Women." In Conservative Judaism and Jewish Law, edited by Seymour Siegel with
Elliot Gertel, 265-280. New York: Rabbinical Assembly,
1977.

This influential argument helped convince Conservative Judaism to allow its congregations the right to honor women
with the privilege of saying the blessings before and after
the reading of the Torah scroll. This problem is not as
difficult to solve as that of women in a prayer quorum since
the traditional reason given for preventing giving women
such an honor is "the honor of the congregation."   Blumenthal contends that since halakha has modified Torah law it
can modify the rabbinic concept of the honor of the congregation which has prevented women from having the honor of an
aliya. Compare entry 500.

503 Feldman, David M. "Woman's Role and Jewish Law." In
Conservative Judaism and Jewish Law, edited by Seymour
Siegel with Elliot Gertel, 294-305. New York: Rabbinical
Assembly, 1977.

This essay not only describes Conservatism's ambivalence
toward women (see entry 230) but also the debate about
including women in public worship (see entries 502, 505-
507, 515, 517, 518, 519, 523, 524). Feldman's position is a
traditional one, arguing that because women are a sexual
distraction they should not be included in public worship.

504 Freehof, Solomon B. "Women Wearing a Talit." In his
Modern Reform Responsa, 52-56. Cincinnati: Hebrew Union
College Press, 1971.

Reform Jewish women seek to take responsible roles in Jewish
life, often adapting traditional practices for men that
Reform had abandoned in the past and revitalizing them.   In
this responsa to a question as to whether women can wear the
prayershawl, Freehof summarizes the talmudic controversy on
this point. He notes that different later authorities are
divided on the question. He also remarks that certain commandments of the same generic type as the prayershawl are
performed by women according to all authorities. He concludes that in our day the wearing of such a garment is
surely permissible.

505 Gertel, Elliot. "Families That Stay Together Pray
Together?" United Synagogue Review 26 (1973): 12-13, 24-28.

The traditional view that the voice of a woman is disruptive
to prayer (see entry 498) echoes in modern Jewish quarters
as well. Conservative Judaism is not completely comfortable
with mixed pews in which men and women sit together. In an
argument against including women with men in worship, Gertel
argues that the family pew obscures the uniqueness of each
member of the family. Women, he claims, do not need to be
with their husbands to worship and indeed may worship better
on their own.

506 Gordis, Robert. "The Ordination of Women." Midstream
26 (1980): 25-32.

Gordis argues that just as the halakha develops, so too the
role of rabbi has changed. Since the rabbi no longer functions as an official in the synagogue, women should not be
excluded on the grounds of laws no longer relevant to the
rabbinic task. Gordis finds that the needs of Jewish survival entail opening doors for women and cannot be satisfied
though Jewish apologetics to women. Note the controversy in
entries 507, 510, 516, 520, 523, 526, 528.

507 Gordis, Robert. "The Ordination of Women: A Short
History of the Question." Judaism 33 (1984): 6-12.

Gordis describes how the ordination of women became a major
concern of American Jews. He includes references to women
in the Reform movement, but focuses on Conservative Judaism,
including mention of Henrietta Szold and her frustrations
with the place given to Jewish women. He traces the most
recent controversies in the Conservative movement.

508 Gottlieb, Lynn. "The Secret Jew: An Oral Tradition of
Women." Conservative Judaism 30 (1976): 69-62.

Gottlieb uncovers hidden rituals that women devised for
themselves in the past. She looks at the prototypical
Jewish woman, Esther, and suggests rituals for the present
and the future of Jewish women. The essay is reprinted in
entry 244, 273-277. Compare the following entry.

509 Greenberg, Blu. "Women and Liturgy." In her On
Women and Judaism: A View from Tradition, 75-104. Philadelphia: Jewish Publication Society, 1981.

This essay provides an insider's glimpse at the woman's
section in a synagogue. The tensions and conflict within
the mind and experience of a pious, but traditional woman
are made clear. Compare entries 508, 511, 521

510 Greenberg, Blu. "Will There Be Orthodox Women Rabbis?"
Judaism 33 (1984): 23-33.

Greenberg looks realistically but also optimistically at the
way changes are made in Jewish Orthodoxy. She suggests that
the signs are not hopeless and expects to see women rabbis
in Orthodox Judaism in her lifetime. Compare entry 506.

511 Gross, Rita M. "Steps Toward Feminine Imagery of Deity
in Jewish Theology." Judaism 30 (1981): 183-193.

Gross notes that the male orientation in Judaism is the
result of cultural programming and not a religious necessity. She claims it is possible to turn to comparative
religious expressions for models in a refashioning of Jewish
views of women. The essay is reprinted in entry 244, 234-
247. Compare the view of images found in 508.

512 Harvey, Warren Zev.   "The Obligation of the Talmud on
Women   According to Maimonides." Tradition 18 (1980): 122-
130.

This essay draws on the teachings of Joseph Soloveitchik to
conclude   that women have specific laws which they are allowed to study.   In contrast see the arguments of some
Orthodox feminists (522) and of other scholars who allow
women the right of study (525).

513 Kasdan, Menachem.   "Are Women Obligated to Pray?" Journal of Halakha and Contemporary Society 2 (1981): 86-100.

Women's spirituality, Kasdan claims, can well be expressed
by the latter.   Men, however, need public prayer.   The
intrusion of women into that setting would benefit neither
them nor the men. Women would be better served by remaining
within the range allowed by traditional Jewish law.

514 Kessner, Carole.   "Kaplan on Women in Jewish Life."
The Reconstructionist 47, 5 (1981): 38-44.

Kessner discovers that although Mordecai Kaplan devotes only
a small chapter in one major work to the problem of women,
he compresses into that study a critique of contemporary
Jewish life.   The problem of integrating women into Jewish
worship demonstrates for Kaplan the problem of Jewish prayer
and folkways in general.

515 Listfeld, Chaim.   "Women and the Commandments." Conservative Judaism 29 (1974): 42-50.

Listfeld's traditionalism leads him to argue that while
women are permitted to choose voluntarily to accept the
positive commandments, they should be satisfied with that
status.   Rather than imitate men they should chose those
voluntary options given to them. Compare entry 503.

516 Mirsky, Norman.   "Preisand Prejudice."   Moment 3,7
(1978): 52-56.

Mirsky notes that the first woman rabbi predated the feminist liberation movement. He suggests that she was ignored,
at best, by her teachers and colleagues and opines that
American Jewry has feminized the rabbinate. Compare specifically Zola (528) and entry 506.

517 Novak, David.   "Who Has Not Made Me a Woman." Law and
Theology in Judaism,   15-20.   New York: Ktav Publishing
House, 1974.

Novak cites talmudic precedent both for the greatness of
peace and for woman's liberation.   He suggests that while
revisions in prayer are not for the individual, authorized
groups could create a liturgy responsive to women's needs.
Compare other views noted in entry 503.

518   Novak,   David.   "Who Has Not Made Me a Woman II."   In
his Law and Theology in Judaism, 2nd Series, 135-147. New
York: Ktav Publishing House, 1976.

Here Novak insists that women have their own time   sequence
and must be different from men. He acknowledges that women
can voluntarily practice some commandments,   emphasizing the
value and need for more female-instituted customs.   At   the
same time he applauds the realism of the tradition in noting
the sexual temptation women represent.

519   Novak,   David.   "Women in the Rabbinate."   Judaism 33
(1984): 39-49.

Novak considers the various arguments for women's ordination
in Judaism. He realizes that women have needs not yet being
filled by traditional Judaism.   He suggests, however, that
the more difficult but more rewarding path leads to renewing
Jewish life through options already available in the   tradition and he counsels caution in making changes.   For this
and the following entry compare entry 506.

520 Petuchowski,   Jakob.   "Halakhic Issues and Non-Issues."
Moment 4:5 (1979): 39-43.

In   a survey of the rabbinic background of women's exclusion
from the rabbinate and the current debate   in Conservative
Judaism,   Petuchowski examines the history of ordination in
relationship to the question of women rabbis.   He suggests
that psychological rather than religious arguments are being
advanced against the ordination of women.

521 Pianko, Arlene.   "Women and the Shofar." Tradition 14
(1974): 53-62.

Pianko, a traditional Jew, demonstrates how one can accept
the framework of Jewish morality while advocating the greater inclusion of Jewish women in Jewish life. The obligation
to hear the Shofar shows the way traditional Jewish law
balanced the needs of women to participate in worship with
the needs of the halakhic system.   The lesson she draws is
that of the need for slow evolution from exemption to participation.   She asserts that a woman's familial role must be
primary, but its nature can be flexible.   She insists that
all change must be halakhic. Compare entries 508, 509, 511.

522 Poupko, Chana K. , Wohlgelernter, Devora L. "Women's
Liberation: An Orthodox Response." In The Dimensions of
Orthodox Judaism, edited by Reuven P. Bulka, 373-379. New
York: Ktav Publishing House, 1981.

This essay presents an argument for women's study of Torah
(compare entries 512, 525) given by two women from within
the framework of Jewish tradition. They claim that in times
of moral crisis such as the present an exception to the rule
excluding women from study must be made. The essay originally appeared in Tradition 15 (1976): 42-52.

523   Rotenberg,   Mark.   "The Buck Stops at the   Seminary."
Moment 4,5 (1979): 27-30.

Rotenberg contends, in the midst of the controversy over
whether Conservative Judaism should ordain women (see entry
506),   that there is no way to deny women their place in the
rabbinate without denying the essence of Conservative Judaism.   He claims that only prejudices, and not legal
prescriptions, prevent women from becoming rabbis.

524 Sigal, Philip. "Women in a Prayer Quorum." In Conservative Judaism and Jewish Law, edited by Seymour Siegel with
Elliot Gertel,   382-392.   New York: Rabbinical Assembly,
1977.

After a survey of various opinions, Sigal asserts the right
of the rigorist to refrain from including women in a minyan
while allowing liberals to include them (see the items noted
in entry 500).   He suggests that the exclusion is only a
custom, a minhag, since various traditional authorities
disagree about it.   Customs should be followed only if they
have religious value, and he claims that this minhag is of
no spiritual benefit.

525 Silver, Arthur A.   "May Women be Taught Bible, Mishnah,
and Talmud?" Tradition 17 (1978): 74-85.

In conjunction with the question of teaching Torah to women
(see entries 512 and 522), Silver notes that scholars from
different periods of the past have given different replies.
He decides that the problem is not to be solved by absolute
decisions but through a study of context.   Today, he concludes, women's study of torah should be cultivated as a bar
to the lures of an immoral secular society.

526 Wisse, Ruth R.   "Women as Conservative Rabbis." Commentary 68,4 (1979): 59-64.

Depicting the debate in Conservative Judaism on women rabbis
(see entry 506), the author suggests that modern feminism
stimulated the decision and complains that the original
intent of the separation of women was to enoble woman's
life.   She warns that pulling down this one pillar of Jewish
tradition may pull down the entire structure of Judaism.

527 Yuter, Alan J.   "Mehitzah, Midrash, and Modernity: A
Study in Religious Rhetoric." Judaism 28 (1979): 147-159.

Yuter analyzes the argument over what type of separation
between men and women is more traditional. While the historical question of whether the requirement is biblical or
rabbinic is interesting, after a summary review Yuter concludes that the issue today is less historical than ideological.   The symbol of separation has become a mark of one's
traditionalism.   In this way ritual becomes a means of
marking certain moral and ethical comittments.

528 Zola, Gary P.   "JTS, HUC, and Women Rabbis." Journal
of Reform Judaism 31 (1984): 39-45.

Zola reflects on the forces that caused the Conservative
movement to accept women for ordination (see entry 506). He
suggests that Reform benefited by its similar move earlier
and predicts that Conservative Judaism will be strengthened
through this decision.

MORAL TREATMENT OF THE ELDERLY

529 Bernstein, Philip. "The Aging," in To Dwell in Unity:
The Jewish Federation Movement in America since 1960, 173-
178.   Philadelphia: Jewish Publication Society of America,
1983.

Bernstein reviews the priorities established by Jewish philanthropies and notes the concern for elderly, poverty
stricken Jews. He suggests the special needs the Jewish
elderly have and the ways Jewish charities deal with those
needs.

530 Blech, Benjamin. "Judaism and Gerontology." Tradition
16 (1977): 63-78.

Blech wonders whether old age is a curse given to those who
observe Torah law. He notes that respect is due to the
elderly even if they are not particularly learned. He
recalls the commandment to honor aged parents and notes the
need for personal security no less than social security. He
enumerates the activities for involving the elderly.

531 Dick, Judah.   "Halacha and the Conventional Last Will
and Testament." Journal of Halacha and Contemporary Society
3 (1982): 5-18.

Dick reviews Jewish inheritance laws concerning bequests,
noting that the law of the land does not overrule Jewish
law concerning wills. He suggests possibilities for Jews
who wish to donate their funds to various causes and persons. This essay is reprinted in Cohen (085), pp. 278-291.

532 Forman, Bernard I. "Attack on Ageism: The Jewish Stake
in the Work Ethic." The Reconstructionist 44 (1979): 17-23.

Forman affirms the work ethic in Judaism since life is
affirmed. He notes that leisure is not equated with pleasure in Judaism and supports the right of the elderly to
work. His contention is that Jewish morality stands against
the pleasure orientation of the modern world. Contemporary
society would learn to value the elderly more if they would
understand Judaic ethics.

533 Freehof, Solomon B. "An Aged Parent to Nursing Home."
In his New Reform Responsa, 92-96. Cincinnati: Hebrew Union
College Press, 1980.

Freehof reviews the duty of honoring parents and suggests that the intention as well as the literal act involved should be taken into account. He uses the precedent of institutionalizing the insane as a basis for permitting such a move by children. The guilt that many feel in institutionalizing a parent should be removed because the Jewish ethics understands the need for different types of actions depending upon different circumstances.

534 Friedman, Maurice. "Aging and the Community of Otherness." In his The Confirmation of Otherness in Family, Community, and Society, 207-224. New York: Pilgrim Press, 1983.

Friedman discusses the existential crisis in aging in our society and the social problems involved. He notes the concerns of both parents and children for nursing home care and the guilt that children often feel. He looks at the various ways individuals have of coping with their responsibilities. He draws on the insights of Jewish tradition and Jewish thinkers like Martin Buber to find a way to reconcile the needs of parents and children.

535 Jung, Leo. "Old Age." In his Between Man and Man, 157-158. 3rd enlarged ed. New York: Board of Jewish Education Press, 1976.

Jung notes Jewish theological views of the elderly. He suggests that old age is a time when one's concern shifts from private good to the public good. He advocates utilizing the elderly for their contributions to society as a whole.

536 Lederman, Sarah. "The Jewish Aged: Traditions and Trends." In The Jewish Family in a Changing World, edited by Gilbert S. Rosenthal, 321-333. New York: Yoseloff, 1970.

In this contribution to an important study of the Jewish family today (see entry 358) Lederman notes that the tradition cannot cope with the medical and economic realities of today's elderly. She points to the low commitment and concern Jews seem to have for the elderly and seeks to change that commitment.

537 Novick, Louis J. "How Traditional Judaism Helps the Aged Meet Their Psychological Needs." Journal of Jewish Communal Service 48:3 (1971): 286-294.

The author suggests that traditional belief enables the Jewish elderly to cope with their situation. He points to the sense of self-worth cultivated by the tradition, the communal warmth of Jewish holiday celebrations and the daily rituals of prayer. He emphasizes that the tradition gives the elderly both a theoretical basis for self-esteem and practical experiences that reinforce that theory.

538 Shapero, Sandford M. "The Vintage Years: General View and Jewish Challenge." Journal of Religion and Health 14 (1975): 130-141.

The author looks at the plight of elderly Jews and condemns society as a whole. The lack of response to the needs of this element in society shows the bankruptcy of our civilization. In order to correct it, all elements in the community, including the young, must be mobilized.

539 Simon, Isador. "La Gerontologie Biblique et Talmudique." Revu D'Historie De La Medecine Hebraique 27 (1974): 77-88

This article presents various Jewish texts concerning the honor and respect due to the aged.

540 Spero, Moshe Halevi. "Death and the _Life Review' in Halakhah." Journal of Religion and Health 19 (1980): 313-319.

Spero notes the psychological value of seeing death as a process in which one is continually engaged. He reviews the talmudic view of the stages of life but recalls as well that one is to repent one day before death. That idea suggests that the aged are part of a process in which all are engaged. Death is thereby linked to life.

541 Stambler, Moses. "Jewish Ethnicity and Aging." Journal of Jewish Communal Service 58 (1982): 336-342.

This survey of empirical data demonstrates the differences between Reform, Orthodox, and Conservative Jews in their relationship to the elderly and suggests ways of enhancing the status of the elderly. The moral code of a communal religion becomes evident in such a review.

MORALITY AND THE RESPECT FOR THE DEAD

542 Bleich, J. David. "Autopsies with the Consent of the Deceased." In his Contemporary Halakhic Problems, 125-126. The Library of Jewish Law and Ethics, 4. New York: Ktav Publishing House, 1977.

Bleich notes that the tradition forbids such desecration of a body and that a person cannot give consent for a transgression. Theological reasons determine how a person looks at his own body. Religious faith should have precedence over human pragmatism. Thus, God, not human beings, controls human life and the human body and divine law, not human whim, should determine how it will be handled after death. See also entries 036, 038, 039 for the concern of Jewish law with respect for a dead body. This essay appeared first in Tradition 12 (1972): 121-122.

543 Bleich, J. David. "Delayed Burial." Tradition 11
(1970): 93-94.

Respect for the dead in Judaism requires immediate burial.
Concern for the mourning, however, and the psychology of
mourning demand that mourning begin as soon as possible.
Usually mourning must wait until burial, out of respect for
the dead, but at times such burial is impossible. Bleich
summarizes the rationale for immediate burial and the problems presented by a gravediggers' strike. He urges that
mourning be begun as soon as possible. See Novak entry 549.

544   Falk, Zeev W.   "The Death of the Righteous." In The
Dying Human, edited by Andre de Vries and Amnon Carmi, 287-
292. Tel Aviv: Turtledove Publishing Company, 1979.

Respect for the dead has a theoretical as well as a practical aspect to it. Falk contributes a theological reflection
to this anthology (see entry 190). He notes that death is
often understood as passing from one room to another in the
same house. He reviews both traditional ideas of death and
that of modern thinkers like Franz Rosenzweig on the meaning
of death and life.

545 Freehof, Solomon B.   "Burial of Cremation Ashes." In
his Reform Responsa for Our Time, 112-115. Cincinnati:
Hebrew Union College Press, 1972.

The reform tradition in Judaism raises new moral questions:
if a family violates traditional law in one way, is it
prevented from the healing benefits of that law in other
ways (compare entry 548). In this case a family wishes to
bury ashes of a relative who has been cremated. Freehof
contends that the burial of such ashes is permitted even
though cremation is against Jewish law. He notes that when
medical need required such cremation it was permitted.

546 Freehof, Solomon. B. "Death and Burial in the Jewish
Tradition." In Judaism and Ethics, edited by Daniel Jeremy
Silver, 192-213. New York: Ktav Publishing House, 1970.

Jewish procedures emphasize concern for the dead and respect
for the dead as representatives of humanity. Freehof
discusses this respect for the dead and how it is exemplified by burial procedures in Judaism and their ethical
importance. The article first appeared in Central Conference of American Rabbis Journal (1968): 85-93.

547 Freehof, Solomon B. "Freezing of Bodies (Cryobiol-
ogy)."   In his Current Reform Responsa, 238-240.
Cincinnati: Hebrew Union College Press, 1969.

Respect for the dead may take the form of refusing to humil-
iate the body for a fantastic hope of living. Can those who
are terminally ill have their bodies frozen in hopes of a
cure being found for them. Freehof notes Jewish opposition
to this practice.

548   Freehof, Solomon B.   "Talit for the Dead and Cremation." In his Modern Reform Responsa,   269-277.   Cincinnati:
Hebrew Union College Press, 1971.

Here, as in other cases (see entry 542) the moral dilemma of
the liberal Jew becomes clear.   How much of traditional
morality can be merged with a non-traditional style of
living and death? Freehof notes this strange combination of
tradition (desiring the prayershawl) and untraditionality
(cremation as forbidden by Jewish law).   He remarks that a
controversy revolves around the burial of the dead in a
talit since it is disrespectful to remind the dead of commandments no longer able to be fulfilled. Since many Reform
Jews have given up the practice of wearing a talit the
gesture in this case may be merely a token given to tradition and even more disrespectful than tradition itself suggests.

549   Novak, David.   "Delayed Burial."   In his Law and
Theology in Judaism,   107-111.   New York: Ktav Publishing
House, 1974.

The problem of reconciling the respect given to the dead by
immediate burial, with concern for those who mourn, is
recognized by both Orthodox and Conservative Jews (see entry
543).   Novak notes the problem of striking grave diggers.
He cites despair as grounds for mourning without a body
present and likens the situation to that of a city under
seige, in which case the tradition allows such mourning. In
this way, he justifies responding to the needs of a very
special situation.

550   Reimer, Jack (editor).   Jewish Reflections on Death.
New York: Schocken Books, 1974.

This useful anthology includes a number of helpful essays.
These range from technical studies on suicide and euthanasia
to investigations of the theology of death and mourning.
See entries 169, 186, 555, 559, 562, 573) In addition to
these studies, the book also includes personal reflections
on the affect of the death of close relatives. The confrontation of Jewish theology and the tragedies of our age--most
particularly that of the Nazi Holocaust and the threat of
nuclear self-destruction--are also represented.

551 Rosner, Fred.   "Autopsy in Jewish Law and the Israeli
Autopsy Controversy." In Jewish Bioethics, edited by Fred
Rosner and J. David Bleich, 331-348.   New York: Sanhedrin
Press, 1979.

This essay declares that respect for the dead precludes
using the corpse even for learning. The rigor of the Orthodox prohibition on mutilation of a corpse is discussed in
great detail. He reviews theological aspects of respect for
the dead.   See also Tradition 11 (1971): 43-63 and entry
19, 132-154. Compare the references given in the annotation
to entry 542.

MOURNING AND ITS MORALITY

552   Ben-Gurion, Arye.   "Memorial Procedures in the Kibbutz."   In The Dying Human, edited by Andre de Vries   and
Amnon Carmi,   487-490.   Tel Aviv: Turtledove Publishing Company, 1979.

Reflecting the inclusive nature of this anthology (see entry
161), this   essay looks at how secular Jews cope with   the
trauma of death.   Continuity of Jewish attitudes can   be
discerned   in this radically different approach to death and
memorializing.   Jewish   ritual is still able to help   integrate   those who mourn into the community as a   whole.   The
symbols   of the people unite the mourner with   a   supportive
group of others.

553   Blank,   Irwin M.   "Truthtelling in Eulogies."   Journal
of Reform Judaism 27 (1980): 27-29.

Ritual reintegrates the dead,   the mourner,   and the living,
sometimes   the   use of a eulogy instead of relating to   life
idealizes the dead and fails in its purpose.   Blank insists
that   the   eulogy should be redemptive.   The whole   of   the
deceased's   life should be reviewed and shown to be   consistent   with the best and highest aspirations the person   held
to be important.

554   Feldman, Emanuel.   Biblical and Post-Biblical Defilement and Mourning: Law as Theology.   New York: Ktav Publishing House, 1977.

This   study provides a detailed description of biblical   and
rabbinic   approaches to death.   The process of purifying   a
dead body,   moral questions concerning death and dying,   the
defilement   associated   with a corpse,   and the   rituals   of
mourning are all included in the study.   The most interesting   aspect of the work is the theological interpretation of
death and mourning offered.   Death is a separation between
the human and life,   as such it desacralizes the dying.   The
procedures   of mourning are understood as a means of   making
life sacred once again.   Compare entries 557, 568, 575.

555   Feldman, Emanuel.   "Death as Estrangement: The Halacha
of Mourning."   In Jewish Reflections on Death, edited   by
Jack Reimer, 84-94.   New York: Schocken Books, 1974.

This essay contributes Feldman's view concerning death to   a
useful anthology (753).   Feldman argues that death desacralizes by separating a person from life, from others, from the
community,   and from observing the commandments.   For contrasting theological views,   one should look at the   other
essays   in the anthology as noted in entry 550.   The   essay
appeared previously in Judaism 24 (1974): 59-66.

556   Freehof, Solomon B.   "Some Kaddish Customs."   In his
Current Reform Responsa,   178-183.   Cincinnati: Hebrew Union
College Press, 1969.

The kaddish prayer is a central feature of Jewish mourning. It represents the moral link between generations, but has often been misunderstood as a prayer for the dead. Freehof summarizes the history of reciting the kaddish and of memorializing the dead. He suggests some misunderstandings in the tradition which, if corrected, liberalize mourning. This interpretation of the prayer should be compared to that of David Novak who views the prayer as a means of reintegration into the community as a whole (entry 565) and to the views of Leo Jung (559) that emphasize its role as an affirmation of faith. The importance of this prayer both in law and lore should be noted.

557 Gerson, Gary S. "The Psychology of Grief and Mourning in Judaism." Journal of Religion and Health 16 (1977): 260-274.

Gerson suggests that Jewish mourning is a means of reintegration into society. His psycholgical interpretation should be compared to entries 568, 570, 571, 573, 575.

558 Goldman, Adolf. "Le Juif Face a La Mort." Recontre 37 (1974): 183-188.

Goldman suggests that Judaism emphasizes life, not death. He interprets Jewish views of death and mourning as a means of stressing the primacy of life itself.

559 Jung, Leo. "The Meaning of the Kaddish." In Jewish Reflections on Death, edited by Jack Reimer, 160-163. New York: Schocken Books, 1974.

This study of a basic prayer in Jewish mourning shows how it sanctifies God's name. Such sanctification is a goal of life and may be said to have been fulfilled through death. The meaning of the prayer is, thus, not mystical but a rededication to the importance of living and life's tasks. Jung's views should be contrasted with those of Solomon Freehof, a Reform rabbi, in entry 556 and of David Novak, a Conservative Jewish rabbi, in entry 565.

560 Kling, Simcha. "Sanctity Even in Death." United Synagogue Review 26,2 (1963): 10-17.

Kling resents the vulgarity of Jewish funerals and their lack of dignity and decorum. He insists that a rabbi should inform Jews of the consensus of the tradition and the offensiveness of such practices that defile the sanctity of death. This essay focuses on practical morality and provides a good counterpoint to other, more theoretical articles, found in this section.

561 Lamm, Maurice. The Jewish Way in Death and Mourning. New York: Jonathan David Publishers, 1969.

This excellent compendium summarizes the entire process of burial and mourning. The moral issues of death and dying are explored as well as all the details involved in considering how to treat the terminally ill, how to prepare a corpse for burial, and how mourning proceeds. The two principles of respect for the dead and therapy for the living are stressed. Lamm sees human dignity rooted in the respect for human life that Jewish mourning provides.

562   Lipman, Eugene J.   "The Minyan is a Community."   In Jewish Reflections on Death, edited by Jack Reimer, 169-172. New York: Schocken Books, 1974.

Lipman offers an interpretation not just of the kaddish, the mourner's prayer, but also of the requirement that it be said with a minyan, that is with a prayer quorum of ten men. He suggests that this requirement aids in the reintegration of the individual to communal life. This essay describes the author's experience with a community minyan that meets with the mourner for the recitation of daily prayers during the period of mourning. Compare entry 565.

563   Novak, David. "Funerals in the Synagogue." In his Law and Theology in Judaism, 94-106. New York: Ktav Publishing House, 1974.

In recent times, some people request funerals to take place in the synagogue. Novak considers this practice and notes that synagogues in the past have reserved this honor for special individuals. The synagogue is a public, not merely a private place and is a legitimate setting for communal meeting. A eulogy is also a public address for which, Novak comments, scholars may abandon their study.

564   Novak, David. "Mourning for a Non-Jewish Parent." In his Law and Theology in Judaism, 71-79. New York: Ktav Publishing House, 1974.

The modern situation has made a decision on this necessary. While a convert has given up past affiliations, the love of a parent may be respected. Kaddish may be said, Novak allows, but a distinction between mourning for a Jew and for a non-Jew should also be made.

565   Novak, David. "A Note on the Mourner's Kaddish." In his Law and Theology in Judaism, 112-113. New York: Ktav Publishing House, 1974.

Novak reviews the laws and the lore concerning the recitation of the mourner's prayer. He recognizes that much that has accrued to the prayer comes from the aggadic rather than legalistic or halakhic side of Judaism. The customs derived from that source, however, are equally important in linking the generations to each other and in reintegrating an individual into the community as a whole. He suggests that an interaction of both law and lore is needed to cope with the trauma of death. Compare entries 556, 559.

566 Reimer, Jack. "After Life." Moment 4,9 (1979): 43-50.

Reimer sketches different views of the afterlife that emphasize life here and now. He uses stories from early modern
and more recent sources to show that Jewish morality has a
double stress on both this life and the next. Of particular
interest is the use Jewish tradition makes of the idea of
judgment at death and of reincarnation.

567 Remson, Michael M. "The Congregational Need to Mourn."
Journal of Reform Judaism 27 (1980): 91-92.

Remson notes that, while a Rabbi may have a personal need to
mourn, the congregation has a public need to do so as well.
He calls for recognition of this problem and for a search to
find solutions to it.

568 Rozwaski, Chaim Z. "On Jewish Mourning Psychology."
Judaism 17 (1968): 335-346.

Rozwaski sketches the problems of the survivor and the way
in which Jewish mourning leads one beyond those problems to
an integration with the community as a whole. He sees self-
identification with the tradition as a healthy way of over-
coming the trauma associated with death. The psychology of
death and mourning is dealt with as well in entries 557,
569-572, 575.

569 Sanua, Victor D. "Coping with Stress and Bereavement
during the Yom Kippur War." Journal of Jewish Communal
Service 55,3 (1979): 235-243.

Sanua notes how rituals, often personal and non-traditional,
enabled survivors to cope after the Yom Kippur War. He
discusses the number of memorial anthologies issues, the
types of literature they contain, and their psychic importance. He suggests that this approach to memorialization is
a modern continuation of the traditional practice of having
a Torah scroll written in memory of departed relatives.

570 Schindler, Ruben. "The Halakhic Framework of Mourning
and Bereavement: Its Implications in Dealing with Crisis."
Tradition 15 (1976): 69-80.

Schindler celebrates the way in which Jewish law structures
mourning and provides a social framework for coping with
grief. He finds that the various stages of grief enable a
person to come to terms with personal loss and with the
supportive community as well. Jewish tradition, he feels,
allows time for personal reflection before forcing the individual out among others. Compare his views in the following
entry.

571 Schindler, Ruben. "The Halakhic Framework of Mourning
and Bereavement and its Implications for the Helping Professions." Journal of Jewish Communal Service 51 (1975): 325-
331.

Schindler shows how the stages of mourning enable an individual to overcome the anger and psychological alienation that accompany an experience with death. His sensitivity to these issues through the helping professions enables him to explain Jewish practice in a more compelling way. Judaism appears as a persuasive tool of social work, enabling people to cope with their personal grief.

572 Schneider, Stanley. "Death as Separation: In Halacha and in the Therapeutic Process." In The Dying Human, edited by Andre de Vries and Amnon Carmi, 417-429. Tel Aviv: Turtledove Publishing Company, 1979.

Schneider argues that Jewish mourning is a therapeutic process. He shows how the elements in Jewish law referring to death help an individual cope with the trauma of death. See the other essays in entry 190 as well as entries such as 555, 557, 568, and 570 for comparative interpretations of Jewish views on death and mourning.

573 Schneider, Stanley. "Mourning Ritual: From Ancient Semitic Antecedents to Modern Applications." In The Dying Human, edited by Andre de Vries and Amnon Carmi, 431-443. Tel Aviv: Turtledove Publishing, 1979.

Schneider demonstrates how Ancient Israel utilized earlier pagan rituals and integrated them into Jewish worship. The way in which these rituals were purified and made therapeutic is a model of the Jewish ability to incorporate the best of non-Jewish culture while retaining its distinctiveness. See the other essays in entry 190 as well as the entire range of interpretations noted with entry 570.

573 Soloveitchik, Joseph B. "The Halakhah of the First Day." In Jewish Reflections on Death, edited by Jack Riemer, 76-83. New York: Schocken Books, 1974.

This exploration of the rituals of the first day of mourning points to the psychological and religious affect of death on individuals. Soloveitchik explores the existential meaning of deep sorrow from the talmudic perspective, discovering that it awakens a sense of guilt and repentance. Although the later stages of mourning move from personal self-introspection to communal affirmation, the first stage is religiously most powerful. This insightful investigation of Jewish halakhic practice shows how law can become a vital agent for psychological self-transformation.

574 Wolowelsky, Joel B. "Self-Confrontation and the Mourning Rituals." Judaism 33 (1984): 107-11.

This essay explores the way in which the rituals of mourning help people confront their values and deepest concerns. Through mourning the Jew learns put life into perspective and discovers the meaning of human action.

5
Political Morality

POLITICAL ATTITUDES

576   "Liberalism and the Jews: A Symposium."   Commentary
69,1 (1980): 15-82.

This symposium consists of the responses of fifty two leading American Jews debating whether the change in the liberal agenda is a crisis for Jews.   May American Jews embrace
conservative politics because they tend to agree that the
interests of Jews and liberals have now diverged.   Liberals
and radicals argue that there is a continuity of values and
no real change in relationship since Jews have always had a
critical and not an unthinking relationship with liberal
politics.   The proposition that Jews have abandoned liberalism for conservatism has aroused much controversy among
American Jews.   The roots of liberalism and the so-called
swing towards conservatism has stimulated discussion and
moral questioning.   Compare entries 578,   584,   589,   590,
594, 595, 597, 603, 609, 611, 612, 630, 632, 634, 636.

577   Ariel, Yaakov.   "Law in the State of Israel and the
Prohibition Against Secular Courts" [Hebrew].   Tehumin 1
(1980): 319-328.

Ariel notes the peculiar predicament of the Jew in Israel
who cannot tolerate a secular system in an independent
Jewish state.   The moral legitimacy of a secular court is
questioned by the Orthodox Jew while the morality of infrin-
ging on their freedom from religion is questioned by the
Israeli secularist.   Particularly repugnant is the idea of
Jew in litigation against the non-Jew in such a legal system.   He insists on the importance of the precept of honoring Torah and suggests that the basic need is to have more
halakhic judges in the civil courts of Israel.   The question
of religious freedom of conscience and of whether government
and religion should be united is a complex one and presents
a major moral dilemma for Jews in the state of Israel.
Compare entries 579, 586, 587, 588, 592, 593, 602, 608, 610,
613, 618, 619, 623-628, 633, 638.

578   Beame, Abraham D.   "A Call for a Reasoned Liberalism."
Judaism 21 (1972): 36-38.

Beame claims, against a growing tide of Jewish political
conservatism, that liberalism is needed to protect minority
rights. While he understands the motivations for shift to
the right, he claims that such a change loses sight of the
history of Judaism which does not do well in such repressive
societies. See the annotation at 576.

579 Berinson, Zvi. "Freedom of Religion and Conscience in
the State of Israel." Israel Yearbook of Human Rights 2
(1973): 223-232.

Berinson argues that human beings should have the right of
conversion out of a religious community as a legal guaran-
tee. He considers religious legislation in Israel as an
attempt to invade the private domain of citizens. In contrast he contends that mutual toleration demands free exercise of religious right to proselytize and to gain converts
by all religious individuals of every persuasion. See the
annotation at entry 577.

580 Bernstein, Philip. "Public Social Policy." In his To
Dwell in Unity: The Jewish Federation Movement in America
since 1960,   225-245. Philadelphia: Jewish Publication
Society of America, 1983.

Berstein emphasizes the importance of taking positions on
political, social issues. He defines what he considers permissible and impermissible lobbying and suggests those areas
of American life in which Jewish should be politically
involved. Compare entries 581, 583, 616.

581   Borowitz, Eugene B.   "Rethinking the Reform Jewish
Theory of Social Action." Journal of Reform Judaism 27
(1980): 1-19.

Borowitz argues that Jewish political morality should be
identified neither with liberalism nor with the politics of
Israeli chauvinism. Instead he contends that ethical ideals
stand in a dialectic relationship to various political alternatives. Compare the entries 580, 583, 616.

582 Bracha, Baruch. "Personal Status of Persons Belonging
to No Recognized Religious Community." Israel Yearbook on
Human Rights 5 (1975): 88-119.

The personal status of individuals who refuse to be catego-
rized in one or another religious community is a problem of
Israeli government. Bracha asks whether personal law can
be considered as an individual's religious law and decides
that such a solution is impossible. He suggests instead
that civil procedures should be instituted for special cases
such as that of the Karaites. Compare entry 577 and the
annotation found there.

583   Brickner, Balfour.   "Social Policy-Making Structures
and the Jewish Community."   In Formation of Social Policy in
the Catholic and Jewish Traditions, edited by Eugene J.
Fisher and Daniel Polish,   5-14.   Notre Dame: University of
Notre Dame Press, 1980.

This passionate defense of how Judaism can contribute to the
political   world order shows the seriousness of the   ethical
tradition in Reform Judaism (compare entry   581).   Brickner
contends   that Judaism can contribute to the general   social
concerns and can add a religious dimension to the discussion
in the context of a pluralism which shares but does not seek
to   dominate.   This policy statement should be compared   to
entries 580, 581, 616.

584   Cohen, Stephen Martin.   "Liberalism as the Politics of
Group   Integration."   In his   American Modernity and   Jewish
Identity,   134-153.   New York: Tavistock Publications, 1983.

Studying   the liberal mentality of American Jewish   politics
can   point to self-interest as well as moral fervor.   Cohen
sees   three constraints on Jewish integration into   America:
traditional subculture,   group survival,   and   assimilation.
He   suggests that these problems appeared to be resolved   by
liberalism,   but   that that appearance was often   deceiving.
This sociological view of liberalism should be compared with
the theological approaches given in the entries found in the
annotation to entry 576.

585   Cohen, Stephen Martin.   "Pro-Israelism as the Politics
of Ethnic Survival."   In his   American Modernity and Jewish
Identity,   154-170.   New York: Tavistock Publications, 1983.

Continuing   his   investigation   into the roots   of   American
Jewish political theory, Cohen notes how American Jews have
changed their political orientation and suggests that it has
arisen   not merely out of concern for survival of the   state
of Israel but as part of a general politics of ethnic asser-
tion even in the face of liberal ideals.

586   Don Yehiya, Eliezer.   "The Politics of the   Religious
Parties in Israel."   In Comparative Jewish Politics: Public
Life in Israel and the Diaspora edited by Sam N. Lehman-Wil-
zig and   Bernard Susser,   110-137.   Ramat   Gan: Bar   Ilan
University Press, 1981.

This   study   reviews   the problems of uniting   religion   and
state   in   Israel (see the annotation to   entry   577).   Don
Yehiya   notes Jewish reactions to modernity and   seculariza-
tion.   He   suggests   a variety of   political   styles   among
Israeli Jews: rational,   pragmatic,   ideological and their
effect on Israeli religious parties.   The moral question of
how   to integrate the identity of the state as a Jewish   one
with the rights of individuals and of how religious   leaders
in   politics   are   to remain true to their   ideals   is   also
raised.

587   Englard,   Itzhak.   "The   Problem of Jewish Law   in   a
Jewish State."   Israel Law Review 3 (1968): 254-178.

Englard notes the place of Jewish law in the Israeli setting
(compare   entry   577).   He discusses the   political   issues
involved in establishing Judaism in the land of Israel.

588 Fein, Leonard. "In Praise of Ambiguity." Moment 10, 8
(1985): 31-34.

Reviewing   the appeal and recognizing the truth inherent   in
the views of Meir Kahane (see entries 600,   601,   615,   626,
629,   637),   Fein suggests that Jews must beware of too much
consistency; ambiguity is the fate of human life.

589   Fein,   Leonard J.   "Liberalism and American Jews." Midstream 19 (1973): 3-18.

Fein   investigates   why Jews were liberal and   whether   that
political posture was rooted in values,   ideology, or history.   He concludes that it was basically self-interested and
now   self-interest and public interest diverge.   He   argues
that   there is a need to rethink what interests should   mold
political decisions. See the annotation to entry 576.

590 Fein,   Leonard J.   "The New Jewish Politics." Midstream
18 (1972): 33-39.

Fein   suggests   that Jews have moved beyond the idea   of   an
American melting pot, but have not yet found a new political
ideology to take its place. While Jewish interests are made
primary   those interests have not been defined beyond a   few
parochial   issues.   In that situation he argues that a   new
liberal politics is now needed. Compare entry 576.

591 Glickstein,   Gary A.   "Religion and the New Left: 1960
to date." American Jewish Archives 26 (1974): 23-30.

Jewish radicalism has fascinated many observers of contemporary politics (see entries 604,   614,   617,   621, 622, 635).
The   roots   of this radicalism have been traced   to   Eastern
Europe   and the disillusionment with it has been examined in
detail.   Here Glickstein charts American Jewry's disillusionment   with the New Left's radicalism and its discovery   not
just   of   Israel but of religion--as an institution   and   as
ideals.   This has led American Jews to work with the system,
to   reject   both   the militancy of groups   like   the   Jewish
Defense   League   and the traditional   leftist   militancy   of
radicalism.

592   Goldberg,   Giora.   "The Israeli Religious Parties   in
Opposition: 1965-1977."   In   Comparative Jewish   Politics:
Public   Life   in Israel and the Diaspora edited   by   Sam   N.
Lehman-Wilzig;Bernard Susser,   138-157.   Ramat Gan: Bar Ilan
University Press, 1981.

The morality of Israel's religious politics has been questioned both for its content and tactics. In the continuing
debate on the place of religion in Israeli morality and
politics (see the annotation to entry 577) Goldberg notes
the readiness of the religious parties to participate in
forming a government. He suggests that the National Religious Party's strategy of negative behavior rather than constructive criticism reaped ideological rewards. It practiced maverick behavior and initiated votes of no-confidence
in the government. Once in power they may face a different
type of challenge.

593 Goldschmidt, Yosef. "Jewish Law in the Legislative
Activity of the Knesset." Dine Israel 5 (1974): xciv-cvii.

Goldschmidt surveys the variety of religious views represented in the Israeli parliament, the Knesset. He notes how
issues such as the raising of pigs, succession and inheritance, contracts, and other specifically halakhic concerns dominate the agenda of the religious parties. He
takes a pessimistic view of the possibility for compromise
and reconciliation of differing elements. Compare this
entry with the previous one and the annotation there.

594 Halpern, Ben. "The Jewish Liberal." Midstream 16
(1970): 31-49.

Halpern traces the liberal hopes of the 19th and 20th centu-
ries and shows how they have been disappointed. In the face
of that disappointment he suggests a need for a new political tradition. Jewish independents, he believes, are biased
toward the _big man' and thus were liberal by inclination,
not ideology. He declares a non-sectarian pose revealed by
Jewish solidarity. His pessimism is not shared by all as a
review of the vast literature on the subject (see the annotation to entry 576) shows.

595 Halpern, Ben. "The Roots of American Jewish Liberalism." American Jewish Historical Quarterly 66 (1976): 190-
214.

While this entry is primarily historical rather than theoretical, it should be compared with the preceding one and the
annotation there. Here Halpern declares that liberalism was
a political response to the promise of enlightenment. He
traces Reform Judaism's leaning towards progressive politics
and the politics of the Yiddish movement.

596 Himmelfarb, Milton. "Jewish Class Conflict."
Commentary 49,1 (1970): 37-42.

The various alignment of Jews according to political causes
is not, according to this article, an outgrowth of Jewish
religion or morality. Himmelfarb notes that Jewish politics
fluctuates in its liberalism. He applauds this fluctuation
since, he believes, Jews stand against all idolatries, even
those of progress and reason.

597 Howe, Irving, and Rosenberg, Bernard. "Are American Jews Turning to the Right?" Dissent 21 (1974): 30-45.

As in the previous entry and in other discussions (see the annotation to entry 576) the vagaries of Jewish politics are explored. The authors note American Jewry's growing disillusionment with liberalism. They find it exacerbated by variety of Jewish traditions, by black anti-semitism, by Israelism, and by ethnicity. They suggest that despite this evidence of political conservatism, the liberal impulse is still strong.

598 Isaacs, Stephen D. Jews and American Politics. Garden City: Doubleday and Co, Inc., 1974.

This political investigation surveys Jewish views of race relationships, demonstrates the limits of power within general politics, and examines liberalism and its limits in Jewish political life. Among central concerns of the book are the views of Jewish radicals, the plight of soviet Jewry and intimations of Jewish power. This work provides a fascinating overview of the issues that motivated American Jewry whether as radicals, liberals or conservatives and how moral questions, political responses, and religious commitment have been intermingled.

599 Kahane, Meir. Our Challenge: The Chosen Land Radnor, Pennsylvania: Chilton Book Company, 1974.

This book and the next entry should be read as examples of an extreme Jewish traditionalism that justifies the existence of the state of Israel only as an exclusively Jewish state in which Orthodox Judaism reigns supreme (on the complexities of this question which Kahane ignores note the entries listed in the annotation to entry 577). Kahane's nationalism voices a strident call for exclusivism and chauvinism. He emphasizes the necessity for religious commitment, exclusivism, and eschatological hope for the future among Jews in Israel. He proposes a radical plan for the extradition of Arabs and declares that the true issue of human rights in Israel is that of the poor Sephardic.

600 Kahane, Meir. They Must Go New York: Grosset and Dunlap, 1981.

Kahane's treatise on the politics of a Jewish State and the problem of having a Muslim majority in the land culminates in his call to expatriate all the Arabs. He denounces what he calls the fraud of Arab acceptance of Israel and details the history of destroyed minorities in Europe as evidence for need of a Jewish majority in the Jewish state. While this is an extremist position, Kahane fully recognizes the dilemma of trying to unite Judaism, an exclusivist religion, and the political process of democracy. The reader should note the controversy around Kahane (see entry 588) as well as entries 717, 718, 722, 728.

601 Kirschenbaum, Aaron. "Jewish Religious Legislation in
the Knesset." Dine Israel 5 (1974): xcvii-cxvii

Kirschenbaum notes that unlike in the United States, Israel's ideology commits it to a particular religious stance,
that of Jewish law. He declares that Jewish family law must
be decisive in Israeli affairs. He notes the problems of
liberal Orthodox interpretations of Jewish law, but contends
that halakha can evolve and be reworked.

602 Krauss, Simcha. "Litigation in Secular Courts." Journal of Halakha and Contemporary Society (1982): 35-53.

Jews, traditionally, are not to use the civil courts to
litigate against fellow Jews.   Does that hold true even for
the State of Israel?   Krauss notes that the prohibition
against Jews using civil courts is only a relative commandment.   In Israel, he suggests, the use of Jewish courts is
certainly permitted to Jews. See entry 577.

603 Lelyveld, Arthur J.   "In Defense of Liberalism." Judaism 21 (1972): 32-35.

Lelyveld notes that Judaism is open to a variety of interpretations but should not be confused with any political
'ism.' He suggests that Judaism eschews politics for an
openness to all new possibilities, standing against authori-
tarian ideologies and the status quo. He contends that
Judaism does best in an open society.   He deplores converting political frustrations into tactics, producing the
political extremes of right and left. See 576.

604 Liebman, Arthur.   Jews and the Left.   New York: John
Wiley and Sons, 1979.

This is a very general but idiosyncratically selective survey of the radical tradition of many Jewish immigrants.   It
includes a good use of the Yiddish newspapers, but presents
a very subjective view of the radical subculture of the
Jewish Left in the 1960s. See entry 591 and 617.

605 Liebman, Charles S. "Changing Conceptions of Political
Life and their Implications for American Judaism." In Comparative Jewish Politics: Public Life in Israel and the
Diaspora, edited by Sam N. Lehman-Wilzig and Bernard Susser,
91-100. Ramat Gan:Bar Ilan University Press,1981.

Liebman contrasts the politics of personal identity with the
politics of collective existence as developed in America in
the 1960s. He finds the radical tradition to be oriented
towards personal self-fulfillment in contrast to Judaism's
nationalism.   He suggests that this presented problems for
many American Jews. See the annotation at entry 577 and the
following two entries.

606 Liebman, Charles S. "The Rise of Neo-Traditionalism Among Moderate Religious Circles in Israel" [Hebrew]. Megamot 27,3 (1982): 231-250;eng.summary p. V.

Liebman notes that many Israelis react against the problems of modernity by returning to tradition. They condemn modernity because of the failure of techniques for adaptation, because compartmentalization of religious and secular life has not worked, and because expansionism of religion into contemporary life has not solved the problems of modernity. The new traditionalism, he suggests, is very different from traditional religious Zionism.

607 Liebman, Charles S. and Don Yehiya, Eliezer. "What A Jewish State Means to Israeli Jews." In Comparative Jewish Politics: Public Life in Israel and the Diaspora, by Sam N. Lehman-Wilzig and Bernard Susser, 101-109. Ramat Gan: Bar Ilan University Press, 1981.

Concentrating on the phenomenon of the power of a religious minority in Israel the two authors explore how Israel's self-image depends upon religious roots (compare entry 577 and the items noted there). The symbols of collective identity unifying Israel are more than a set of beliefs. The political problem in Israel is that of reflecting Jewishness in a civil, secular setting.

608 Lipstadt, Deborah E. "Religious Politics in Israel." Midstream 27,5 (1981): 41-47.

This article notes the conflict arising when Orthodox Jews seek to make Israel more halakhic. It suggests the ferment within Israeli orthodoxy, the growing Jewishness of Israelis, and moral issues arising from the woman's movement. Compare the annotation at entry 577.

609 Lowenberg, Robert. "The Theft of Liberalism-A Jewish Problem." Midstream 23,5 (1977): 19-33.

Lowenberg suggests that modern Jews face an Identity crisis: they must choose between being a Jew or being a Liberal (compare the works noted in the annotation to entry 576). He traces the history of Jewish liberalism from the time of Baruch Spinoza and contrasts Jewish universalism from Liberal universalism. He combines preference for a liberal state with an attack on liberalism as a type of idolatry.

610 Meron, Simha. "Freedom of Religion As Distinct from Freedom from Religion in Israel." Israel Yearbook on Human Rights 4 (1974): 219-240

Meron declares that free conscience applies to thought whereas freedom of religion includes providing the opportunities and environment in which it is possible to perform the commandments. He contends that the validity of a social norm, as opposed to a religious dictum, lies in the motiva-

tion for its enforcement. In the case of Israel he provides
examples of cases in which religious Jews were denied their
rights to free exercise of the halakha.   See the annotation
at entry 577.

611 Miller, Alan W. "Liberalism is Indispensable." Judaism
21 (1972): 20-23.

A representative of Reconstructionist Judaism who holds that
Jewish thought supports and requires liberal political action, Miller is concerned with growing American Jewish conservatism.   He places the blame not on Jewish theology, but
on practical political events. He claims that the trend away
from liberalism is due to Christian silence during the June
1967 day war, to third world pro-Arabism and to black anti-
semitism. He notes the rush to establish Jewish day schools
and claims that Jews are no longer passive under duress. He
offers a theological contribution to a general discussion
(see the next entry and the annotation to entry 576).

612 Neusner, Jacob.   "Judaism, Jews, and the Liberal Outlook." Judaism 21 (1972): 39-42.

Neusner, a noted scholar of rabbinic Jewish sources, avers
that Judaism speaks to the contemporary world and that sound
historical reasons explain Jewish liberalism. He notes that
while support for Israel is a dominant concern, an identi-
fiably Jewish approach to politics is unclear, ambiguous and
complex.

613 Oren, Stephen. "Continuity and Change in Israel's Religious Parties." Middle East Journal 35:4 (1973):36-54.
Oren outlines the traditional religious issues of Israel's
religious parties: concern for Shabbat legislation, opposition to autopsies, determination of Jewish identity according to traditional law. He notes new questions based on a
messianic religious politics stressing the sacredness of the
territories captured in the 1976 war. He contrasts the
various understandings of military victories by the theologians Isaiah Liebowitz, J.B.Soloveitchik, and Z.Y.Kook. See
the annotation to entry 577.

614 Perlmutter, Nathan and Ruth Ann Perlmutter. "The Left
and the Jews." In their The Real Anti-Semitism in America,
112-140. New York: Arbor House, 1982.

This is a passionate and compassionate examination of the
moral impetus for Jewish political involvement. The authors
trace the relationship of Jews and leftist movements.   They
review the changes in both the left and the right that have
alienated Jews and suggest the dangers those changes bring.
Jewish politics, in their view, is neither leftist nor conservative. Compare entry 591.

615 Reich, Walter. "The Kahane Controversy." Moment 10,1
(1985): 16-24.

Reich notes the growing stridency of Israeli militant Orthodoxy (see entries 577 and 588). He suggests that the danger
of extremism is a real one and points to important questions
facing the State of Israel.

616 Robison, Joseph B. "Issues Troubling America: What Involvement for the Jewish Community." Journal of Jewish
Communal Service 51 (1974): 52-57.

Robison notes the changing involvement of Jews in American
politics since the Second World War. He suggests as contributing factors the lesson of the Nazi Holocaust, the 1972
election, the impact of the Yom Kippur War, and the question
of personal security versus Jewish liberalism. He sees
little support for the hopeful conclusion of a return to the
views of 1950s and 60s. Both the policies of organized
Judaism and the views of individual Jews are considered. A
program for the community as a whole is offered. Compare
entries 580, 581, 583.

617 Rothman, Stanley, and Lichter, S. Robert. The Roots of
Radicalism: Jews, Christians, and the New Left. New York:
Oxford University Press, 1982.

This investigation of Jewish radicalism notes that the
upper-middle class urban Jewish professional is usually a
democrat. The authors see a continuity of radicalism between Jewish generations which is supported by case histories
and the contention that non-Jews are less radical. See the
annotation at entry 591 and entry 604.

618 Rubenstein, Amnon. "The Enforcement of Morals In A
Secular Society." Israel Yearbook of Human Rights 2 (1972):
57-98.

The rationale of this study grows out of the religious
nationalism of Orthodox Jews who insist that Israel must
enact the laws of Judaism as civil legislation. These Jews
claim that since Israel's identity and self-understanding
imply fidelity to traditional Jewish religion laws enforcing
that religion do not infringe upon private, personal rights.
They argue that Judaism commands social and political as
well as ritual and cultic behavior; they claim that a Jewish
state must make all aspects of Jewish religious behavior
mandatory. Since Judaism provides the rationale of existence it must also become the structure of the state.
Rubenstein agrees with this argument but only to a limited
degree. He investigates what minimum standards a society
can demand. He compares religious commands and social prohibitions and regulations governing sexual and economic
life, noting the requirement for consent and the limits of
enforcement of morality without an individual's consent. He
studies areas in which morality can be imposed such as the
rights of paternal protection for minors and society's right
to educate its youth as it sees fit. compare entry 577.

619   Rubenstein, Aryeh.   "Religious Parties in Israel."
Midstream 22 (1976): 27-41

Since the Orthodox contend that Israel must be a Jewish
state, it is important to know exactly what they mean.
Rubenstein looks at the religious issues which the Orthodox
see as essential in establishing a Jewish state.   Among
their concerns are the prohibition against raising unclean
animals, the enforcement of sabbath laws, the preservation
of Jewish family law, and determination of Jewish identity
for the sake of the law of return. He notes the compromises
given by the parties in order to keep power and their ex-
cuses justifying them. See the annotations at entry 577.

620   Rubenstein, Richard L.   "Liberalism and the Jewish
Interests." Judaism 21 (1972): 16-19.

Richard L. Rubenstein, a radical theologian who expresses
what many Jews think but are afraid to say, rejects the idea
that Judaism and liberalism support one another. He suggests that Jews deluded themselves when they became liberals
and denies that there was ever an alliance between Jews and
liberalism. While he admits that a democratic coalition may
be still possible, suggests that Jews now have the same
interests as other middle class Americans. He points to
black anti-semitism and to the changing socio-economic reality to prove that Jewish liberalism will soon be at an end.
See the annotation at entry 576.

621 Rubenstein, W. D. The Left, the Right, and the Jews.
London: Croom Helm, 1982.

This extensive study of Jewish political involvement in
America shows how Jews have been utilized by the American
system, how they have attempted to use it, and the misconce-
ptions that exist concerning the Jewish role in American
political life. Rubenstein uses facts and data to dispel
myths about the Jews. Jews do not have omnipotent political
power and the anti-semitic images of Jews by the Left are
false. He shows that Jews excluded from corporate capitalism. See the following entry and entry 591.

622 Rubenstein, W. D. "The Left, The Right and the Jews."
Midstream 25 (1979): 3-7.

Rubenstein summarizes in brief compass the major points made
in his major work. This article notes the irony that the
establishment has become philosemitic and the left antisemi-
tic. Rubenstein argues that Jewish interests are tied dis-
proportionately to capitalism .

623 Sandler, Shmuel. "The National Religious Party:
Towards a New Role in Israel's Political System?" In Comparative Jewish Politics: Public Life in Israel and the
Diaspora, edited by Sam N.Lehman-Wilzig and Bernard Susser,
158-170. Ramat Gan: Bar-Ilan University Press, 1981.

Sandler reviews Israeli political history from Ben Gurion through Menachem Begin. He notes the problems of a diluted religious party and its move from from a satellite of Labor to independence and from concentration on specifically religious issues to broad political concerns. Compare entry 577

624 Shava, Menashe. "Legal Aspects of Change of Religious Community in Israel." Israel Yearbook of Human Rights 2 (1973): 256-269.

Shava notes the previous privileges and liabilities of the various religious groups in Israel before its becoming a state. He discusses the impossibility of being a person without a religious affiliation in Israel and the problems of marriage and divorce possibilities.

625 Shava, Menashe. "Matters of Personal Status of Israeli Citizens Not Belonging to A Recognized Religious Community." Israel Yearbook on Human Rights 11 (1981): 238-254.

Shava notes that status attributed through belonging to a religious community is for the purpose of determining jurisdiction, does not represent a choice of which law one seeks to live under. He advocates a clear separation between the two types of status attribution through the creation of territorial administration based upon geography and not upon religious commitment. Compare entry 577.

626 Shenker, Hillel. "Kahanism: A Clear and Present Danger." New Outlook (1984): 13-15.

Drawing on the lessons of Kahane's victories, Shenker points to both the positive response liberals can take and to the dangers in Kahane's appeal. Compare entry 588.

627 Shetreet, Shimon. "Freedom of Conscience and Religion in Israel." In Essays on Human Rights: Contemporary Issues and Jewish Perspectives, edited by David Sidorsky with Sidney Liskofsky, Jerome J.Shestack, 179-192. Philadelphia: Jewish Publication Society of America, 1979.

Shetreet argues that state imposed religious practice does not violate religious freedom because it expresses the will of the nation as a whole. The enforcement of religious norms is illegitimate only if it violates the _secular primacy purpose' test to see if it is motivated by the will of the nation as a cultural body or by a small group of people out of their private interests. Compare entry 577.

628 Shetreet, Shimon. "Some Reflections on Freedom of Conscience in Israel. Israel Yearbook on Human Rights 4 (1974): 194-218.

Admitting the lack of separation of religion and state in Israel, this article defends this imposition of religious norms as having a pragmatic rationale. Contrast Meron (611) and compare 677.

629   Shotat,   Orit.   "The Flipside of Meir   Kahane."   New Outlook (1985): 11-14.

After   touring with Kahane (see entry 588) Orit shows how he manipulates audiences with a religio-political message.   The danger of a national religion clearly emerges here.

630 Siegel, Seymour.   "An Anatomy of Liberalism: A Conservative View." Judaism 21 (1972): 24-31.

As   part   of   the continuing debate   about   American   Jewish politics,   Siegel   contends   that liberalism is   opposed   to Judaism.   To   oppose   liberalism,   in his view,   is not   to oppose justice, but the idolatry of a liberal ideology which he   defines as valuing liberty over order,   government   over private involvement, the power of the environment over freedom   of the will,   of possession over   opportunity,   and   of universal   over   particularism.   He finds religious   values more closely aligned with the non-liberal   stance.   Compare entry 576.

631   Siegel,   Seymour.   "On   Jews,   Terror   and   Political Morality." Midstream 26 (1980): 42-44.

Siegel extends his views of conservatism into an analysis of the basis for anti-semitism.   The political position of Jews is most often, according to Siegel, that of a catalyst which reveals   the   hidden   agenda of terrorists.   Judaism   is   a lightning rod attracting those who hate freedom,   democracy, and morality.   He contends that terrorism is a rejection of that civilization which Judaism represents.   He sees antisemitism   as   a   reaction against that morality   which   Jews symbolize.   Thus because Jews accept Sinai, others face them with sina, that is hatred.

632 Smith,   Morris.   "The Jew and Liberalism." Jewish Life 37,2 (1969): 26-40.

In   a   traditionalist response to the   on-going   controversy over Jews and liberalism (see the annotation at entry   576), Smith   contends that an alternative to Liberalism is   needed in   the   face of growing Communism and new Left.   He   notes that   black   power   is hostile to the Jew and   contends   that Jewish attitudes are spiritual and not political.   He contrasts   liberalism   as Greek and philosophical   with   Jewish theological   views.   He condemns liberalism for its lack of appreciation of particularistic and communal values, its ambivalence to family, and its misguided view of education.

633 Tabory, Ephraim.   "Religious Rights as a Social Problem in Israel." Israel Yearbook on Human Rights 11 (1981): 256-271.

Tabory   points   to the conflict between   individual   rights, collective rights, and the public welfare that underlies the struggle between religious and secular factions in Israel.

He reviews controversies over education, legislating religious observances, and permitting archeology on suspected
grave sites as examples of social problems arising from a
lack of sensitivity to religious rights. The moral dimension of Israel's religious conflicts lies in the bitterness
with which these controversies divides the country. See the
annotation at entry 577.

634   Teller, Judd L.   "The Jewish Experience with
Liberalism." Judaism 21 (1972): 43-50.

Not all observers think that Jews have either deserted
liberalism or embraced conservatism (see the annotation at
entry 576). Some feel that Jews have always been independent. Thus Teller notes that the liberal coalition has been
an inconstant one. He contends that Jews do not seek redemption from politics only from God and so are skeptical of
all ideologies. He remarks that the American Jewish experience has been checkered and diverse. Looking at Meir
Kahane and his discovery of lower class Jews, he declares
that a new respectable alliance needs to be forged.

635   Whitfield, Stephen J.   "The Legacy of Radicalism." In
his Voices of Jacob, Hands of Esau: Jews in American Life
and Thought, 73-95. Hamden: Archon Books, 1984.

Whitfield offers an elegant and beautifully constructed
essay exposing the Jewish political tradition in American
Jewish life. He traces the relationship of Abbie Hoffman
and other radicals to earlier Jewish political tradition.
He finds in both the tactics and approach a legacy from the
Yiddish theater. Jewish politics is not only religious but
evokes a morality and ethos of an ethnic tradition. Thus he
suggests that the politics of radicalism has roots in ethnic
self-identification. Compare entry 591. The essay first
appeared in Judaism 32 (1983): 136-152.

636   Whitfield, Stephen J.   "The Persistence of Liberalism."
In his Voices of Jacob, Hands of Esau: Jews in American
Life and Thought, 97-112. Hamden: Archon Books, 1984.

In another well written and perceptive essay Whitfield
surveys the liberal tradition in Judaism from Spinoza to
Leslie Fiedler and Will Herberg. Despite the differences
between these thinkers a continuity of belief and morality
can be discerned. It may appear that Jews are becoming
disillusioned with liberalism. Such a view looks only at
the changing environment and voting patterns, factors that
Whitfield contends do not tell the whole story. See the
annotation at entry 576.

637   Yishai, Yael.   "Challenge Groups in Israel." Middle
East Journal 35 (1981): 544-556.

Politics in Israel has a moral dimension to it. The religious parties in Israel, and particularly the extremely

militant ones, cloak their extremism in apocalyptic and moralistic terms. Yishai looks at Meir Kahane's Kach group and the campaign for Arab emigration from Israel. She notes the problem of Zionism as a radical religion for some Israelis. See the annotation to entry 577 and look especially at the debate concerning Meir Kahane (entry 588 and the references there).

638 Zucker, Naomi Flink, and Zucker, Norman I. "Piety and Politics." Present Tense 3,2 (1976): 63-69.

The problem of religious political power worries these two authors. The Orthodox have an emotional and religious stake in making Israel an ideal halakhic country. Secular Israelis, however, have moral rights as well, especially that of personal conscience. The two authors seek to find a modus vivendi between secularists and religionists in Israel despite the problems of Jewish identity, public education, and religious legislation. They lament that you can tell a Jew by his butcher not his moral behavior.

639 Zukerman-Bareli, Chaya. "Religion and its Connection to Consensus and Polarization of Opinions Among Israeli Youth" [Hebrew]. Megamot 22,1 (1975): 62-81.

This essay points out common concerns among all Israelis: the importance of democracy, the need for welfare legisla- tion. Significant differences do occur, however, on ques- tions of Israel's relationship to the Diaspora, on treatment of the Arabs and on the image of Israel as a Jewish state.

THE MORALITY OF WAR AND PEACE

640 Arieli, Shameryahu. Jewish Military Law. Jerusalem: Reuben Maas, 1971.

Arieli provides a detailed description the types of war traditionally permitted and forbidden, the age of conscrip- tion, exemptions from military service, and modern problems in the Israeli army. He contends that Israeli wars are commanded wars and Jews of the diaspora must support them. Compare entries 645 646, 647, 651, 658, 666.

641 Bleich, J. David. "Judea and Samaria: Settlement and Return." In his Contemporary Halakhic Problems 2, 189-221. The Library of Jewish Law and Ethics, 10. New York: Ktav Publishing House, 1983.

The dilemma of Israeli wars and the captured territory has concerned many Jews (see entries 643, 647, 648, 649, 649, 653, 655, 657, 660, 663, 664, 667, 670, 671). Bleich, in the tradition of militant Orthodoxy, justifies nationalism as religiously imperative. He notes the conflicting theologi- cal viewpoints but ends by supporting the use of military means to support the state of Israel. The article originally appeared in Tradition 11 (1970: 91-93; 12 (1972): 91-92.

642   Bleich,   J.   David.   "Nuclear Warfare."   Tradition 21
(1984): 84-88.

Bleich   surveys   traditional Jewish law and notes   that   only
limited   war   is   permitted.   A nuclear war with   its   vast
devastation is,   thus,   forbidden.   The use of a nuclear for
purely deterrent purposes, however, may be accepted.

643   Bleich,   J.   David.   "Pre-Emptive War in Jewish   Law."
Tradition 21 (1983): 3-11.

The Israeli invasion of Lebanon occasioned much Jewish self-
searching.   Here Bleich examines whether Jewish law permits
such   a war.   He concludes that Israel's centricity and its
importance   for the final redemption of all   humanity   makes
such a war not only justified but also imperative.

644   Bleich,   J. David.   "The Sanctity of the Liberated Territories."   In his Contemporary Halakhic Problems 2,   169-
188.   The Library of Jewish Law and Ethics,   10.   New York:
Ktav Publishing House, 1983.

Bleich   reviews the religious sanction for wars of attrition
and provides a theological justification for Jewish   refusal
to   negotiate concern the territories in the Land of Israel.
He sounds a familiar note of nationalism and   traditionalism
that is characteristic of militant Orthodox Jews.   The essay
appeared first in Tradition   15 (1975): 119-135.

645   Bleich, J. David.   "War and Non-Jews." In his Contemporary   Halakhic Problems 2,   159-166.   The Library of Jewish
Law and Ethics, 10.   New York: Ktav Publishing House, 1983.

War is not only a question for Jews to answer concerning the
State of Israel.   Other wars are equally important in Jewish
thought,   those conducted by non-Jewish   states.   Bleich
examines   war in relationship to the commandments   given   to
humanity   as a whole,   that is to the Noahides.   He details
their obligations to engage in certain types of war.

646   Bleich,   J.   David.   "War and Peace."   In his   Contemporary Halakhic Problems,   180-182.   The Library of Jewish
Law and Ethics, 4.   New York: Ktav Publishing House, 1977.

War itself must be conducted according to certain prescribed
patterns of behavior.   In this essay Bleich explains   the
distinction between obligatory,   permissible,   and defensive
wars   and   the   the mandatory setting forth of   peace   terms
according   to   Jewish law.   He studies conscription   and
exemptions from military service in Jewish law.   This   essay
first appeared in Tradition 11 (1970): 95-96.

647   Bleich,   J.   David.   "War and the State of Israel."   In
his Contemporary Halakhic Problems,   13-18.   The Library of
Jewish Law and Ethics,   4.   New York: Ktav Publishing House,
1977.

Bleich reviews traditional arguments against wars to regain
possession of the land of Israel. He notes the aggadic
tradition of oaths sworn not to take land by force and not
to rebel against the gentiles, but does not consider it
binding in the present situation. While noting that most
wars require permission from the Sanhedrin, defensive wars
are an exception. Bleich holds up the biblical command to
eradicate the Amalekites as warrant for wars against Arab
aggression. See Tradition 12 (1972): 114-117.

648 Cohen, S. Y., et al. "The Religious Meaning of the Six
Day War." Tradition 10 (1968): 5-20.

In this symposium Israeli thinkers and reflect on the six
day war and its victory; many see it in eschatological
terms. The reader will find both the extremely nationalistic and the less enthusiastic Orthodox Jew represented in
this discussion. It provides a good point of departure for
a study of the controversy within modern Orthodox Judaism
concerning political wars, particularly those carried on in
the state of Israel.

649 Dinstein, Yoram. "Terrorism and Wars of Liberation
Applied to the Arab-Israeli Conflict: An Israeli Perspective." Israel Yearbook on Human Rights 3 (1973): 78-92.

Dinstein contends that the term people is subjective and in
the case of Israel and the Arabs must be used with caution.
He claims that war as such is illegal, but that a people's
self-defense is a credible justification. While he admits
that there are more Jews outside Israel than inside, he
notes there are more Arabs outside Palestine than those who
claim territorial rights there. He considers terrorism as a
legitimate threat to any sovereign power and considers a
state that tolerates it responsible for terrorism. See the
annotation at entry 641.

650 Gazit, Shlomo. "Policy in the Administered Territories." Israel Yearbook on Human Rights 1 (1971):278-282.

Gazit claims that the aim of Israeli policy in the occupied
territories is to develop a close relationship between Arabs
and Jews, to overcome irrationality, and demonstrates concern for the way of life of the non-Jewish residents.
Israel's treatment of minorities is justified as moral and
respectful of human rights. See the annotation at entry 641
as well as entries 717, 718, 722, 725, 727, 728.

651 Gendler, Everett E. "War and the Jewish Tradition."
In Contemporary Jewish Ethics, edited by Menahem Marc
Kellner, 189-210. Sanhedrin Jewish Studies. New York:
Sanhedrin Press, 1978.

Because of the diversity within Jewish law controversy
arises over Judaism's approach to pacifism. Here Gendler
discovers a concern for conscience and personhood that can

provide the basis for a contemporary pacifism. He shows how the moral impetus in Jewish thought, whatever the particular details of Jewish legal thinking about war and peace, led to a limitation and reduction in the legitimacy of war. Compare entries 650, 658, 661, 665, 666.

652 Hoenig, Sidney B. "The Orthodox Rabbi as A Military Chaplain: A Bicentennial Retrospect." Tradition 16 (1976): 35-60.

This article is both a practical message to rabbis serving in the Armed forces and a theoretical defense of rabbinical assistance in such a case. Hoenig raises questions of kashrut, marriage and tevilah, and religious discrimination in the army. He notes the problems that arise from consulting a Rebbe unfamiliar with army routine. He gives a detailed case study concerning the traditional wearing of the beard and army codes of personal appearance. This essay should be read in conjunction with other essays focusing on the relevance of a Jewish chaplaincy (see entries 672, 673.)

653 Isaac, Erich, and Isaac, Raul J. "The Siren Song of Peace: Israel's Dissenting Intellectuals." Conservative Judaism 26 (1972): 3-19.

This article condemns those non-Israelis and even some Israelis who call for peace at all costs. Such a moral stance relies upon others to defend the very basis upon which the moral claims are being made. Thus the authors claim that the intellectuals who call for peace are allowing themselves a dishonest luxury since they depend upon the army for protection while speaking against the waging of war. Morality demands an honesty of approach and not just pious mouthing of peaceful sentiments.

654 Kirschenbaum, Aaron. "A Cog in the Wheel: The Defense of Obedience to Superior Orders' in Jewish Law." Israel Yearbook on Human Rights 4 (1974): 165-193.

The morality of war and peace includes the moral dimension of agreeing to participate in a war not of ones own making. Can Judaism support dissent from an authority who demands the performance of an immoral deed? Kirschenbaum explores the rabbinic principle that there is no agency for illegal acts. The agent and not the principle who commands the agent is ultimately responsible for a deed. The originator of the act, however, does have liability as the examples of Abner standing against Saul's execution of priests of Nob, the case of minors and of David's instigation of the death of Uriah the Hittite show.

655 Kriegel, Annie. "Les Juifs, La Paix et Les Guerres du XXe Siecle." In her Les Juifs et Le Monde Moderne: Essai Sur Les Logiques D'Emancipation, 137-164. Paris: Edition Du Seuil, 1977.

The author explores Jewish thinking about war from the perspective of Jewish experience as a subjected people. War is never desirable from that standpoint. In the twentieth century war has been associated with the liberation of peoples and Jews have shared in that through the rebirth of Israel. Nevertheless Kriegel is sensitive to the problems of modernity and the way in which Israel's rhythms of life have been shaped by the reality of war.

656 Lamm, Maurice. "After the War: Another Look at Pacifism and SCO." In Contemporary Jewish Ethics, edited by Menachem Marc Kellner, 211-238. Sanhedrin Jewish Studies. New York: Sanhedrin Press, 1978.

Jews were deeply divided on the morality of the American war in Southeast Asia. Here one perspective is offered (see also entries 668, 669). On the basis of traditional theory and approach to the State Lamm defends the power of the nation to invoke its citizens for war. He shows that despite arguments for conscientious objection Judaism invariably supports decisions made by a civil government to engage in war. The essay first appeared in Judaism 20 (1971): 416-430.

657 Leibowitz, Isaiah. "The Spiritual and Religious Meaning of Victory and Might," trans. by Isaac Gottlieb. Tradition 10 (1969): 5-11.

Leibowitz describes the spiritual meaning of bravery in Judaism. He suggests that the spiritual problems of Israel remain even after military victory. He cautions that the empirical fact of victory is not to be given any special religious significance. This approach to war is one strand in modern Israeli thinking; other strands emphasize the eschatological importance of retaining all lands conquered from the Arabs. Leibowitz's views should be seen in the context of the modern debate in Israel and compared to contrasting views.

658 Novak, David. "A Jewish View of War," in Law and Theology in Judaism, 125-135. New York: Ktav Publishing House, 1974.

Novak admits that Jewish thinking about war, its division of war into three legitimate types, and its restrictions on war all apply only to a Jewish government. He claims, nonetheless, that Judaism is an appropriate resource for American thinking about war. He finds that the Noahide code places restrictions on war-making by non-Jews. He examines one paradigm used to justify war--that of self-defense in the presence of a pursuer--and suggests its uses and its limitations. Compare the discussion at Gendler (651).

659 Olan, Levi I. "The Mission of Israel in a Nuclear Age." Judaism 32 (1983): 27-33.

The threat of nuclear disaster has caused many Jews to find in their tradition a means of averting that tragedy. Olan contends that secularism cannot cope with the problems of morality in the nuclear age. Instead he calls upon the prophetic idea of monotheism to confront the science of atomism and monism. He calls upon Jews to recapture the prophetic mission that can save humanity from itself. Compare entry 614.

660 Pa'il, Meir. "The Dynamics of Power: Morality in Armed Conflict After the Six Day War." In Modern Jewish Ethics: Theory and Practice, edited by Marvin Fox, 191-220. Columbus: Ohio University Press, 1975.

This defense of the Israel Defense Force and its moral approach is both convincing and illuminating. Pa'il suggests that there are minimum ethical values present in the waging of any war that include minimizing the loss of life, establishing a brotherhood of warriors, and mitigating the mentality of an eye for an eye retribution. In Israel, facing the danger of national-racism, other safeguards and moral restraints have been built into the conduct of war. He cites novels, first hand reports, and interviews with soldiers to show how Israeli soldiers attempt to maintain "purity of arms" and morality while engaged in war.

661 Polak, Joseph. "Torah and the Megabombs." Judaism 32 (1983): 303-308.

Polak finds the modern situation radically different from that of any previous generation. In the light of the nuclear catastrophe threatening the entire world a pacifism is required not because of war itself but because of the weapons involved. This essay should be compared to that of Levi Olan (entry 659).

662 Rackman, Emanuel. "Violence and the Value of Life: The Halakhic View." In Violence and Defense in the Jewish Experience, edited by Salo W. Baron, George S. Wise, and Lenn E. Goodman, 113-141. Philadelphia: Jewish Publication Society of America, 1977.

Together with a general discussion on the value of life and the opposition to violence in Judaism Rackman studies the question of war, civil disobedience, and the Israeli wars of defense, noting the divergence between hawks and doves among Orthodox in Israel.

663 Rosenak, Isaiah. "The Mitzvot, the Messiah, and the Territories." Tradition 10 (1968): 12-40.

Rosenak offers a compromise between extremists who see Israeli victories as redemption or as merely secular. He stands against the arguments of the maximalists-they negate moral mitzvoth, and against the minimalists--they negate the task of redemption. Compare entry 641.

664   Rubenstein,   Amnon.   "War and the Rule   of   Law: The
Israeli Experience."   Israel   Yearbook on Human   Rights   1
(1971): 322-326.

The moral stress of war may lead to a hardened and   insensitive attitude.   Rubenstein disagrees that this is the case
in Israel.   He contends that Israel has become more liberal
and tolerant since Israel cannot accept the excesses of war.
He notes   the concern that Israelis have for   the   minority
population.   He also suggests that Israel's   self-criticism
and   its   willing limitation in the use of emergency   powers
shows   a   restraint and tendency   towards   peace.   See   the
annotation at entry 641.

665   Saperstein,   David,   editor.   Preventing the   Nuclear
Holocaust.   New   York: Union of American Hebrew Congregations, 1983.

This   is   a compendium of Jewish responses   centered   on   an
article   by Maurice Lamm with rejoinders by Immanuel Jakobovits,   and Michael Wyschogrod focused on the Jewish view   of
war   and peace.   Special perspectives are offered by   Louis
Jacobs,   Arthur   Waskow,   and   David Novak on the threat   of
nuclear War,   the permissibility of war, and other issues in
Jewish morality concerning the waging of war.   Compare   entries Gendler (651).

666   Shapiro,   David S.   "The Jewish Attitude Toward War and
Peace."   In   his   Studies   in   Jewish   Thought   1,   316-363.
Studies   in   Judaica.   New York,   Yeshiva University   Press,
1975.

This   detailed review of the major Jewish   options   together
with its emphasis on life calls Christians to look to Jewish
halakha   for   guidance in policy.   The essay   is   primarily
meant   as   a theoretical study and is not addressed   to   the
particular   issues of Israel and Israeli wars that have been
of   basic   concern to contemporary Jewish   moral   thinking.
Compare this entry with the previous entry.

667   Urofsky,   Melvin I.   "Looking Beyond Peace: The Family
at Odds."   Judaism 28 (1979): 324-333.

The moral questions of war and peace,   Urovsky contends, are
often   overlooked in the immediate needs of the   hour.   The
moral dimension,   however,   is essential if Jews are to confront   the meaning of the state of Israel and its   relationship   as   a religious center for all Jews in   the   diaspora.
Thus Urovsky declares that the problem of the   Arab-Israeli
conflict   involves   not merely the question of war   but   the
relationship of Israeli needs and Diaspora ideals.   He considers   the crisis atmosphere to be debilitating for ethical
concerns   and notes as contributing factors to   the   problem
the   centrality of Israel for American Judaism and the   fac-
tionalism   arising from divergent Orthodox and liberal religious views.

668 Wein, Berel. "Jewish Conscientious Objectors and the Vietnamese War." Jewish Life 37 (1969): 22-31.

Wein declares that the thrust of the Jewish spirit is anti-war but should not be confused with pure pacifism. Judaism considers self-defense a commandment, even while forbidding aggressive, selfish wars. He summarizes the general halak-hic view: loyalty to country overrides one's personal qualms: the law of the land must be obeyed. Compare entry 656 and the following entry as well as the discussion of disobedience to governmental orders found in entry 654.

669 Winston, Diane. "Vietnam and the Jews." In The Sociology of American Jews, edited by Jack Nusan Porter, 189-209. Washington, D.C.: University Press of America, 1978.

Winston argues that the Jewish love of Israel has been manipulated into militant Americanism. She points to Michael Wyschogrod as Orthodox representative of this mili-tancy. She admits the dilemma of Abraham Heschel who found that his friends with whom he protested the war in Vietnam refused to help Israel in its time of trouble. Compare this view with the previous entry and with entry 654.

670 Wisse, Ruth R. "Peace Now and American Jews." Commen-tary 70,2 (1980): 19-22.

Wisse claims that Jews often sacrifice the welfare of other Jews in order to make the needed gentile look good. She thinks that this syndrome is at work in American Jewish support of "Peace Now," an Israeli pacifist group. She claims that supporting peace now makes the American Jew feel morally right, recreates the enemy in a better light, but is dangerous for Jewish survival. Compare this view with the traditionalists as in entry 641; see the annotation to that entry. This article is special in its emphasis on the vicarious ethics of American Jewish sympathizers with the peace movement in Israel.

671 Yehoshua, Abraham B. Between Right and Right, trans. by Arnold Schwartz. Garden City: Doubleday and Company, 1981.

Yehoshua claims that only an exile mentality separates religious and national systems. In Israel, he contends, the two must be united. That unification is threatened by the state of siege in which Israelis exists. He sees the shadow of war as a moral and psychological reality in Israel that must be confronted and overcome. This balanced study shows the sensitivity that an Israeli has for the delicate moral questions raised by the double rights that clash over the land of Israel.

672 Zahn, Gordon Z. "The Scandal of the Military Chaplaincy." Judaism 18 (1969): 313-319.

Zahn claims that the chaplain has guidelines as military personelle but needs to be independent. Zahn feels that he can support the individual soldier without supporting the system of which the soldier is a part. He claims that the role of religious leadership should be to question the morality of war even in the military itself. Contrast this view with the following entry and with entry 652.

673 Zimmerman, Sheldon. "Confronting the Halakhah on Military Service." Judaism 20 (1971): 204-212.

Zimmerman claims that Jews must support the law of the land including the wars of the land. He cites the medieval authority Moses Maimonides on the legitimacy of non-Jewish kings and their wars, noting that even the profanation of the Sabbath either under duress or to prove loyalty to the king was permitted. Modern Jews may chafe at this approach, but Zimmerman finds it part of the halakhic tradition.

RACE AND MORALITY

674 Bleich, J. David. "Black Jews: A Halakhic Perspective." In his Contemporary Halakhic Problems, 297-324. The Library of Jewish Law and Ethics, 4. New York: Ktav Publishing House, 1977.

The morality of race relationships has many dimensions. While American Jews have focused on the question of Black anti-semitism, Israelis focus on the problem of the Black Jews, the Falashas. According to Bleich Judaism is color-blind and the approach the Falashas, reflects Jewish law concerning women taken captive, legislation on divorce laws, and conversion concerns, not racism. Bleich considers American black Jews as converts. He considers Harlem's Jews as Noahides who are rewarded for their practices but are not identified as Jews even if they do practice circumcision. This essay is found in Tradition 15 (1975): 48-79.

675 Cohen, Naomi Werner. "You Know the Heart of a Stranger." In her Not Free to Desist: The American Jewish Committee 1906-1966, 383-497. Philadelphia: Jewish Publication Society of America 1972.

Cohen notes that Jews have identified with the cause of equal rights and the Black struggle. They led in the pressure for public school integration and fair housing. Because of this involvement they have felt bitterness at the rise of Black anti-semitism that threatens to destroy the former coalition. The combination of continued ethical concern and sense of disillusionment that many Jews feel is captured in this survey and analysis.

676 Dubin, David. "Community Involvement and Traditional Priorities Compatible objectives of the Jewish Community Center." Journal of Jewish Communal Service 47 (1970): 37-42.

Morality often goes against self-interest. In this case the double problem for Jews and Blacks threatens to erupt into hostility. Dubin looks at cases of rent control, of the role for a youth center in a public housing project and stands against the philosophy of _Jews First'. He notes that the Jews often isolate themselves in a community, and that Black anti-semitism is sometimes provoked.

677 Fein Leonard J. "Thinking about Quotas." Midstream 19 (1973): 13-17.

The morality of race relations may sometimes overcome the practical concerns. Thus Fein argues that while Jews will be displaced by affirmative action, merit as an enlightened ideal is an indefensible proposition for a minority group. Jews have a moral responsibility to recognize the limits of that ideal. Compare the various views on this subject in entries 678, 682, 684, and 697.

678 Fishman, Howard, Fishman, Walda Katz. "Blacks and Jews and Affirmative Action." The Humanist 40 (1980): 24-27.

The authors claim that neither quotas nor merit should exercise the thinking of Blacks and Jews. What is needed is rather joint efforts to correct the maldistribution of power, wealth and opportunity. This article draws attention to the need to look at moral questions rather than self-interest in solving social problems such as race relationships. See also entries 677, 682, 684, 697.

679 Forster, Arnold. "The Defunis Case and the Jewish Organizations." United Synagogue Review 27,2 (1974): 5, 7, 25.

In discussing this classic case challenging affirmative action Forster notes that Jewish organizations were originally organized not just to fight anti-semitism but to gain full freedoms for all individuals. Jews, the author feels, have a moral obligation to support all aspirations for freedom and equality, even if some Jews may suffer in the process. See also entries 693, 694.

680 Ginzberg, Eli. "The Black Revolution and the Jew." Conservative Judaism 24 (1969): 3-19.

While many Jewish leaders have rejected civil rights because of their disappointment with Black anti-semitism, not all agree. Ginzberg reviews the Jewish experience with anti-semitism is reviewed as well as the areas of conflict in urban ethnic areas. He calls for a contextual understanding of black anti-semitism. See entry 683.

681 Glazer, Nathan. "Blacks, Jews, and The Intellectuals Question." Commentary 47:4 (1969): 33-39.

Jewish fear of the blacks may be exaggerated. Glazer asks
Jews whether are actually threatened by black Power. His
investigation suggests that Jewish perception of the problem
is biased. He contends that the establishment coalition
with blacks includes Jews as well as non-Jews. He notes
that all members of the middle class and not just Jews
suffer the effects of affirmative action. Jews, he feels,
should respond by educating blacks about Judaism and Jews
about dangers of black extremism.

682 Halpern, Ben. "The _Quota' Issue." Midstream 19
(1973): 3-12.

The problem of quotas, reverse discrimination, and the general victimization of the middle class has made Jews ap-
prehensive. This apprehension has many causes, some of them
affecting Jews as Jews, some of them affecting Jews as
members of other middle class grouping. Halpern suggests
that Jewish and black self-interests have diverged. Jews,
he thinks, must respond first as Jews and only then as
academics, suburbanites, or liberals who are also threatened
but in different ways. See entries 677, 678, 684, 697.

683 Halpern, Harry. "Reply to Eli Ginzberg: Facts, Feelings, Fears." Conservative Judaism 24 (1969): 20-23.

This response to Eli Ginzberg (entry 634) rejects his appeal
to understanding and suggests that Jewish self-interest and
plain justice stand against affirmative action. Morality
from this standpoint implies concern for Jews and their
interests no less than it implies a caring for blacks and
their historical problems in the United States. This essay
reflects the popular stand of many former liberals who have
decided that Jewish interests must take precedence over
liberalism.

684 Hertzberg, Arthur. "Merit, Affirmative Action, Blacks
and Jews." Present Tense 7,2 (1980): 27-28.

The question of quotas and affirmative action goes beyond
who is victimized and who is not. The problem involves the
theory of how to distribute goods and maintain civil rights.
Hertzberg notes the move from liberalism in Jewish politics.
He suggests that the real moral problem is not how to gain
rights but how to share with others--a lesson both blacks
and Jews need to learn. See also entries 677, 678 , 682,
697.

685 Hochbaum, Jerry. "Black and Jew: Re-Appraising the
Emerging Relationship." Jewish Life 36 (1969): 6-13.

The author considers black anti-semitism evidence of deep-
seated hatred, not just for whites, but specifically for
Jews. He suggests that anti-semitism is an expression of
the same pathology as that leads whites to be anti-black.
He thinks that Jewish self-interest includes working to help
change the social situation that causes black deprivation.

686 Hofmann, Justin. "Racism in Jewish View." Jewish Life
38 (1970): 42-48 .

This emotional response to a social problem suggests that
Jews look at more than the political reality of racism.
Hoffman calls racism a basic American problem. He adds that
it is inconceivable to be both a Jew and a racist.   Citing
biblical and talmudic statements on human equality, he affirms the Jewish tradition against racism and quoting the
blessing to be said on seeing a wise non-Jewish scholar he
notes that Jews have a positive view of the non-Jew.

687 Kallen, Horace M.   "Black Power, White Power, and
Education." Judaism 20 (1971): 134-140.

Kallen claims that education should be seen as an alternative to power.   While some equate power with force and
violence, true power is self-mastery, attained through self-
knowledge.   He suggests, however, that education must be
digested to become power.

688 Mandelbaum, Bernard. "A Jewish Response to Black Anti-
Semitism." Conservative Judaism 24 (1969): 24-29.

This essay argues that morality not only takes precedence
over self-interest but may also be more effective. The true
Jewish response, according to Mandelbaum, is to love the
enemy more than before. Following the example of that
precept, he suggests, Jews should act responsibly in urban
areas and not flee from them. The example of Moses and
Jethro's daughter may held up as an ideal for black-Jewish
relationships and cooperation. See also entries 689, 692.

689 Perlmutter, Nathan, Perlmutter, Ruth Ann. "Blacks and
Jews." In their The Real Anti-Semitism in America, 182-203.
New York: Arbor House, 1982.

The authors, clearly writing from personal experience, note
the emotional investment Jews have in civil rights and
freedom of speech.   Jews have been in the vanguard of movements to insure the civil rights of blacks and of other
minority groups. The authors suggest that minority communication must be reciprocal; understanding cannot flow in only
one direction.   Blacks need to listen responsively to the
"souls" of other people, including Jews. The danger is not
from discrimination as such but rather from insularity of
minority groups. See also entries 688, 692.

690 Rabb, Earl. "The Black Revolution and the Jewish
Question." Commentary 47,1 (1969): 23-34.

Rabb examines the contemporary situation, the paranoia of
conspiracy theories and threats to Jewish security.   He
considers the new black politics dangerous for Jews but
affirms the Jewish will to survive.

691 Rabinowitz, Dorothy. "Blacks, Jews and New York Politics." Commentary 66,5 (1978): 42-47.

Rabinowitz claims that the talk of violence among blacks is directed not just against whites or the Koch administration but against the Jews generally and the Hasidim specifically. She deplores the rhetoric of death, violence, and the one-sided reporting that made this an issue.

692 Roth, Sol. "Black Anti-Semitism: Diagnosis and Treatment." Judaism 30 (1981): 283-289

This rather conservative approach laments that blacks have deserted their erstwhile friends. Roth claims that anti-semitism is rooted in economic and political myths. Jewish conduct is prompted by universal principles of morality and justice and should transcend those myths. See also entries 688, 689.

693 Singer, Howard. "The Defunis Case and the Jewish Organizations." United Synagogue Review 27,2 (1974): 4-6, 22-23.

Singer declares that the Jewish organizations defending Marco Defunis appear to be ganging up on blacks and minorities He feels that the court had the sense to say this is not a time to take a public stand. He urges Jewish organizations to do likewise. See also entries 679, 694.

694 Vorspan, Albert. "The Defunis Case and the Jewish Organizations." United Synagogue Review 27,2 (1974): 4-7, 24-25.

Vorspan claims that this was the wrong case for an investigation of reverse discrimination and affirmative action. He felt that Washington University seemed to be trying to fulfill its obligations to all parties involved. He urges Jewish organizations not to _gang up' against the minorities but denies that this was the case. Rather he sees the problem to have been mistaken tactics. Political dilemmas often obscure the moral concerns that are at the basis of the problem. See also entries 679, 693.

695 Vorspan, Albert. "Race Relations," in Great Jewish Debates and Dilemmas: Jewish Perspectives in Conflict in the Eighties, 1-17. New York: Union of American Hebrew Congregations, 1980.

Vorspan argues the need to change self-perception and one's perception of others in order to improve race relationships. He notes the problems and possible solutions to bridge the gap between blacks and Jews. He feels that the perception of self-interest on both parts needs to be altered. His application of this approach to a particular case of affirmative action can be found in the preceding entry.

696   Weinberger, Bernard.   "The Interracial Crisis: How
Should Jews Respond." Journal of Jewish Communal Service 46
(1969): 38-44.

Weinberger takes a conciliatory approach noting that Jews
show collective impotence dealing with blacks. He claims
that the Hasidic dictum that love is knowing what the other
needs should apply in this case. He stands against the
Jewish Defense League and its tactics. He recognizes the
threat to Orthodox Jews from black anti-semitism but suggests projecting an unassuming image since the best policy
is, in his view, one of disengagement.

697 Weitz, Marvin.   "Affirmative Action: a Jewish Death
Wish?" Midstream 25 :1 (1979): 9-17.

The author claims that Judaism emphasizes a time for the
self as well as for others. He suggests such a time is now
when blacks and Arabs have a coalition against the Jews.
After reviewing the history of the relationship between
American Jews and American blacks he concludes that it is
time for a change. Compare entries 677, 637, 682, 684.

CAPITAL PUNISHMENT AND THE JUDICIAL SYSTEM

698 Bleich, J. David. "Capital Punishment in the Noachide
Code."   In his Contemporary Halakhic Problems 2, 341-367.
The Library of Jewish Law and Ethics, 10.   New York: Ktav
Publishing House, 1983.

Bleich explains the Difference between the Noachide code and
the Sinaitic code.   He notes the authorities who contend
that Noahides must impose capital punishment for violations
of their legislation.   He reviews the validity of cir-
cumstantial evidence in such cases and whether Jews are to
be tried under such a process.

699 Bleich, J. David. "Imprisonment or Death for Convicted
Terrorists." In his Contemporary Halakhic Problems, 25-27.
The Library of Jewish Law and Ethics, 4.   New York: Ktav
Publishing House, 1977.

Convicted terrorists clearly deserve the death penalty
according to Bleich's thinking. While he admits that in the
modern world the absence of a Sanhedrin makes implementation
of the halakhic procedures for trying capital crimes impossible, he offers another solution. He suggests that the
death penalty is appropriate for non-Jews especially when
violations of the Noahide laws are involved. See Tradition
14 (1973): 122-126.

700 Blidstein, Gerald J. "Capital Punishment: The Classic
Jewish Discussion." In Contemporary Jewish Ethics, edited
by Menahem Marc Kellner, 310-325. Sanhedrin Jewish Studies.
New York: Sanhedrin Press, 1978.

Blidstein provides a review of the debate in rabbinic Judaism between those favoring and those opposed to capital punishment. He notes that there is no clear tradition one way or the other and that there are sound arguments on both sides of this question.

701 Carmi, Amnon. "On Death Sentencing." In The Dying Human, edited by Andre de Vries and Amnon Carmi, 373-379. Tel Aviv: Turtledove Publishing Company, 1979.

Carmi notes in his anthology (190) that the question of the death penalty is difficult to resolve. If it is legitimate it must meet three criteria: does the community demand it, the judges who lead the community should seek to create conditions under which it might be abolished, and love should be made the root of human culture. While the argument that the death penalty is needed for self-defense is an important one it must never be allowed to dehumanize or desensitize a community.

702 Cohn, Haim H. "Torture and Cruel Punishments." In his Human Rights in Jewish Law, 217-224. New York: Ktav Publishing House, 1984.

Cohen raises serious concerns about the death penalty. He examines the types of death penalty found in Jewish law and their justification. He investigates other types of penalties where death is not involved.

703 Falk, Zeev W. "Forensic Medicine in Jewish Law." Dine Israel 1 (1969): xx-xxx.

See annotation at entry 014.

704 Freudenstein, Eric G. "A Swift Witness." Tradition 13 (1973): 114-123.

Analyzing the biblical injunction for a swift witness, Freudenthal suggests that having the witness throw the stones is an example of both the right to a speedy execution and the need for witnesses to take responsibility for the consequences of their testimony.

705 Herring, Basil F. "Capital Punishment." In his Jewish Ethics and Halakhah For Our Time: Sources and Commentary, 149-173. The Library of Jewish Law and Ethics, 11. New York: Ktav Publishing House and Yeshiva University, 1984

Herring reviews the debate about the appropriateness of capital punishment both in classical sources and in modern times. He shows how society requires such a punishment even if moral questions can be raised about it.

706 Kazis, Israel J. "Judaism and the Death Penalty." In Contemporary Jewish Ethics, edited by Menahem Marc Kellner, 326-329. Sanhedrin Jewish Studies. New York: Sanhedrin Press, 1978.

Kazis provides an important counterpoint to the view of Blidstein (entry 700). Many Jews are opposed to the death penalty and argue that the general tendency in Judaism is to stand in opposition to the practice even if it is necessitated by the state of human society.

707 Priest, James E. Governmental and Judicial Ethics in the Bible and Rabbinic Literature. New York: Ktav Publishing House, 1980.

This book provides a comprehensive study of Jewish judicial law including a careful look at crime and punishment. The case for and against capital punishment is also examined.

708 Sasso, Dennis C. "Capital Punishment Re-Examined." The Reconstructionist 47,4 (1981): 12-16.

Sasso presents the classic Jewish sources and argues the case against capital punishment. He expresses concern lest justice miscarry without being able to reverse the decision.

709 Vorspan, Albert. "Crime and Punishment." In his Great Jewish Debates and Dilemmas: Jewish Perspectives in Conflict in the Eighties, 183-204. New York: Union of American Hebrew Congregations, 1980.

Vorspan traces the development of Jewish law and the modification of its penal views from the biblical period until the present time with special reference to modern concerns of crime and punishment.

710 Warhaftig, Itamar. "The Ethics of Using Prisoners for Experimentation" [Hebrew]. Tehumin 1 (1980): 530-536.

The element of coercion on prisoners raises moral questions about their participation in experimentation and about the judicial process itself; see entry 070.

711 Warhaftig, Itamar. "Self Defense in Murder and Accident" [Hebrew]. Sinai 81 (1977): 48-78.

Warhaftig reviews modern Israeli law, talmudic and classical sources to define the ideas of the "pursuer", self-defense, and the significance of circumstances such as the age of the pursuer, unintended pursuit, and compulsion when judging the inflicting of death as "self-defense."

THE MORALITY OF HUMAN RIGHTS

712 Bayer, Abraham J. "American Response to Soviet Anti-Jewish Policies." American Jewish Yearbook 74 (1973): 210-225.

Bayer analyzes the impact of the movement to work of Soviet Jews in American Jewry, noting the participants, tactics, and the ethical issues involved. See entries 713, 714, 715, 716, 719, 720, 721, 723, 724, 730.

713 Bernstein, Philip. "Soviet Jews in Crisis." In his To
Dwell in Unity: The Jewish Federation Movement in America
Since 1960, 67-84. Philadelphia: Jewish Publication Socie-
ty of America, 1983.

Bernstein shows how American Jews mobilized to the defense
of the rights of Soviet Jews. He provides details on the
strategy, tactics, and universal importance of the movement.
See the annotation of the previous entry.

714 Cohen, Naomi Werner.   "Behind the Iron Curtain." In
her Not Free to Desist: The American Jewish Committee,
1906-1966 , 496-510.   Philadelphia: Jewish Publication Society of America, 1972.

Cohen sketches the history of American Jewish involvement
with Soviet Jews and the socio-moral dimensions of that involvement.   She shows how a concern for human rights developed into a major Jewish movement.   See the annotation at
entry 712.

715 Dinstein, Yoram.   "Soviet Jewry and International
Rights." Israel Yearbook on Human Rights 2 (1972): 194-210.

Dinstein points to the ethics of shared suffering illustrated by American Jewish concern for the Soviet Jews.
Those Jews suffer cultural and religious deprivation and are
victims of an official violation of educational rights,
racial discrimination, and the right to emigrate.   See the
annotation at entry 712.

716 Friedberg, Maurice. "Trying to Save Soviet Jewry."
Present Tense 6,1 (1978): 46-50.

This essay traces the change of tactics in the effort to
save Soviet Jews from peaceful protest to activism. It also
documents the continued efforts on behalf of Soviet Jews
that were engaged in after Soviet Jews emigrated to the
United States. See the annotation at entry 712.

717 Gershuni, Jehudah.   "Minority Rights in the State of
Israel in the Light of Halacha" [Hebrew]. Tehumin 2
(1981): 180-192.

Gershuni struggles with the rights of non-Jews in the state
of Israel. He examines the three types of non-Jew --ger
toshav, benai noach, and idolater-- and the regulations
applied to each by Jewish law. He concludes that in the
modern world in which many laws can no longer practiced and
in which the transfer of of lands cannot be said to be for
perpetuity, the importance of the paths of peace outweighs
the disabilities that Jewish law once placed on minorities
in the land of Israel. On the moral question of Israel's
minorities see entries 718, 722, 725, 727, 728.

718 Herzog, Yitzhak Isaac Halevi. "Minority Rights According to Halacha" [Hebrew]. Tehumin 2 (1981): 169-179.

Herzog examines the status of non-Jews and the application of this status to Christians and Muslims. He suggests that there is a need to compromise in modern times for the sake of general good will. Morality demands treating minorities well. See the annotation at entry 717.

719 Lurie, Walter A. "Jewish in the Soviet Union." In his Strategies for Survival: Principles of Jewish Community Relations, 99-101. New York: Ktav Publishing House, 1982.

Lurie deplores the use of violence and activism and prefers the use of diplomacy in achieving rights for Soviet Jews. He suggests that public outcry is more effective than militancy. While the human rights issue of Soviet Jewry is central to his concerns, he is equally concerned with the means by which he attains those rights. See the annotation at entry 712.

720 Orbach, William W. The American Movement to Aid Soviet Jews. Amherst: University of Massachusetts Press, 1979.

It is no accident that Orbach who has evolved a theology of non-violence organizes his study of the movement to aid Soviet Jewry around the theme that the tactics of non-violence are more effective than those of violence. He charts the changing strategies and tactics of the movement and contrasts the student leaders with the Jewish Defense League, which he claims accomplished little other than alienating important allies to the cause. See the annotation at entry 712.

721 Porath, Jonathan. "The Challenge of Soviet Jewry." United Synagogue Review 27,1 (1974): 6-7.

While the rights of Soviet Jews for emigration and free practice of Judaism are important goals, Porath sees a different challenge facing the American Jew. That challenge is how ready we are to become serious about Judaism and to live so that Soviet emigrees to United States will find their trials and struggles worth the rewards they reap. See the annotation at entry 712.

722 Rabinowicz, Aaron K. "Human Rights Problems in the United States and in Israel." Jewish Social Studies 34 (1972): 207-242.

This fascinating essay presents an extended comparison of civil liberties issues of voting, housing, due process, freedom of thought, religion, press and association in each context. The problem of the Black in America is contrasted with that of the Arab minority within Israel. See the annotation at entry 717.

723 Rubin, Ronald I. "American Jews and Soviet Jews." Jewish Life 38 (1970): 7-21.

Rubin explains the moral reasons for Jewish concern, the Student Struggle for Soviet Jews, and the moral issue which motivated the students. It also explains why students were activists but rejected the tactics of the Jewish Defense League as alien to the purposes of their cause. See the annotation at entry 712.

724 Schnall, David J. "Soviet Jewry: Malaise Within the Movement." Midstream 26 (1980): 8-13.

Schnall analyzes why the movement to aid Soviet Jewry goes through periods of latency as well as activism. It languishes, he suggests, when Soviet Jews elect to come to the United States and not Israel. They do not appear to live up to expectations of Jews here in their practice of Judaism. He urges that Israelis as well as Americans work for the rights of Soviet Jews. See the annotation at entry 712.

725 Shestack, Jerome J. "Human Rights Issues in Israel's Rule of the West Bank and Gaza." In Essays on Human Rights: Contemporary Issues and Jewish Perspectives, edited by David Sidorsky, 193-209. Philadelphia: Jewish Publication Society of America, 1979.

Shestack laments that critics magnify minor incidents so that the treatment of minorities in Israel is misunderstood. In fact, he explains, freedom of access to holy places and to the media is granted to minorities. Some restrictions are imposed for the sake of national security, but these apply only to elections, demonstrations, and security offenders. See the essays in the following entry and the annotation at entry 717.

726 Sidorsky, David. Essays on Human Rights: Contemporary Issues and Jewish Perspectives, in collaboration with Sidney Liskofsky and Jerome J. Shestack. Philadelphia: Jewish Publication Society of America, 1979.

This is a collection of thoughtful and provocative essays. Many of the essays are dealing with general human rights and not just Jewish morality. Nevertheless they are important reading. See entries 724 and 627.

727 Smooha, Sammi. "Arabs and Jews in Israel: Minority-Majority Group Relations." Megamot 22 (1976): 397-423.

Smooha reviews the various options open to Israeli society. He notes that either Israel is committed to democracy or it is not. He charges that current practice fails to meet either Arab or Jewish needs. What he suggests as the most moral response is to offer citizens a choice of national identity either as Israelis or as Palestinians. See the annotation at entry 717.

728 Stendel, Ori. "The Rights of the Arab Minority in Israel." Israel Yearbook of Human Rights 1 (1971): 134-155

The keenest challenge of morality, Stendel claims, is to tolerate extremist groups who exploit freedom. He claims that equality requires organic integration of the minority, an ideal that has not yet been achieved in Israel. See the annotation at entry 717.

729 Vorspan, Albert. "Civil Liberties." In his Great Jewish Debates and Dilemmas: Jewish Perspectives in Conflict in the Eighties, 35-52. New York: Union of American Hebrew Congregations, 1980.

Vorspan surveys the problems concerning civil liberties, particularly those in which Jews and Nazis have clashed. He notes the vulnerability of Nazi survivors but also the importance of free speech. He investigates the issues of censorship and privacy in that connection.

730 Vorspan, Albert. "Soviet Jewry." In his Great Jewish Debates and Dilemmas: Jewish Perspectives in Conflict in the Eighties, 96-122. New York: Union of American Hebrew Congregations, 1980.

Vorspan provides a summary of the history of the movement, disappointment because of dropouts by emigrees and the current state of concern. He remarks that a human rights program entails becoming aware of the issues and familiar with literature reflecting the conditions of Soviet Jewry. See the annotation at entry 712.

731 Wyschogrod, Michael. "Religion and International Human Rights: A Jewish Perspective." In Formation of Social Policy in the Catholic and Jewish Traditions, edited by Eugene J. Fisher and Daniel F. Polish, 123-141. Notre Dame: University of Notre Dame Press, 1980.

Wyschogrod provides biblical and talmudic sources to show the values of Judaism and and their relevance to human rights. This theoretical study should be read in conjunction with the two practical issues that are the most prominent human rights questions for the modern Jew: the plight of Soviet Jewry and the dilemma of the state of Israel in dealing with its Muslim minority.

6
Morality and Valuation

POVERTY

732 Bar Ilan, Naphtali. "The Needy Person's Right to
Zedakah" Tehumin 2 (1981): 459-465.

Bar Ilan asks whether the duty to give charity is personal
or communal. He concludes that making sure each person has
satisfied basic minimal needs is a communal duty. On the
other hand, support enabling a person to maintain a former
life-style while fallen on hard times demands individual
zedaka. Compare entries 739, 741 and 742.

733 Bernstein, Phillip. "Poverty." In his To Dwell in
Unity: The Jewish Federation Movement in America Since 1960,
242-244. Philadelphia: Jewish Publication Society of America, 1983.

Bernstein focuses on the Jewish concern with all poor. He
notes that all levels of help must be considered and that
one important task is that of supplementing income from
government aid.

734 Cohen, Jack Simcha. "Jewish Poverty: Measurement Problems." Journal of Jewish Communal Service 49 (1973): 210-
213.

Cohen describes the special needs of the Jewish poor: kosher
food, two sets of dishes, and problems arising from the
desire for education and lack of transportation. He contends that the Jewish poor need special attention.

735 Cottle, Thomas J. Hidden Survivors: Portraits of Poor
Jews in America. Englewood Cliffs: Prentice-Hall, Inc.
1980.

This anecdotal and passionate book describes the sense of
desertion plaguing the Jewish poor and elderly. Cottle
shows that they do not see just society at fault but, more
especially, blame their families. He notes that the

marginality of such people is two-fold, springing from their age and their Jewishness.

736 Cowan, Paul. "Jews Without Money, Revisited." In Poor Jews: An American Awakening, edited by Naomi Levine and Martin Hochbaum 39-58. New Brunswick: Transaction Books, 1974.

Cowan contends that the Jewish poor are not merely past memories from a "once upon a time" immigration to the Lower East Side of New York's Manhattan. Instead, they are part of the current fabric of a society that has abandoned its elderly and victims whose social support has warn thin. The article contains case studies. See entry 422.

737 Efron, Mark. "Left Behind, Left Alone." In A Coat of Many Colors: Jewish Subcommunities in the United States, edited by Abraham Lavender, 167-174. Westport: Greenwood Press, 1977.

This examination of the problems of the poor Jew in America discloses the need for a response by organized American Jewry. As problematic as the economic situation of the Jewish poor may be the sense of being abandoned is even more pressing a problem (compare entry 735).

738 Franck, Phyllis. "The Hasidic Poor in New York City." In Poor Jews: An American Awakening edited by Naomi Levine and Martin Hochbaum, 59-69. New Brunswick: Transaction Books, 1974.

This article reviews the problems of running welfare prog-rams in a Hasidic community with the restrictions of shab-bat, work with women, and dietary laws. Not only are there difficulties in job training in such a setting, but the special needs of the Jewish poor become clear.

739 Freehof, Solomon B. "Order of Sustenance." In his Reform Responsa For Our Time, 63-66. Cincinnati: Hebrew Union College Press, 1971.

Freehof shows how Jewish law sets priorities in helping the poor. Differences in temperament and needs are taken into account. He notes that the needy at home have first prior-ity for aid. Compare entries 732, 741 and 742.

740 Hochbaum, Martin, editor, with Levine, Naomi. Poor Jews: An American Awakening. New Brunswick: Transaction Books, 1974.

This collection of essays on the facts, the ethics, and possibilities for helping the Jewish poor is an invaluable guide to the moral consciousness of contemporary Jews when confronting poverty. Essays from this anthology can be found in entries 732, 734, 737.

741   Jung,   Leo.   "The Concept of Tzedakah in Contemporary
Jewish Life."   In Poor Jews: An American Awakening, edited
by Naomi Levine and Martin Hochbaum, 96-104.   New Brunswick:
Transaction Books, 1974.

This essay in a sensitive collection (see entry 740)   notes
the ethical priorities in Judaism, its emphasizes upon
grace, kindness and pity, and the centrality of zedaka as a
moral virtue.   Other theological treatments of the question
can be found in entries 732, 739, and 742.

742   Jung,   Leo.   "The Poor."   In his Between Man and Man,
3rd enlarged ed.,   6-14.   New York: Board of Jewish Education, 1976.

Jung contends that the Jewish approach to poverty extends
beyond handouts to the poor.   The poor need self-respect and
Judaism suggests that the true obligation is that of teaching them so that they can prevent poverty itself.

743 Shava, Menashe.   "Maintenance of Young Children: Jewish
Laws of Zedakah and Israeli Law" [Hebrew].   Dine Israel 4
(1973): 181-217.

This essay reviews the principles of zedaka in Judaism and
in Israeli law as applying to the maintenance of children
below age of 15 and children above that age in cases of
divorce.   The obligation comes as an extension of zedaka to
relatives and those in the household.

744   Sprafkin,   Benjamin R.   "The Jewish Poor: Who are They?
Are we Helping Them Enough?" Journal of Jewish Communal
Service 49 (1973): 206-209.

Sprafkin offers special proposals to help alleviate certain
problems unique for the Jewish poor such as the formation of
a "Passover League," to supply provisions for that holiday.
He declares that the fact of Jewish communal help for these
poor does not exonerate the government from its obligations.

745   Wolfe,   Anne G.   "The Invisible Poor."   Journal of
Jewish Communal Service 48 (1971): 259-265.

This classic article uses various tests and sociological
measures to define the problem of the Jewish poor and to
suggest appropriate responses.   See the response to this
article in Journal of Jewish Communal Service 48 (1971):
348-359.   The essay is reprinted in A Coat of Many Colors:
Subcommunities in the United States, edited by Abraham Lavender, 137-144. Westport: Greenwood, 1977.

BUSINESS ETHICS

746 Bick, Ezra.   "Payment of Income Taxes: Halakhic Guide-
lines."   In Contemporary Jewish Ethics, edited by Menahem
Marc Kellner, 343-346. Sanhedrin Jewish Studies. New York:
Sanhedrin Press, 1978.

This essay shows little complexity and fails to note the controversial exemptions for religious bodies (see entries 771, 781, 790). The problem of the payment of taxes includes more than the ethics of deductions or the morality of the government to which they are paid. Jewish thinkers have sought to define both the limits of responsibility to a central government and the necessity for supporting one.

747 Bleich, J. David. "Automatic Banking Machines." In his Contemporary Halakhic Problems 2, 16-19. The Library of Jewish Law and Ethics, 4. New York: Ktav Publishing House, 1983.

Bleich notes the various halakhic problems faced because of the prohibition on usury and the fact that daily interest accrues on festivals and holidays. He adds that such machines are a temptation for use on Jewish holidays. Compare the interaction of ritual proscriptions and Jewish business morality in entry 752.

748 Bleich, J. David. "Business and Commerce." In his Contemporary Halakhic Problems 2, 120-138. The Library of Jewish Law and Ethics, 4. New York: Ktav Publishing House, 1983.

This is a general summary of views on the ethics of business, including a review of copyright, loans, the black market and severance pay. Taken as a whole this group of essays suggests the range of Jewish concern for moral business practice.

749 Bleich, J. David. "Copyright Laws." Tradition 19 (1981): 248-253.

Laws of copyright are particularly problematic in Judaism since the spread of education is taken as an important value. Thus business ethics and the priority of Jewish study, come into conflict. Bleich stresses the importance of disseminating learning and the medieval tradition of liberal use of the works of earlier writers. In the modern period, questions of honesty are involved that make the situation slightly different. Compare entry 785.

750 Bleich, J. David. "Hetter Iska." In his Contemporary Halakhic Problems 2, 276-384. The Library of Jewish Law and Ethics, 4. New York: Ktav Publishing House, 1983.

Jewish law rigorously forbids lending on interest to other Jews or lending on exorbitant interest to anyone. In the modern period, contemporary banking has presented problems in this regard which Jewish legalists have sought to resolve (see entries 783, 786, 788). Bleich reviews the Jewish prohibition on usury and the legal fictions used to legitimate certain types of loans. He notes the special case of home mortgages. The essay first appeared in Tradition 19 (1981): 149-162.

751 Bleich, J. David. "Organized Labor." In his Contemporary Halakhic Problems 186-189. The Library of Jewish Law and Ethics, 2. New York: Ktav Publishing House, 1977.

The Jewish approach to organized labor and strikes has occasioned considerable debate as has the relevance of Jewish tradition to the modern marketplace (see entries 757, 762, 764, 772, 773, 794). Bleich summarizes the sources concerning the rights of workers to organize and strike as well as other relevant views on Jewish law and contemporary labor relationships.

752 Bleich, J. David. "Sale of Commercial Enterprises to Sabbath Violators." In his Contemporary Halakhic Problems, 35-36. The Library of Jewish Law and Ethics, 2. New York: Ktav Publishing House, 1977.

Bleich affirms that permitting a business to be used for a transgression is forbidden. He also prohibits any profiting from that transgression. This essay shows how Jewish ceremonial concerns become morally relevant to business life (compare entry 747).

753 Bleich, J. David. "Sale of Israeli Real Estate to Non-Jews." In his Contemporary Halakhic Problems, 27-32. The Library of Jewish Law and Ethics, 2. New York: Ktav Publishing House, 1977.

The sanctity of Land of Israel for the Jew is reflected in the biblical prohibition of sale of that land to the non-Jew. Bleich limits this prohibition, however, to cases in which the land is sold in perpetuity. The lack of clarity concerning the definition of permanence limits the applicability of the law.

754 Bokser, Ben Zion. "Religion and Economic Policy: A Jewish Perspective." In Formation of Social Policy in the Catholic and Jewish Traditions, edited by Eugene J. Fisher and Daniel F. Polish, 67-76. Notre Dame: University of Notre Dame Press, 1980.

Bokser claims that religion is not a direct agent of social change, but rather acts to stir the human conscience which then prompts new policies. The debate concerning the meaning of Judaism for current economic life can be traced in entries 758, 763, 768, 772, 784.

755 Cohen, Alfred S. "Gambling in the Synagogue." Tradition 18 (1980): 319-326.

The question of the permissibility of gambling has been studied by Jewish thinkers (see entries 759, 760, 770). This article reviews the rabbinic disapproval of gambling and argues that a good deed achieved by evil means has no value. The author laments the fading of Jewish ideals in modernity.

756 Cohn, Haim H. "The Right to Property." In his Human
Rights in Jewish Law, 87-95. New York: Ktav Publishing
House, 1984.

Cohn notes the theological presupposition that God possesses
the world and its expression in the sabbatical year. He
draws upon its implications for limitations on the power of
kings and political leaders as well as for judicial expro-
priations of land.

757 Cohn, Haim H. "The Right to Work and Renumeration."
In his Human Rights in Jewish Law, 96-102. New York: Ktav
Publishing House, 1984.

Cohn emphasizes that, for the Jew, work is a privilege, not
a punishment. He reviews the mutual obligations of workers
and employers, remarking on the right of workers to unionize
and support for the idea of a minimum wage. Compare entry
751 and the entries listed in the annotation there.

758 Freddy, Raphael. Judaism et Capitalism: Essai Sur La
Controverse Entre Max Weber et Werner Sombart. Paris:
Presses Universitaire France, 1982.

This basically sociological work surveys different views and
explores economic ethics of Judaism in talmudic and medieval
as well as modern times. Freddy reviews modern Jewish
thinkers and theologians on Judaism and economic questions.
Compare the discussion at entry 754.

759 Freehof, Solomon B. "Gambling For Benefit of the
Synagogue." In his Current Reform Responsa, 52-62. Cincinnati: Hebrew Union College Press, 1969.

The debate about gambling involves economic as well as moral
relevance since many synagogues seek to emulate other religious groups in using gambling (such as bingo) to raise
funds. Freehof declares that both traditional Jewish law
and Reform Judaism oppose such a practice as utilizing an
immoral means for a putatively moral end. Compare the
following entry as well as entry 755 and the other entries
included in the annotation there.

760 Freehof, Solomon B. "Occasional Gambling and State
Lotteries." In his Reform Responsa for Our Time, 229-232.
Cincinnati: Hebrew Union College Press, 1971.

Freehof repeats the talmudic warning that gamblers are
cheaters. While distinguishing between the occasional gambler and the professional or compulsive one, he remarks that
state lotteries are to be respected as the law of the land.

761 Freehof, Solomon B. "Unfair Competition." In his
Modern Reform Responsa, 281-285. Cincinnati: Hebrew Union
College Press, 1971.

Freehof summarizes the talmudic discussion opposing en-
croachment of one competitor in the territory of another.
He notes the liberal tendency of capitalism in contrast to
the limits in the middle ages. Nevertheless, he contends
that one Jew does not have the right to endanger the liveli-
hood of another. The question of fairness in business and
the protection of the consumer is debated at length in
Jewish sources (see entries 779, 782, 787, 791, 792).

762   Friedman, Hershey H.   "Talmudic Business Ethics."
Akron Business and Economic Review 11 (Winter 1980): 45-49.

Friedman contends that there are current needs for defini-
tive guidelines for business ethics. He notes that Jewish
law and ethics are united and summarizes basic laws concerning buying and selling, pricing, employee-employer relationships, and deception. He concludes that commercial
honesty is the foundation of Jewish business ethics. Compare entries 751, 754, 761, 786.

763 Herberg, Will. "Business Enterprise in Moral Perspective." In Business, Religion and Ethics: Inquiry and Encounter, edited by Donald G. Jones, 57-67. Cambridge: Oelgeschlager, Gunn and Hain, 1982.

This theological study examines the paradox of capitalism:
even base motives can be turned into social well being. He
notes the danger in the idea of an economic calling: voca-
tion can lead to the idolatry of work. Compare entry 754.

764 Jacobs, Harold. "Torah Ethics in Business: Is Honesty
Really _The Best Policy?'" Jewish Observer 4 (1967): 5-7.

This is a popular presentation of Jewish business ethics.
Jacobs examines both the obligations and expectations of the
Jewish business man. He contends that success needs to be
reevaluated in terms of ethical achievement.

765 Jung, Leo.   "The Ethics of Business." In his Between
Man and Man, 89-100.   3rd enlarged ed. New York: Board of
Jewish Education, 1976.

This essay investigates Judaism's concern for every aspect
of life. Judaism stands against monopolies and economic
exploitation. He particularly emphasizes that business must
avoid fraud for any type. See Menahem Marc Kellner, ed.
Contemporary Jewish Ethics, 332-343. Sanhedrin Jewish
Studies. (New York: Sanhedrin Press, 1978).

766   Jung, Leo.   "Jewish Foundations of the New World
Order." In his Judaism in a Changing World, 1-63.   The
Jewish Library, 4. London: Soncino Press, 1971.

In this survey of relevant source material, Jung presents
Jewish texts related to social questions including business
ethics and political ethics.

767   Krafetz, Gerald. Jews and Money: The Myths and the
Reality. New York: Ticknor Fields Press, 1982.

Krafetz examines the facts and myths about Jewish business
life. He examines Jews in crime, the condition of nursing
home care, and the plight of the Jewish poor.

768 Kriegel, Annie. "Les Chemins Du XXe Siecle: Judaism et
Socialism."   In her Les Juifs et Le Monde Moderne: Essai
Sur Les Logique D'Emancipation, 25-42.   Paris: Editions Du
Seuil, 1977.

This study of Karl Marx, of Moses Hess, and nationalism as
the achilles' heel of Soviet Marxism shows how Judaism is
superior to, although an inspiration for, Marxism. Compare
entry 754 and the following entry.

769   Kristol, Irving.   "The Spiritual Roots of Capitalism
and Socialism." In Capitalism and Socialism: A Theological
Inquiry, edited by Michael Novak, 1-14. Washington: American
Enterprise Institute For Public Policy Research, 1979.

Kristol launches a polemic against gnostic dualism which he
identifies with Christianity's approach to business.   In
contrast, he finds that Judaism sees business as a moral
enterprise in which even the poor are morally responsible.

770 Landman, Leo. "Gambling in the Synagogue." Tradition
10 (1968): 75-86.

Landman, reviewing the talmudic distinction between professional, compulsive, occasional, and charitable gambling,
notes that while the compulsive gambler is disqualified from
Jewish law and shunned as morally reprehensible, limited
gambling for charitable purposes is permitted.   Compare
entry 755.

771 Landynski, Jacob W.   "Tax Exemptions for Religious
Institutions." Jewish Life 37 (1969): 5-11.

Landynski notes that the exemption is a product of the
establishment cause.   Since the state cooperates with religion and benefits from it in significant ways tax exemption
is to be defended.   Compare entries 746, 781, 790.

772 Leister, Burton M. "The Rabbinic Tradition and Corporate Morality." In The Judeo-Christian Vision and the Modern
Corporation, edited by Oliver F. Williams and John W. Houck,
141-158. Notre Dame: University of Notre Dame Press, 1982.

Leister relies on the musar tradition and on the Hafetz Haim
(died in 1933) to criticize contemporary business
practices.   He reviews civil restraints placed on business,
the prohibition of deceptive advertising, the rejection of
unfair competition, the discussion of fringe benefits,
theft, and unemployment. Compare entry 754.

773 Levine, Aaron. Free Enterprise and Jewish Law: Aspects
of Jewish Business Ethics.   New York: Ktav Publishing
House, 1980.

Levine comments upon the permissibility of strikes, regulations on pricing and advertising, problematic business practices, and related issues. Compare entries 751 and 754.

774 Levine, Aaron. "Advertising and Promotional Activities
as Regulated by Jewish Law" Journal of Halacha and Contemporary Society 1 (1981): 5-37.

Levine studies the ethics of persuasion, the obligations for
disclosure, and regulations to maintain good practices of
business.   He provides a detailed examination of all types
of fraud and deception.   Compare entries 761 and 776.

775 Levine, Aaron.   "Opportunity Cost as Treated in Talmudic Literature." Tradition 15 (1975): 153-172.

Levine demonstrates that cost should include recompense for
opportunities lost.   He notes that a mitzvah often includes
expectation of loss for sake of religious gain.   He surveys
how this applies to judicial fees and to restrictions placed
on restitution for opportunity lost.

776 Merling, Bernard.   "Advertising and the Jewish Problem." Jewish Life 38,5 (1971): 22-27.

Merling looks at the facts of Jewish advertising and finds
that they are neither appropriate to their causes nor re-
flective of Jewish business ethics. Compare 774.

777 Merling, Bernard. "The Ben-Torah Businessman: Profits
and Losses." Jewish Life 36,4 (1969): 26-36.

Merling insists that the tradition of joining study and
business should not be misconstrued as an ideal; only the
full time scholar, in his view, represents that ideal.

778 Rakover, Nahum. "Business Procedures in Hebrew Law."
[Hebrew] Sinai 80 (1977): 217-244.

Rakover examines both contemporary Israeli business legislation and the classical tradition of consumer protection. He
studies the limits of such protection and the principle of
considering the good of the community. Compare the following entry and entries 751 and 761.

779 Rakover, Nahum.   "Consumer Protection in Hebrew Law"
[Hebrew]. Sinai 74 (1974): 210-238.

Rakover summarizes the prohibition against injuring another
person and its various implications, discussing fraud, deceit, price-fixing, strikes, and boycotts from the standpoint of Jewish law. Compare entry 761.

780   Shapiro,   Edward S.   "American Jews and the   Business
Morality."   Judaism 27 (1978): 214-223.

Shapiro   points out that capitalism was key to the   rise   of
the   Eastern European Jew and it is unwise for   contemporary
Jews   to romanticize the earlier period which was,   in fact,
often opportunistic and unethical.

781   Shaviv,   Yehuda.   "Equitable   Taxation"   [Hebrew].
Tehumin 3 (1983): 298-306.

Shaviv traces Jewish taxation law to the time of the   monar-
chy.   He claims that taxes are justified because they serve
the general good.   They form a theoretical partnership between the citizens and the government.   Since the rabbis see
are   a   spiritual necessity for any country they   should   be
free from taxation, as they already fulfill a vital national
task.   Compare entries 746, 771, 790.

782   Shohatman,   Eliav.   "Consumer   Protection   in   the
Halakhah."   Dine Israel 2 (1971): 227-237.

Shohatman studies the meaning of deception,   its harm to the
consumer   and seller alike,   and instances of _stealing   the
mind' of the consumer.   He also looks at obligations to the
non-Jew   and the ethical principles behind Jewish laws   pro-
tecting the consumer.   Compare entry 761.

783 Shurin, Jacob.   "Hetter Iska"   Tradition 18 (1980): 357-
364.

Shurin   explains the ethics of the prohibition   on   interest
and   ways of transforming a loan into a joint business   ven-
ture   so as to avoid the prohibition.   Compare the discussion at entry 750.

784 Siegel,   Seymour.   "A Jewish View of Economic Justice."
In Business,   Religion,   and Ethics: Inquiry and Encounter,
edited by Donald G.   Jones, 89-98. Cambridge: Oelgeschlager,
Gunn, and Hain, 1982.

Siegel   declares that Jewish law restrains human   sin   while
fulfilling   the task of improving nature.   He distinguishes
between permitted profit and price-gorging and analyzes   the
creation of monopolies,the rights of the laborer,   and other
details   of   commercial ethics from the   Jewish   standpoint.
Compare entry 754.

785   Silver,   Arthur Jay.   "Copyright in Jewish Law."   Tradition 14 (1974): 28-36.

Silver   traces   the historical precedent for using the   writings of others in ones own work, citing rabbinic and medieval examples.   He claims that delicate ad hoc decisions are
needed to balance the protection of a claimant with the need
to disseminate Jewish knowledge.   Compare entry 749.

786   Silver, Arthur Jay.   "Prohibition   Against   Interest
Today."   Tradition 15 (1975): 97-109.

Silver explains the biblical prohibition against interest in
terms of its context.   He traces the talmudic extensions of
the   idea   to   types of partnership   and   explores   medieval
methods   of coping with the problem.   Today,   new types   of
iska   agreement   are   needed because of   controversies   over
savings banks, paper money, and checks.   Compare entry 750.

787 Silverstein,   Arthur Jay.   "Consumer Protection in Talmudic Law" Commercial Law Journal 79 (1974): 279-282.

Silverstein   traces   the talmudic and   biblical   sources   on
weights and measures,   fraud, and pricing.   He suggests that
discretion   is left to the consumer except for regulation in
areas beyond the consumer's cognition.   Compare entry 761.

788 Stern, Joseph.   "Ribit: A Halakhic Anthology."   Journal
of Halacha and Contemporary Society 4 (1972): 46-69.

This   compendium   of sources studies the varieties   of   forbidden and permitted interest, the hetter iska document, and
more dilemmas such as the personal mortgage loan,   buying on
time,   corporations,   partnerships,   and charitable bodies.   The
essay also appears in Cohen (085), pp. 167-190.   Compare the
discussion in entries 750, 783, 786.

789   Tamari,   Meir.   "Competition,   Prices and Profits   in
Jewish Law" [Hebrew].   Bar Ilan Annual X (1972): 130-145.

This   discussion   of Jewish commercial ethics   both   at   the
specific   injunctions   of Jewish law and the general   inten-
tions   of   those commandments to find an ethical   basis   for
them.   Tamari declares that Judaism creates a moral climate
limiting misrepresentation,   theft,   and uses legal   regulations to enforce subjective values.   Compare entry 761.

790   Vorspan,   Albert.   "Proposition #13, Tax Revolt, Econo-
mic   Justice."   In his Great Jewish Debates and   Dilemmas:
Jewish Perspectives in the Eighties,   168-182.   New   York:
Union of American Hebrew Congregations, 1980.

Vorspan   notes the conflict between liberal and Jewish needs
in   American   Judaism's response to poverty and   its   public
policy on welfare and welfare institutions.   Compare entries
746, 771, 781.

791 Warhaftig,   Itamar.   "Consumer Protection in the Light
of Halacha: Wage and Price Guidelines" [Hebrew].   Tehumin 1
(1980): 444-488.

Warhaftig   presents a general approach to limits on   profits
and to the imperative that vital necessities be available to
all,   noting both market conditions and religious   factors.
Compare entry 761.

792 Warhaftig, Itamar. "Consumer Protection in Light of Halacha II: Laws of Deceit and Fraud" [Hebrew]. Tehumin 2 (1981): 470-492.

Warhaftig contrasts Judaism to the Roman principle of caveat emptor. Limits are set on profits, wages for workers must be just, treatment of non-Jews must be fair as well as rules of deceit and their modern application.

793 Warhaftig, Zerah. "The Basic Principle of Responsibility of Damages in Hebrew Law" [Hebrew]. Bar Ilan Annual 13 (1976): 132-148.

Warhaftig points to two theories of responsibility: either implying guilt or not implying guilt. He notes that business is often undertaken as a known risk so that there should be no-fault responsibility.

794 Wolkinson, Benjamin A. "Labor and the Jewish Tradition: A Reappraisal." Jewish Social Studies 40 (1978): 231-237.

Reviewing the controversy over the Steiger bill for open shops, Wolkinson pits the Jewish libertarian ethics against talmudic permissiveness of organized action by workers. Compare the discussion in Bleich (751).

795 Zipperstein, Edward. Business Ethics in Jewish Law New York: Ktav Publishing House 1983.

This is an apologetic summary of Jewish business law drawing on a variety of modern and classical sources. Zipperstein claims that the well being of the individual and the community are central Jewish concerns.

INTERRELIGIOUS DIALOGUE

796 Bamberger, Henry. "Some Difficulties in Dialogue." Judaism 32 (1983): 176-183.

Various modern crises have raised the question of whether interreligious dialogue is an ethical enterprise (See 797, 799, 801, 807, 810, 813, 816, 818). Bamberger investigates this issue by analyzing the idea of Noahides and by using the theology of Franz Rosenzweig.

797 Berkovits, Eliezer. "Facing the Truth." Judaism 27 (1978): 324-326.

Berkovits contends that Christian ethics or rather lack of it presents an obstacles to dialogue. He calls for missionizing to end and insists that interfaith dialogue be restricted to matters of moral conscience. See the comment at the previous entry.

798 Bleich, J. David. "Teaching Torah to Non-Jews." In his Contemporary Halakhic Problems 2, 311-340. The Library of Jewish Law and Ethics 4. New York: Ktav Publishing House, 1983.

Bleich summarizes the principles restricting how and what Jews should teach the non-Jew. The ethics of interfaith conversation must be for the sake of improving the world. The essay first appeared in Tradition 18 (1980): 192-211.

799 Blidstein, Gerald. "Jews and the Ecumenical Dialogue." Tradition 11 (1970): 103-110.

Blidstein reviews the questions of Jewish-Christian dialogue from the standpoint of an enlightened traditional Jew. See the annotation at entry 796 and below.

800 Cohen-Sherbok, Dan. "Jewish-Christian Relations: A New Development." Conservative Judaism 38 (1985): 30-35.

The author notes that part of the problem in interfaith communications lies in a lack of shared symbols. He suggests using the Exodus story and the motif of standing against the powerbrokers of the world as such a symbol. This new development in interfaith relationships will enable the religious groups of America to stand against the exploitation of third world countries by the superpowers. Compare the annotation at entry 796.

801 Cytron, Barry D. "Nostra Aetate, the Jews and the Future of Dialogue." Conservative Judaism 38 (1985): 21-29.

Cytron surveys twenty years of interfaith relationships. He notes that fear encounter has thwarted many attempts at religious communication. He looks at responses given both by Jews and Christians to interfaith activities and calls for greater openness and willingness to take risks.

802 Drachman, Bernard. "Jewish-Gentile Relations Considered from the Jewish Viewpoint." In Judaism in a Changing World, 106-123. The Jewish Library, 4. London: Soncino Press, 1971.

Drachman notes that Israel's election emphasizes humility and sympathy for the non-Jew. He contends that Jews have been misunderstood as elitest. Rather Jews use the concept to understand their mission and purpose in relationship to all other nations; they are servants, not an elite group.

803 Edelheit, Joseph A., with Arthur Meth. "Accepting Non-Jews as Members of the Synagogue." Journal of Reform Judaism (1980): 87-92.

The authors argue for a sympathetic response to non-Jewish partners in an intermarriage and describe how one synagogue approached and solved the problem; contrast the following entry.

804 Freehof, Solomon B. "Gentile Membership in a Synagogue." In his Reform Responsa For Our Time, 221-223. Cincinnati: Hebrew Union College Press, 1971.

Freehof contends that while mixed marriages are not encouraged the partners should not be penalized. He suggests that the family as a whole be accepted into the synagogue in the name of the Jewish spouse.

805 Freehof, Solomon B. "Interfaith Services." In his Modern Reform Responsa, 69-78. Cincinnati: Hebrew Union College Press, 1971.

Freehof will not compromise belief for the sake of ecumenicity. He declares that only those prayers, symbols, or rituals which all can share should be used and insists that all prayers must be spoken with a clear conscience.

806 Friedman, Norman. "Boundary Issues for Liberal Judaism" Midstream 19 (1973): 47-52.

The test of interreligious tolerance and its limits is one boundary issue on which liberals must choose between their liberalism and Judaism. Compare entries 289, 381, 830.

807 Greenberg, Irving. "New Revelations and New Patterns in the Relationship of Judaism and Christianity." Journal of Ecumenical Studies 16 (1979): 247-267.

Greenberg contends that both Judaism and Christianity supplement the originating revelatory event with later orienting ones. The Holocaust is such an event, teaching the need for unity among religions in the struggle to make human life more precious. Compare entry 796.

808 Haberman, Joshua O. "Universalism and Particularism in Interreligious Dialogue." Central Conference of American Rabbis Journal 24 (1977): 59-74.

Haberman traces the history of interfaith dialogue, its connection with Zionism and new realities obstructing the process. He reinterprets the ideas of covenant and election in terms of Franz Rosenzweig's paradigm of two legitimate religious traditions. Compare entry 796.

809 Kasimov, Harold. "Abraham Joshua Heschel and Interreligious Dialogue" Journal of Ecumenical Studies 18 (1981): 423-434.

Kasimov traces Heschel's involvement in interfaith dialogue and the humility springing from regarding reality as a puzzle before which human beings stand amazed. He looks at both Christian and non-Christian religions and seeks a basis for future dialogue. Compare the annotation at entry 796.

810 Lookstein, Joseph H. "The Vatican and the Jews 1975." _Tradition_ 15 (1975): 5-24.

Lookstein defends the ethics of Orthodox Jewry's dialogue with Roman Catholics. He suggests that a new basis has been created for interfaith communication that should not be rejected out of hand. Compare entry 796.

811 Matt, Hershel. "How Shall a Believing Jew View Christianity?" _Judaism_ 24 (1975): 391-405.

Matt affirms the two covenant theory which legitimizes both Judaism and Christianity in contrast to the traditional Christian belief that the "new" covenant replaced the "old." Judaism is a covenant made with a people and Christianity is a revelation by a person. Both share a high valuation of life and human dignity. Compare entry 796 and particularly entries 807-809.

812 Novak, David. "The Prohibition of Gentile Wine." In his _Law and Theology in Judaism, 2nd Series_, 174-183. New York: Ktav Publishing House, 1976.

Novak investigates the ethical and religious reasons for prohibiting Jewish use of Gentile wine and suggests that in today's world there is no reason to relax the prohibition.

813 Sarnat, David I. "Fresh Dimensions in Inter-Group Relations." _Journal of Jewish Communal Service_ 50 (1974): 98-103.

Sarnat calls upon Jews to examine their own self-interest and the pitfalls of isolationism. He claims that both principles and constituencies must be taken into account. Compare entry 796 and the following entry.

814 Sklare, Marshall. "The Conversion of the Jews." _Commentary_ 56,4 (1973): 44-53.

This pessimistic view of the growth and decline of Jewish-Christian dialogue provides an interesting perspective on how Jews have viewed both missionizing and dialogue.

815 Teichman, Zvi Y. "Chukat Ha'Akum: Jews in a Gentile Society." In _Halacha and Contemporary Society_, edited by Alfred S. Cohen, 243-264. New York: Ktav Publishing House, 1983.

Teichman presents the traditional Jewish objection to following in the ways of the Gentiles, including participation in interdenominational worship. Compare Freehof (805) and Novak (812).

511 Vorspan, Albert. "Interfaith Relations." In his _Great Jewish Debates and Dilemmas: Jewish Perspectives in Conflict in the Eighties_, 79-95. New York: Union of American Hebrew Congregations, 1980.

Since interfaith dialogue and conversion are interrelated, Vorspan suggests the continuation of interfaith relationships and the creation of a special havura or worshiping community, just for the newly converted.

817   Warhaftig, Jacob.   "_Lo Techanaym': Its Meaning in Modern Israel" [Hebrew].   Tehumin 2 (1981): 193-212.

Warhaftig struggles to understand the halakhic rule not to favor the non-Jew. He concludes that the rule is derivative from commands having to do with the Jewish relationship to the land of Israel and idolatry.   His survey includes a study of general business relationships and of the specific problems arising from the creation of the State of Israel.

818   Wigoder, Geoffrey.   "Interfaith in Israel."   Midstream 26 (1980): 16-20.

Wigoder recognizes that the existence of the modern state of Israel is a theological challenge to Christianity. He notes that a tension develops between Israeli Christians and those abroad because the former are favorable to Israel.   He laments Orthodox Jewish suspicion of Christianity and thinks that good Jewish-Christian relationships are valuable.

CONVERSION TO JUDAISM

819   Angel, Marc D.   "A Fresh Look at Conversion."   Midstream 29 (1983): 35-38.

Angel is a bit of a maverick in traditional Jewish views of conversion (compare entries 820, 825, 832, 837, 840). He acknowledges the historical background and the classical texts that preach a reticence in seeking conversions to Judaism.   On the other hand, he suggests that an openness to the non-Orthodox is needed in the modern period.

820   Angel, Marc D.   "Another Halakhic Approach to Conversions."   Tradition 12 (1972): 107-113

Angel liberalizes Orthodox stringency by suggesting new leniency and recognition of Jewish children of mixed marriages.   His view should be compared to the other traditional positions noted in the previous entry as well as to that of the non-Orthodox.

821   Berger, Peter L.   "Converting the Gentiles."   Commentary 67,5 (1979): 35-39.

Berger presents a positive Christian perspective on Reform Judaism's decision to missionize (See entries 826, 828, 833, 836, 838). He suggests that missionizing reflects a realistic view of the pluralistic competition of modernity.

822   Berkovits, Eliezer.   "Clarifications in the Laws of Conversion" [Hebrew].   Sinai 77 (1976): 28-36.

Berkovits notes that the purpose of conversion is for the sake of performing all the commandments. While Jewish law suggests that a new convert be informed only of some of the laws, in principle all are accepted. Berkovits also probes the question of motivation for conversion.

823 Berkovits, Eliezer. "Conversion According to Halakha: What is it?" Judaism 23 (1974): 467-478.

Berkovits claims that conversion implies acceptance of the Sinaitic commandments. Since only a fully orthodox conversion does this, it alone is acceptable. Compare entry 819.

824 Bleich, J. David. "The Conversion Crisis: A Halakhic Analysis." In his Contemporary Halakhic Problems, 270-296. Library of Jewish Law and Ethics, 2. New York: Ktav Publishing House, 1977.

Bleich questions the motivation of many conversions to Judaism, especially that of marriage, as well as the problems arising from civil ceremonies and insincere conversions. This essay first appeared in Tradition 11 (1971): 16-42; compare entries 832, 837, 840 and contrast 819, 820.

825 Bulka, Reuven P. "The Psychology of Conversion." Midstream 29 (1983): 32-35.

Bulka's study of the psychology of conversion raises the questions of sincerity and of the obstacles placed before conversion by Jewish law, concluding that Jewish law is a safeguard against ill considered haste in conversion. His clearly traditional and Orthodox viewpoint is bolstered by appeal to the psychological process by which a conversion is initiated and completed.

826 Cohen-Sherbok, Dan. "The Paradox of Reform Conversions." Journal of Reform Judaism 27 (1980): 83-85.

The paradox of Reform conversion is that while theology stresses a change of heart, the process demands almost no theological commitment. He seeks new symbols symbolizing conversion's seriousness. Compare the discussion in 821.

827 Crawford, Yael. "Convert to Judaism." United Synagogue Review 24,2 (1971): 10-11, 30-31.

Crawford testifies to the total change of life that a conversion to Conservative Judaism entails. She shows how Conservative Jews integrate a convert into their midst. Her practical experience should be contrasted with the theoretical considerations of leading Conservative theologians;compare entries 831 and 834.

828 Freehof, Solomon B. "Circumcision of Proselytes." In his Reform Response For Our Time, 71-79. Cincinnati: Hebrew Union College Press, 1971.

Freehof reviews the debate within liberal Judaism as to whether circumcision is needed for conversion to Judaism. He concludes that the test is the conscience of the rabbinic group involved. He notes that if the man is sickly then even tradition does not require circumcision. This rationale, however, would hardly be accepted by most non-Reform Jews.

829 Freehof, Solomon B. "An Incomplete Conversion." In his New Reform Responsa, 75-78. Cincinnati: Hebrew Union College Press, 1980.

Freehof seeks to decide whether a conversion holds if a course has been completed but certain rituals or symbols have been left undone. He concludes that since intention is most important, if the most essential parts of the process have been carried out then the conversion is valid. This leniency is one reason that Orthodox Jews are suspicious of conversions carried out by the non-Orthodox.

830 Friedman, Norman. "Boundary Issues for Liberal Judaism." Midstream 19:9 (1973): 47-52.

The question of conversion to Judaism is yet another area in which the liberal must choose between Judaism and liberalism. See entries 289, 381, 806.

831 Gordon, Albert I. "Inner and Outer Conversion." United Synagogue Review 21,1 (1968): 12, 30.

Gordon notes that conversions undertaken for the sake of intermarriage often look only at the externals of Jewish behavior. He advocates, instead, a focus on inner changes. Conversion, he contends, must be religiously significant. This view should be compared to the personal experience of a convert to Conservative Judaism in entry 827.

832 Jung, Leo. "The Sincere Proselyte." In his Between Man and Man, 78-80. 3rd enlarged ed. New York: Board of Jewish Education Press, 1976.

The general and theoretic approach of Judaism to the treatment of converts is clearly humanitarian (see entries 837, 840). Here Jung insists that converts should be treated with respect and given every consideration as a Jew.

833 Kallin, Gilbert. "The Advisability of Seeking Converts." Judaism 24 (1973): 49-57.

Gilbert suggests reviving Judaism's early positive orientation towards making converts, an orientation that changed, according to him, because of historical accident. Compare the views noted in entry 821.

834 Lear, Elmer N. "On Inter-Racial Conversions." The Reconstructionist 40,9 (1974): 22-29.

This open minded essay declares that the Jewish heritage accepts all individuals who seek to join the Jewish people, despite social and economic obstacles.

835 Meron, Simha. "Law of Proselytes" [Hebrew]. Dine Israel 1 (1969): 67-74.

The definition of a convert, discussions of those permitted or forbidden to convert to Judaism, and a description of the conversion ceremony make this a valuable essay.

836 Polish, David. "Jewish Proselyting--Another Opinion." Journal of Reform Judaism 26 (1979): 1-9.

Polish disapproves of seeking converts to Judaism since it has none of the theological necessity for conversion of Christianity. His approach contrasts with that of other Reform Jews who advocate making conversions and compares with traditional Jews who voice concern about an active Jewish mission of seeking converts. See the discussion at entry 821.

837 Riskin, Steven. "Conversion in Jewish Law." Tradition 14 (1973): 29-42.

While clearly in the restrictive mode of traditional Judaism (compare entry 824 and contrast entries 820, 821), this essay shows deep sympathy for the proselyte (compare entries 825, 832). Riskin points to a variety of problems involved in seeking to make converts to Judaism, but notes that converts are to be treated with kindness.

838 Schindler, Alexander. "Reaching In; Reaching Out." Moment 4,4 (1979): 17-19.

Schindler launched the modern movement for Jewish prose-lytism (see the discussion in 821). He gives both practical reasons (the declining Jewish birth rate) and ideological ones (Judaism's spiritual worth) to support his case. See the responses by Wolfe Kelman, Leo Pfeiffer, Harold Schul-weis, and Daniel Schwartz, pp. 24-28.

839 Shaki, Avner. "Reform Conversion Abroad: Its Validity in Israel" [Hebrew]. Dine Israel 4 (1973): 161-179.

Shaki notes the differences in official conversions in Is-rael and those performed abroad. He suggests that at issue is the definition of being a Jew and the law of return.

840 Zemel, Ephraim. "Thou Shalt Love the Convert" [Hebrew]. Tehumin 2 (1981): 232-235.

Zemel cautions against rejecting the convert and teaches love for the non-Jew. He suggests that teaching a prospec-tive convert does not transgress the prohibition against teaching a stranger since the interest in Judaism of the convert brings him near to Judaism.

Author Index

The index that follows contains only the primary authors or editors appearing in citations or in the Introductory Survey. References to the Introductory Survey are indicated by page number; references to the Bibliographical Survey are indicated by citation number.

Title Index

The references in this index are to the citation numbers of entries in which the title occurs as the primary citation; anthologies are noted only if they are the primary citation; Journal titles are not included.

7

228 TITLE INDEX

Subject Index

This index includes subjects discussed in the Introductory Survey and in the Bibliographical Survey. References to the former are by page number; references to the latter are by entry number. Hebrew words are in underlined.

About the Compiler

S. DANIEL BRESLAUER is Associate Professor of Religious Studies at the University of Kansas, Lawrence. He is the author of *Contemporary Jewish Ethics: A Bibliographical Survey* (Greenwood Press, 1985) and a contributor to *A Dictionary of the Jewish-Christian Dialogue,* edited by Leon Klenicki and Geoffrey Wigoder.